Aesthetes and Decadents OF THE 1890's

AN ANTHOLOGY OF BRITISH POETRY AND PROSE

Aesthetes and Decadents OF THE 1890's

AN ANTHOLOGY OF
BRITISH POETRY AND PROSE.
EDITED, WITH AN
INTRODUCTION AND
NOTES, BY *Karl Beckson*

WITH 16 ILLUSTRATIONS
BY *Aubrey Beardsley*

VINTAGE BOOKS
A Division of Random House
New York

ACKNOWLEDGMENTS: Oriole Press, for selected poems of John Barlas;
Edward Colman Esq., Executor of the Lord Alfred Douglas Literary
Estate, for selected poems and footnotes from *Lyrics 1935* by Lord
Alfred Douglas; The Bodley Head Ltd., for selected poems from
Silverpoints by John Gray, selections from *The Works of Max Beerbohm* and letter to editor of *The Yellow Book*, The Society of Authors as the literary representative of the late Richard Le Gallienne,
for selected poems from *English Poems*, an essay from *Prose Fancies*
and a short extract from *Retrospective Reviews* by Richard Le Gallienne; The Macmillan Co. (USA) and the Macmillan Co. of Canada,
for selected poems from *Collected Poems of William Butler Yeats*,
Copyright 1906 by The Macmillan Co., Copyright renewed 1934 by
William Butler Yeats; The Pierpont Morgan Library, for a passage
from a letter to Arthur Moore by Ernest Dowson; Gerald Duckworth
& Co., Ltd., for a passage from *Letters to the Sphinx* by Ada Leverson; Ian Fletcher, for his translation of "In Honorem Doriani Creatorisque Eius" by Lionel Johnson; The Richards Press, for selected
poems of Theodore Wratislaw; The Owner of the Copyright and John
Baker Ltd., for selections from *The Green Carnation* by Robert
Hichens.

VINTAGE BOOKS
are published by
Alfred A. Knopf, Inc. and Random House, Inc.

To my wife, Estelle,
and
To my sons, Mace and Eric,
who are neither Aesthetes nor Decadents

PREFACE

To most students of the period, the 1890's in England—more specifically, London—are less a chronological designation than a state of mind. For some, the decade conjures yellow visions of Decadence, of putrescence in life and art, with its loss of the "complete view" of man in nature, perhaps best symbolized by fetid hothouses where monstrous orchids, seemingly artificial, are cultivated as a challenge to nature and an assertion of man's cunning. For others, the 1890's suggest the artist's protest against a spiritually bankrupt civilization, his imagination striving for the unattainable to restore his wholeness.

Limited as the phenomenon of Decadence was—one writer has rightly referred to it as but a single stone in the mosaic of the Nineties[1]—in recent years it has attracted the attention of critics who see in its curious posing, its desire to shock with excursions into perversion, its devotion to artifice, and its desire to pull down the decaying temples of Victorian respectability, not only an absorbing chapter in literary history and taste but also a significant prelude to and major influence on contemporary literature. In both the Decadence of the Nineties and in our current literature, one encounters a similar quest for new experience and for new forms of expression in a world bereft of unassailable truths.

The attempt to state precisely what Decadence and Aestheticism mean has led numerous literary historians to dash themselves on the semantic rocks. For most modern critics, the term "Decadence"—when used to describe certain nineteenth-century works—does not carry pejorative con-

[1] This was also the period, one recalls, of Shaw, Wells, Kipling, and Thomas Hardy, among others.

notations. In the Nineties, however, it generally implied marked condemnation and on many occasions was used to characterize the artist's moral and spiritual depravity.[2] In 1893, Arthur Symons turned its pejorative suggestions into praise by describing Decadence as a "beautiful and interesting disease," though later in the decade he limited the term to style alone. (There was confusion in the Nineties—and to some extent today—in the use of "Decadent" to characterize the artist, his work, or both; Ernest Dowson is still widely referred to as a Decadent because of his erratic life, though his poems reveal few decadent qualities.) Similar problems exist with the term "Aesthete," which in the 1880's evoked visions of effeminate poets holding various floral displays in characteristic poses, as in the case of Wilde, who welcomed the label. However, Aestheticism implies certain attitudes rather than forms of behavior, attitudes associated with the concern over aesthetic form and experience divorced from moral judgment. Despite the attendant difficulties, both terms can be usefully employed to delineate attitudes, style, and subject matter.

In the Introduction that follows, I have attempted to set down some main lines of the "Aesthetic Movement"—the term "movement" is itself misleading, for actually it refers to a great number of writers who subscribe, with varying degrees of assent, to some loosely defined aesthetic principles. In choosing selections, I have been generally guided by the dual principle of quality and relevance.[3] Consequently, I have included such works as the imitative verse of Theodore Wratislaw, whose representative decadent poems occupy as

[2] Max Nordau's *Degeneration* (1892), which attacked such writers as Baudelaire, Ibsen, Tolstoy, and Zola as degenerates, discovered evidence of madness in their works. "Who but a 'decadent' would treat all these alike?" quipped Nicholas Butler, then a young professor at Columbia University. In the Nineties, Shaw's *The Sanity of Art* and A. E. Hake's *Regeneration: A Reply to Max Nordau* argued against Nordau's thesis.

[3] I have omitted William Morris and John Ruskin from the discussion, for though they are certainly a part of the movement they are at the same time apart from it since they were animated primarily by the desire to reform society's tastes for moral ends, believing not in "art for art's sake" but in art for society's sake.

much space here as the early verse of Yeats, whose work in the Nineties is associated with Aestheticism. In the Appendix, I have included selections from two works that inspired the English Aesthetes and Decadents (Pater's *Renaissance* and Huysmans' *A Rebours*), as well as two satires (one of Wilde and Lord Alfred Douglas, and one of *The Yellow Book*) which indicate late nineteenth-century attitudes toward the Aesthetes and Decadents.

Since no editor is infallible (one recalls the motto that Symons, as editor of *The Savoy* used in the July, 1896, number: *Ne Juppiter Quidem Omnibus Placet*—"Not even Jupiter pleases everybody") and since limitations of space are a major consideration, the reader may be disappointed by certain inclusions or omissions; to have included all that I wished would have resulted in a volume at least twice its present length.

In the preparation of this volume, several friends and colleagues generously offered their assistance whenever textual problems arose. To my colleagues in the City University of New York—namely, Konrad Gries, of Queens College; Gloria Glikin and Jules Gelernt, of Brooklyn College—I wish to express my gratitude. To John M. Munro, of the American University of Beirut, I am especially grateful for his careful reading of the Introduction (which remains my responsibility) and for enlightening me on several troublesome allusions in the text. I should also like to thank Miss Berenice Hoffman, of Random House, for her patience and helpfulness in the preparation of the manuscript.

The co-operation of the New York Public Library and the Butler Library of Columbia University in reproducing various works has saved me countless hours of tedious copying. And, finally, I am grateful to the Princeton University Library for providing me with a copy of the text of Aubrey Beardsley's *Venus and Tannhäuser*, which had been available only in a privately printed edition prior to its appearance in this volume.

KARL BECKSON

Brooklyn College,
The City University of New York,
November 1, 1965

CONTENTS

INTRODUCTION   XVII

John Barlas ❁

OBLIVION   1

THE MEMPHIAN TEMPLE   1

THE DANCING GIRL   2

BEAUTY'S ANADEMS   3

THE CAT-LADY   3

TERRIBLE LOVE   4

MY LADY'S BATH   4

Aubrey Beardsley ❁

THE BALLAD OF A BARBER   6

THE STORY OF VENUS AND TANNHÄUSER   9
   [with illustrations]

Max Beerbohm ❁

A DEFENCE OF COSMETICS   47

A LETTER TO THE EDITOR   63

DIMINUENDO   66

Olive Custance (Lady Alfred Douglas) ❀

PEACOCKS: A MOOD 74

THE MASQUERADE 75

HYACINTHUS 75

THE WHITE STATUE 76

STATUES 77

CANDLE-LIGHT 78

Lord Alfred Douglas ❀

APOLOGIA 79

TWO LOVES 80

IMPRESSION DE NUIT 82

REJECTED 83

ODE TO MY SOUL 85

THE DEAD POET 85

Ernest Dowson ❀

NUNS OF THE PERPETUAL ADORATION 87

NON SUM QUALIS ERAM BONAE SUB REGNO CYNARAE 88

O MORS! QUAM AMARA EST MEMORIA . . . 89

VILLANELLE OF SUNSET 90

EXTREME UNCTION 91

EXILE 92

BENEDICTIO DOMINI 93

SPLEEN 94

A LAST WORD 94

Michael Field ❀

FROM BAUDELAIRE 96

THE POET 96

A DANCE OF DEATH   97

LA GIOCONDA   100

A DYING VIPER   100

John Gray ❀

From SILVERPOINTS   101

On a Picture   102

Poem   102

A Crucifix   103

Parsifal Imitated from the French of Paul Verlaine   104

Femmes Damnées   104

The Barber   105

Le Voyage à Cythère   106

Mishka   108

Lionel Johnson ❀

THE CULTURED FAUN   110

THE CHURCH OF A DREAM   113

MYSTIC AND CAVALIER   114

TO A PASSIONIST   115

IN HONOREM DORIANI CREATORISQUE EIUS   116

THE DESTROYER OF A SOUL   118

THE DARK ANGEL   118

NIHILISM   120

A DECADENT'S LYRIC   121

Richard Le Gallienne ❀

From ENGLISH POEMS   122

To the Reader   122

The Décadent to His Soul   123

Beauty Accurst   125

Sunset in the City   126

A Ballad of London   127

THE BOOM IN YELLOW   128

Arthur Symons ✿

THE DECADENT MOVEMENT IN LITERATURE   134

EMMY   151

MAQUILLAGE   152

MORBIDEZZA   152

PROLOGUE: BEFORE THE CURTAIN   153

PROLOGUE: IN THE STALLS   154

TO A DANCER   154

LA MÉLINITE: MOULIN ROUGE   155

JAVANESE DANCERS   156

BY THE POOL AT THE THIRD ROSSES   157

HALLUCINATION: I   158

VIOLET: PRELUDE   158

From STÉPHANE MALLARMÉ: HÉRODIADE   159

PREFACE TO THE SECOND EDITION OF *Silhouettes:*
   Being a Word on Behalf of Patchouli   161

PREFACE TO THE SECOND EDITION OF *London Nights*   164

Oscar Wilde ✿

THE DECAY OF LYING: AN OBSERVATION   167

SALOMÉ   194
   [*with Beardsley's illustrations*]

PHRASES AND PHILOSOPHIES FOR THE USE OF
   THE YOUNG   238

SYMPHONY IN YELLOW   240

THE HARLOT'S HOUSE   241

IMPRESSION DU MATIN   242

HÉLAS!   242

Theodore Wratislaw ✿

From CAPRICES   244
   Opoponax   244

Satiety   245
Frangipani   245
Palm Sunday   246
From ORCHIDS   247

Orchids   247
White Lilies   247
Sonnet Macabre   248
Hothouse Flowers   248

William Butler Yeats ✿

THE LAKE ISLE OF INNISFREE   250

THE WHITE BIRDS   251

ROSA MUNDI   252

TO THE ROSE UPON THE ROOD OF TIME   252

O'SULLIVAN RUA TO MARY LAVELL   253

THE SECRET ROSE   254

THE SONG OF WANDERING AENGUS   255

AEDH WISHES FOR THE CLOTHS OF HEAVEN   256

APPENDIX

Walter Pater:
From STUDIES IN THE HISTORY OF THE RENAISSANCE   258

Joris-Karl Huysmans:
From AGAINST THE GRAIN   270

Robert Smythe Hichens:
From THE GREEN CARNATION   281

The Second Coming of Arthur
[a satire of *The Yellow Book*]   294

BIOGRAPHICAL NOTES   297

SELECTED BIBLIOGRAPHY   304

INTRODUCTION

Oh Wilde, Verlaine, and Baudelaire,
their lips were wet with wine;
Oh poseur, pimp, and libertine! Oh
cynic, sot, and swine!
Oh voteries of velvet vice! . . . Oh
gods of light divine!

ROBERT SERVICE

When *The Yellow Book* appeared in April, 1894, a "universal howl" went up, wrote John Lane, its publisher, because of Beardsley's cover and title page designs. The London *Times* decried Beardsley's efforts as "repulsive and insolent" and labeled the entire enterprise "a combination of English rowdyism and French lubricity," despite the fact that such contributors as Henry James, Edmund Gosse, and George Saintsbury—little known as rowdies or libertines— provided proper balance to Beardsley and Beerbohm. Reacting to the latter's "Defence of Cosmetics," the *Westminster Gazette* clamored for an "act of Parliament to make this kind of thing illegal." In the United States, the prominent literary journal *The Critic,* heading its initial review "A Yellow Impertinence," called *The Yellow Book* "the Oscar Wilde of periodicals,"[1] and later referred to a subsequent

[1] Wilde, furious at not being invited to contribute to *The Yellow Book,* wrote to Lord Alfred Douglas on the appearance of the first number: "It is dull and loathsome: A great failure—I am so glad."

number as "A Yellow Bore," both "indecent and dull." By February, 1895, *The Critic*, its hostility increasing, declared that the fourth number pandered to "depraved tastes." [2] Though for much of the press the daring of *The Yellow Book* was interpreted as a deliberate and dangerous assault upon respected codes of decency, for *Punch*, less inclined to hysteria, this newest expression of Decadence provided comic inspiration for doggerel verse.

Not since the publication of Swinburne's *Poems and Ballads* (1866), attacked for its paganism and satanism, had there been such a sensation in the literary world. Swinburne had been charged with perversity, unwholesomeness, and morbidity—terms later flung at the Aesthetes and Decadents, who wore them as badges of their sensitivity and superiority. In this they had been instructed by their counterparts in France, who declared that the bourgeoisie was not only their natural enemy but also their sport, for in order to demonstrate their moral superiority, they would have to shock and dazzle the dull and muddy mettled middle classes—*épater le bourgeois*.[3] For a brilliant exponent of the pose, the English needed only to turn to Théophile Gautier (1811–72), who, more than any other figure of the nineteenth century, had

---

[2] In 1897, *The Critic*, commenting on the apparent suicide of Hubert Crackanthorpe, a contributor to *The Yellow Book*, wrote that it was not "surprised": "No young man, or old one, for that matter, could write such morbid, loathsome stories as he wrote and have a sane mind. He was the most pronounced type of the decadent. . . . There is, after all, a good deal of truth in some of Nordau's theories. A man must have a diseased mind who finds pleasure in writing of diseased morals."

[3] In 1894, *The Chameleon*, a journal with distinctly homosexual preoccupations, appeared in England, with Wilde and Lord Alfred Douglas as contributors. Its first number was its last. In an anonymous essay titled "On the Appreciation of Trifles," the writer argues: ". . . if the average Philistine were to be civilized and were suddenly to become enamoured of the beauty of those trifles that today are the exclusive enjoyment of the artist, we should feel the loss of his quaint antics very keenly. It would be very sad if we were to lose that great delight to which I alluded earlier: it would be very sad if there were no one left to shock." (See Wilde's "Phrases and Philosophies for the Use of the Young.")

publicized the idea of "art for art's sake"—*l'art pour l'art*[4] —and who had developed shocking as a fine art.

At the age of nineteen, Gautier attended the stormy premiere of Hugo's anticlassical drama *Hernani* (1830) dressed in a bright pink waistcoat, to which he later ironically attributed his fame as a young man. He was, however, not in complete sympathy with Hugo's belief in art for progress' sake. Gautier felt that Hugo, like other leading Romantics, such as Vigny and Lamartine, was debasing art by lending his pen to humanitarian causes. In the introduction to his second volume of poems, *Albertus* (1832), he wrote: "In general, when a thing becomes useful, it ceases to be beautiful," an idea he developed in the celebrated preface to his novel *Mademoiselle de Maupin* (1835), which advanced the idea that art was concerned only with itself in opposition to the idea of *l'art utile* held by political radicals and bourgeois writers. In an attempt to force a cleavage between art and social reform, he contended that beauty and usefulness were mutually exclusive:

> *Nothing is really beautiful unless it is useless; everything useful is ugly, for it expresses a need and the needs of man are ignoble and disgusting, like his poor weak nature. The most useful place in a house is the lavatory.*

As the foremost inspiration in the "Aesthetic Movement," Gautier established what was to become a central concept of Parnassianism: the supremacy of form. In his *Victor Hugo* (1835), he announced that the difference between a block of stone and a statue lay in its form, that the poet, too, was a sculptor, for he carved ideas and images out of words. The separation of form from content was, he contended, incomprehensible, for "Une belle forme est une belle idée."

By stressing the analogy with the plastic arts, Gautier attempted to make poetry objective and impersonal. In his poem "L'Art," which he added to his 1858 edition of *Emaux*

---

[4] First used in 1804 by writers to indicate disinterestedness in art, a concept which the German philosopher Kant had expressed as "purposiveness without purpose." By the late 1820's, however, it designated a movement which expressed hostility to the intrusion of moral, political, and social ideas in art.

et camées (*Enamels and Cameos*), he issued a manifesto urging poets to avoid easy rhythms and to forge hard, clear lines. Only an art purified of irrelevant intrusions of morality and social-political ideas could resist time.[5] Spontaneity, he cautioned, was the reckless outpouring of emotion without suitable control, a fault he noted in the Romantics. Art required the chisel and the file.

To achieve the impression of hardness and clarity, Gautier employed such images as exquisitely carved cameos, porcelains, marble statues, and gems. The lapidary quality of his verse was sufficiently distinctive and attractive to influence both the French and English Parnassians.[6] To preserve artistic purity and autonomy, Gautier employed what the Romantics had called *transposition d'art*, by which poetry, for example, attempted to suggest the effects produced by the other arts. Sonnets were called pastels; and pastels sonnets. Thus, in *Emaux et camées*, "Symphonie en blanc majeur" is designed to suggest a musical composition.[7]

Though the English Parnassians agreed with Gautier that

[5] The English Parnassian Arthur O'Shaugnessy was later to write:

> What is eternal? What escapes decay?
> A certain, faultless, matchless, deathless line
>   Curving consummate . . .

[6] Théodore de Banville (1823–91), who titled a volume of poems *Améthystes* (1862), announced in his *Petit traité de poésie française* (1872) that the sharply defined image should be the poet's major concern; that poetry was "at the same time music, statuary, painting, and eloquence"; and that poets should return to older fixed forms of verse, such as the ballade, rondeau, and triolet. Influenced by Banville, Austin Dobson, whose free translation of Gautier's "L'Art" provided the English Parnassians with a manifesto, titled a series of poems "A Case of Cameos" (1876) and in 1893 published *Proverbs in Porcelain*. Like Andrew Lang, Edmund Gosse, and W. E. Henley, Dobson followed Banville's example in using the older French fixed forms.

[7] The influence of *transposition d'art* is apparent in the American painter Whistler, who painted "harmonies" and "nocturnes." When he contributed an illustration to the second number of *The Yellow Book* titled "Symphony in White," the critic for the *Saturday Review* wanted to know why the title should be used for a picture with so many colors. Whistler replied: "And does he then believe that a Symphony in F contains no other note, but shall be a continued repetition of F, F, F? . . . Fool!" (See Wilde's "Symphony in Yellow.")

form and craft were of primary importance, the doctrine of *l'art pour l'art* was alien to their temperaments. Essentially moral in their attitude toward art, they adopted the poetic fashions and ignored the slogans, for the aestheticism they were attracted to did not imply hostility to the bourgeoisie. They wished to avoid the unrestrained verbal fleshliness of Swinburne, who, like the earlier Spasmodics, valued spontaneity. Traditional form and restraint, the English Parnassians agreed, were suitable to a British man of letters, an ideal expressed by Dobson in "In After Days," which he regarded as his epitaph: "He held his pen in trust/To Art, not serving shame or lust."

Dobson's declaration of purity was an attempt to dissociate himself from French Decadence as well as from "The Fleshly School of Poetry" in England. The latter phrase, coined by Robert Buchanan in an article which appeared in the *Contemporary Review* in 1871, had ignited a controversy that involved Dante Gabriel Rossetti, one of the primary targets of the moralists. As leader of the Pre-Raphaelites, Rossetti was attacked for his fleshliness in verse ("fleshly all over from the roots of his hair to the tips of his toes"), his lack of wholesomeness, his erotic daydreams and for his aestheticism. Preferring medievalism to materialism, he was both poet and painter who, like Gautier, saw the possibility of combining the arts. Though he held ideas somewhat similar to those of the French Aesthetes, he was convinced that subject was more important than mere form and that *l'art pour l'art* was a meaningless doctrine. The sensuality of Rossetti and other aesthetic poets, Buchanan raged, was "shooting its ulcerous roots deeper and deeper, blotching more and more the fair surface of things."[8] For many young Aesthetes, however, Rossetti, despite his hostility to Aestheticism and artifice, provided inspiration rather than discoloration.

Though the Pre-Raphaelites were far from being apostles of amorality in art, they were regarded by their later worshippers as the archetypes of anti-Philistinism. Rossetti, the

[8] In 1887 Buchanan, revising his estimate, declared that "those who assert that Rossetti loved Art 'for its own sake' know nothing of his method."

cloistered dreamer devoted to beauty, appealed to those young writers who saw nineteenth-century science and progress, industrialism and prosperity as forces destructive to the imagination.[9] Yeats considered him a "subconscious influence" on the Rhymers' Club (1890–95), which included Ernest Dowson, Lionel Johnson, Arthur Symons, Richard Le Gallienne, and Yeats himself, who had helped to found it.

Buchanan's other major target in his attack was Swinburne, who deserves more than anyone before him the distinction of being called "the first Decadent in England." Already hailed by an anonymous reviewer for the London *Saturday Review* as "the libidinous laureate of a pack of satyrs," Swinburne was amused by Buchanan's fulminations over *Poems and Ballads* and the evil influence of Baudelaire, whom Buchanan referred to as "a fifth-rate *littérateur*" and "the godfather of the modern Fleshly School."

When Gautier died, Swinburne was asked to contribute to a memorial volume, *Le Tombeau de Gautier* (1873; the only other English contributor was John Payne, a minor Parnassian poet). Swinburne's contribution—which Tennyson called "poisonous"—was a sonnet in praise of Gautier's novel *Mademoiselle de Maupin*, about which he wrote: "This is the golden book of spirit and sense,/The writ of beauty . . ." The novel, which Mario Praz has called "the apologia of lesbian love" and "the Bible of the Decadence," reveals Gautier's love of physical beauty and his interest in sexual perversion. (Gautier himself took up weight-lifting and spent much time in the Greek rooms at the Louvre.) The Chevalier d'Albert, its hero, suffers from a feeling of spiritual impotence and ennui. In his craving for the impossible— which Gautier believed was a central characteristic of the decadent sensibility—he yearns to be a woman in order to taste new experiences. At the estate of his mistress, d'Albert falls in love with a handsome young man who he suspects is a woman in disguise. The "young man" is, of course, Mademoiselle de Maupin, who confesses to her epistolary confi-

---

[9] In a famous pronouncement, the Pre-Raphaelite painter Burne-Jones declared, "The more materialistic Science becomes, the more angels shall I paint."

dant that she cannot love either a man or a woman completely. Before leaving the estate, she appears in d'Albert's
room. Disrobing before d'Albert, she poses like a Greek goddess at the Louvre; enthralled by the perfection of her body,
he studies her as though she were a work of art, reluctant to
take his eyes from the vision. After a night of love, she leaves
d'Albert, but not before spending some time with his mistress
as well.[10]

Though Swinburne's *Poems and Ballads* was universally
condemned—*The Athanaeum* said that Swinburne was "un-
clean for the sake of uncleanness" and a letter from Dublin
threatened him with castration—it did not suffer legal prosecution as had Baudelaire's *Les Fleurs du mal*. In the first
essay on Baudelaire to appear in England, Swinburne in 1862
defended him by taking the position of *l'art pour l'art*, thus
becoming the first English exponent of the idea: "The critical
students there in France, as well as here . . . seem to have
pretty well forgotten that a poet's business is presumably to
write good verses, and by no means to redeem the age and
remould society." Countering the charge of immorality, to
which Baudelaire had been subjected in France—and to
which *Poems and Ballads* would be subjected later—Swinburne saw "not one poem of the *Fleurs du mal* which has not
a distinct and vivid background of morality to it," despite
the fact that it was, admittedly, poetry of "strange disease
and sin." Most Englishmen, including Swinburne, did not
grasp the complexities of Baudelaire, but they acknowledged
his power and originality. Though Swinburne believed he

---

[10] In his early twenties, Swinburne, under the spell of Gautier's novel,
wrote *The Chronicle of Tebaldeo Tebaldei*, a tale of the Borgias in
which Swinburne totally disregarded the Victorian conviction that the
primary function of art was moral instruction. In addition to his fascination with perverse and androgynous figures, Swinburne was pre-
occupied with the theme of the fatal woman—the *femme fatale*.
Mario Praz has pointed out in *The Romantic Agony* that the Romantics, such as Byron, were absorbed with the idea of the fatal man, but
from mid-century the image of the destructive woman dominates much
of the work written by the Aesthetes and Decadents, as indication,
some critics believe, of the change from masculine assertion to decadent passivity.

was doing in English what Baudelaire had done in French, T. S. Eliot has remarked that "had Swinburne known anything about vice or sin, he would not have had so much fun out of it." [11]

The most perceptive essay on Baudelaire in the century was unquestionably Gautier's, which appeared as the "Notice" to the 1868 edition of *Les Fleurs du mal.* As A. E. Carter states in his important study, *The Idea of Decadence in French Literature* (1958), Gautier was in reality summing up his own work while discussing Baudelaire's, for he had anticipated virtually all that one may find in *Les Fleurs du mal.* Gautier perceived that Baudelaire's concern with artifice —which had developed into a cult by mid-century—was of metaphysical significance—that man in a state of nature was evil and that virtue, since it was artificial, was good. In his "Eloge du maquillage" ("Praise of Cosmetics"), Baudelaire had written:

> *All that is beautiful and noble is the result of reason and calculation. Crime, the taste for which the human animal draws from the womb of his mother, is natural in its origins. Virtue, on the contrary, is artificial and supernatural, since gods and prophets were necessary in every epoch and every nation to teach virtue to bestial humanity, and man alone would have been powerless to discover it. Evil is done effortlessly and naturally by fate; the good is always the product of some art.*

The employment of make-up, therefore, results in the transcendence of nature:

> *Woman performs a kind of duty when she endeavors to appear magical and supernatural; she should dazzle men and charm them; she is an idol who should be covered with gold in order to be worshiped. She should therefore borrow from all the arts the means of rising above nature in order to better subjugate all hearts and impress all minds.*

[11] Swinburne was, however, not unaware of his own posturing:

> Some singers indulging in curses,
>   Though sinful, have splendidly sinned;
> But my would-be malefient verses
>   Are nothing but wind.

Similarly, the Decadents' fascination with such drugs as hashish and opium and their preference for absinthe—the official beverage of the movement—enabled the ego to transcend itself and thus improve its natural state.

The artist, too, must proceed from nature to a transcendent reality in order to invest his art with spiritual beauty. For Baudelaire, unlike the earlier Romantics, nature was not an inspiration to his creative genius but the material from which to forge new images; it existed only because it had its origins in the spiritual world. Under the influence of the mystic Swedenborg, Baudelaire adopted the Platonic idea of the universal analogy between the natural and spiritual worlds and Swedenborg's belief that forms, numbers, colors, and perfumes in both worlds were reciprocal. The latter idea was not new, for there had been experiments with synaesthesia in the previous century.[12] Baudelaire's sonnet "Correspondences," which had an enormous influence on the Symbolist movement, sets forth the doctrine that nature is a "forest of symbols" and that perfumes, colors, and sounds "answer one another." The imitation of nature was to be avoided; the poet must interpret the vast storehouse of symbols which revealed the spiritual world, the source of all beauty. Asked to write nature poetry, Baudelaire replied in a famous letter to Fernand Desnoyers in 1855 that he was incapable of being moved by vegetables, adding, to indicate his preference for artifice, that he preferred to swim in a bathtub rather than in the sea and that a music box pleased him more than a nightingale.

A believer in original sin, Baudelaire had contempt for humanitarian ideals and the nineteenth-century faith in progress. As a dandy, he cultivated a cold, precise exterior which masked intense suffering brought about by a perverse will. He said that Milton's Satan was just such a figure; and indeed Baudelaire's admirers were attracted to the Satanic elements of his dandyism. In his vision of man and nature, Baudelaire inspired the cult of artifice, a challenge to Rousseau's cult of nature, to which most Romantics subscribed. In this connection, Carter describes the paradox of the revolt:

[12] See G. L. Van Roosbroeck's *The Legend of the Decadents* (New York, 1927), pp. 21–39.

> The decadents, even when they refused to live by Rousseau's gospel, never denied its truth. They were like unfrocked priests celebrating the Black Mass—perfectly aware that their cult was blasphemous. They accepted Nature as their norm, and primitivism as synonymous with virtue. They admitted, either tacitly or enthusiastically (depending on the individual writer's desire to shock or astonish) that anything different, anything civilized or "artificial" was a priori unnatural and depraved. From the very beginning, decadent sensibility is thus self-consciously perverse; and its cult of the artificial distinguishes it sharply from Romanticism, whatever traces of depravity may be found in certain Romantics.

Indulgence in the abnormal became, moreover, "proof of man's superiority to natural law." The exercise of individual will thus superseded adherence to universal principles. The Romantic—emotional and flamboyant—pursued an ideal love rooted in the natural relations of the sexes; the Decadent—intellectual and austere—sought new sensations in forbidden love, for sexual depravity revealed a desire to transcend the normal and the natural.

Gautier himself did not identify artifice with Decadence, though he had suggested as much in *Mademoiselle de Maupin*. He was, like many Decadents, absorbed by paganism and exoticism (such as one finds in *Une Nuit de Cleopâtre*), which for Baudelaire held no interest. Baudelaire did, however, see that modernism, artifice, and Decadence were intimately related. As a Decadent, he envisioned the decay of civilization and the horrifying, seductive evils of men in a style which, as Gautier has described, contains

> the morbidly rich tints of decomposition, the tones of mother-of-pearl which freeze stagnant waters, the roses of consumption, the pallor of chlorosis, the hateful bilious yellows, the leaden gray of pestilential fogs, the poisoned and metallic greens smelling of sulphide of arsenic, . . . the bitumens blacked and browned in the depths of hell; and all that gamut of intensified colors, correspondent to autumn, to the setting of sun, to overripe fruit, and the last hours of civilization.[18]

[18] In "Langeur," Verlaine, regarded as a leader of the Decadents at the end of the Second Empire (1852–1870), announced: "Je suis l'Empire

All the themes and images which had absorbed the Decadents from Gautier on are to be found in the novel that was to have a profound effect upon the English Decadents—Joris-Karl Huysmans' *A Rebours* (1884), usually translated as *Against the Grain*, which Arthur Symons called "the breviary of the Decadence." Its sexually perverse hero, Des Esseintes, like many fictional Decadents, is an aristocrat, the last of his tainted line, who suffers from severe neurosis, later complicated by indigestion, for which he takes—with considerable pleasure—enemas to provide nourishment. His genius and delight is to cultivate an interest in artifice and the abnormal. Thus, in his strange house outside of Paris, where he has secluded himself from a hated bourgeois society, he becomes absorbed in the authors of the Latin Decadence, and exotic gems, diseased flowers and monstrous orchids that look artificial.[14] Suffering from boredom, he seeks new sensations which are *à rebours*: he builds a "mouth organ" which instead of musical tones releases various liquors in symphonic arrangements to suit changing moods; he collects and mounts precious gems on the back of an enormous turtle that dazzles the eye.

In "The Decadent Movement in Literature" (1893), Symons wrote that Huysmans "has concentrated all that is delicately depraved, all that is beautifully, curiously poisonous, in modern art." Barbey d'Aurevilly, the dandy whom

à la fin de la Décadence." For an attempt—perhaps satirical—to imitate Baudelaire's images without grasping their function, see below, Michael Field's "From Baudelaire."

[14] Though Baudelaire's *Les Fleurs du mal* is largely responsible for the strange, exotic flowers that grow in decadent literature—hothouses and orchids becoming central images of the Decadents' disdain of nature—Gautier's *Fortunio* (1837) anticipates both Baudelaire's and Huysmans' works. The hero, who resembles Des Esseintes, lives in a windowless house with a greenhouse of tropical plants in the courtyard. In 1878, George Moore's feeble attempt to imitate Baudelaire resulted in *Flowers of Passion*, which one critic has called "infantile diabolism." Maurice Maeterlinck titled a volume of verse *Les Serres chaudes* (1890), or "Hothouses," and in the Nineties Theodore Wratislaw wrote highly derivative decadent verse with such titles as "Orchids" and "Hothouse Flowers" (see below). See also Symons' "Violet," which restates the decadent devotion to the hothouse.

Mario Praz calls "a Holy Father of the Decadent Movement," wrote of *A Rebours*: "After such a book, it only remains for the author to choose between the muzzle of a pistol or the foot of the cross." Like Des Esseintes, who at the end of the novel returns to bourgeois society to embrace the Church, Huysmans became a devout Catholic.

Though young Aesthetes found in Rossetti and in Keats, whom the Pre-Raphaelites had "discovered," a devotion to beauty and to the world of the imagination, and in Swinburne an extraordinary sensibility which had dramatically widened the area of subject matter in Victorian literature, it was in *Studies in the History of the Renaissance* (1873) by Walter Pater, the Oxford don, that they discovered their "golden book." The famous "Conclusion" talked of the flux of life and of the necessity of experiencing with intensity the constantly fleeting impressions: "To burn always with this hard, gemlike flame, to maintain this ecstasy, is success in life." And the equally ambiguous: "Not the fruit of experience, but experience itself, is the end." And finally, what earned Pater a reputation as the foremost Aesthete of his day: "For art comes to you professing frankly to give nothing but the highest quality to your moments as they pass, and simply for those moments' sake."

Pater's subtle, evocative prose, with its sinuous ambiguities and attention to strangeness, had brought to criticism a new sensibility. His admirers saw in *The Renaissance* an unmistakable manifestation of Decadence: in his essay on Leonardo da Vinci, for example, Pater writes that the artist's life was one of "brilliant sins and exquisite moments" and finds that in his work "the fascination of corruption penetrates in every touch of its exquisitely finished beauty." The famous description of Leonardo's *La Gioconda* is Pater's impression of that corruption. Wilde is reported by Yeats to have said of *The Renaissance*: "It is my golden book. I never travel without it; but it is the very flower of decadence: the last trumpet should have sounded the moment it was written." Arthur Symons, who had become friendly with Pater in the late 1880's and to whom he dedicated his volume of poems *Days and Nights* (1889), wrote that *The Renaissance* seemed to him "to be the most beautiful book of prose in our literature. Nothing in it is left to inspiration: but it is all inspired. Here is a writer who, like Baudelaire, would better nature. . . . An almost oppressive quiet, a quiet which seems to exhale an atmosphere heavy with the odour of tropical flowers, broods over these pages; a subdued light shadows them."

Pater became known as the apostle of art for art's sake— he had unfortunately used the term in his "Conclusion"— with all the misunderstandings which that term is heir to. He was, however, concerned with moral development through art, and was not—as some of his professed disciples were— opposed to moral considerations in art. Aware that he was misinterpreted by those who claimed him as their spokesman, Pater removed the "Conclusion" from the second edition (1877), but restored it in the third edition (1888) after he believed that his position had been made clear in his novel *Marius the Epicurean* (1885). In restoring the "Conclusion," he wrote:

> *This brief "Conclusion" was omitted in the second edition of this book, as I conceived it might possibly mislead some of those young men into whose hands it might fall. On the whole, I have thought it best to reprint it here, with some slight changes which bring it closer to my original meaning. I have dealt more fully in* Marius the Epicurean *with the thoughts suggested by it.*

Pater was indeed far less decadent than his disciples. When someone once tried to convince him of the excellence of Huysmans and his style, he is reported to have said, "Beastly man!" One of Pater's unwelcome disciples was George Moore, who in 1888 sent Pater a copy of his *Confessions of a Young Man*, a semi-autobiographical account of his adventures in Paris during the 1870's, which Moore seems to have envisioned as the English equivalent of Huysmans' *A Rebours*.[15] In a letter to a friend, Moore referred to his *Confessions* as "satiric," but whether it is a satire of the Decadence or of himself he does not say. Pater, too, re-

---

[15] In the French edition of the *Confessions*, Moore declared: "I am effeminate, morbid, perverse. But above all perverse. Everything that is perverse fascinates me."

garded it as satirical, but he subtly perceived in a letter to Moore, who published it in a preface to the *Confessions*, that the pretense was too thin to escape detection: " 'Thou com'st in such a questionable shape!' I feel inclined to say on finishing your book; 'shape' morally, I mean; not in reference to style . . ."

Moore, though a professed Paterian, was more bewitched by the French. Staggering under the influence of Gautier and Baudelaire, Moore had published *Flowers of Passion* in 1878, which included among its "pale passion flowers" [16] the "Ode to a Dead Body," containing the memorable line: "Poor breasts! whose nipples sins alone have fed . . ." Attacked as immoral, the volume was withdrawn by the publisher. In 1881, he published *Pagan Poems*, which contained—not unexpectedly—"The Hermaphrodite" (after Gautier and Swinburne) and "Chez Moi":

*My white Angora cats are lying fast
Asleep, closely curled together, and my snake,
My many-coloured Python,[17] is awake
Crawling about after a two-months' fast.*

Characteristically, Moore assumed the appropriate poses which he thought might startle his readers—and perhaps himself. Having been dazzled by the "grand barbaric face" of Gautier, he was then attracted to the satanic Baudelaire, whom he little understood:

"Les Fleurs du Mal!" beautiful flowers, beautiful in sublime decay, What great record is yours, and were Hell a reality how many souls would we find wreathed with your poisonous blossoms. The village maiden goes to her Faust; the children of the nineteenth century go to you, O Baudelaire, and having tasted of your deadly delight all hope of repentance is vain. Flowers, beautiful in your sublime decay, I press you to my lips . . .

[16] See Olive Custance's "Candlelight" and Wilde's "The Decay of Lying," which talks of a club of "Tired Hedonists" who wear faded roses in their button-holes. The weariness of the Decadent is his mark of sophistication and moral superiority: it is both cause and effect of his quest for new experiences, preferably abnormal.

[17] The pet Python—named "Jack"—appears in the *Confessions*.

By the late eighties he had abandoned his fastidiously cultivated decadence, his devotion to Pater, and had become a disciple of Zola.[18]

The Rhymers' Club, Yeats tells us in his autobiography, "looked consciously to Pater for [its] philosophy"; elsewhere, Yeats, paraphrasing Pater, says that the Rhymers "wished to express life at its intense moments and at these moments alone." [19] Among the Rhymers, Lionel Johnson was perhaps the only poet who grasped Pater's intent, for, in temperament, he had many affinities with the "Sage" at Oxford. As an undergraduate, Johnson had met Pater and had spent much time in his company. Writing to a friend in 1889, he reported that he "lunched with Pater, dined with Pater, smoked with Pater, walked with Pater, went to mass with Pater, and fell in love with Pater." Johnson later wrote that Pater—far from being the poseur or the effeminate Aesthete depicted by popular journalists and satirists—was "never more characteristically inspired than in writing of things hieratic, ascetic, almost monastic." On Pater's death in 1894, Johnson wrote:

> Stern is the faith of art, right stern, and he
> Loved her severity.

Johnson shared Pater's attraction to church ritual, which for both was an intensely aesthetic though not unreligious experience, for ritual provided order and symbol.[20] Whether in religious ritual or in a work of art, as Ian Fletcher states in his monograph, Pater sought "through intense experiences the unification of personality" and ultimately moral perfection.

Few of these qualities are to be found in Pater's most

[18] Zola and other realists of the period were habitually referred to as "Decadents" because of the subject matter of their fiction and their insistence that it be free of moral judgment.

[19] In *The Romantic 90's*, Richard Le Gallienne recalls that the young men of the time were urging one another "to burn with a hard gemlike flame."

[20] Johnson's "favorite phrase," Yeats says, was "Life is ritual," which he conducted with "great dignity of manner."

vocal and perhaps most unwelcome disciple, Oscar Wilde, who sought fame by offering himself as a willing object of satire. When Wilde published *The Picture of Dorian Gray* (1891)—part of which had been serialized the year before —it provided Pater with an opportunity to publicly disavow himself from the extreme aestheticism expressed in the Preface and in the novel itself. In the Preface, Wilde had listed— whether seriously or whimsically—such apothegms as "No artist has ethical sympathies" and "All art is quite useless." In the novel, which the London *Daily Chronicle* called "a tale spawned from the leprous literature of the French Décadents, a poisonous book," Dorian Gray is the extraordinarily beautiful young man, an *homme fatal* who attracts others— both male and female—and destroys them. "Made out of ivory and rose leaves" with lips of scarlet, Dorian is counseled by Lord Henry Wotton, his aristocratic, dandified, evil genius: "Be always searching for new sensations. Be afraid of nothing. . . . A New Hedonism—that is what our century wants. You might be its visible symbol." Filled with such distortions from Pater and familiar motifs from Huysmans (Dorian, fascinated by *A Rebours,* attempts to emulate Des Esseintes' love of artifice), Wilde's novel owes its curious tenets and its conventional ending to the flawed sensibility of its author. In reviewing it, Pater wrote:

> *Clever always, this book seems intended to set forth anything but a homely philosophy of life for the middle-class— a kind of dainty Epicurean theory, rather—yet fails, to some degree, in this, and one can see why. A true Epicureanism aims at a complete though harmonious development of man's entire organism. To lose the moral sense therefore, for instance, the sense of sin and righteousness, as Mr. Wilde's heroes are bent on doing as speedily, as completely as they can, is to lose, or lower, organisation, to become less complex, to pass from a higher to a lower degree of development.*

Pater's "hedonism"—aesthetic, intellectual pleasure—was concerned with the "expansion and refinement of the power of perception." This, Wilde never grasped, nor did he attempt to, for in the isolation of his own genius, he was concerned with the expansion of his public personality. His originality—aside from *The Importance of Being Earnest,* which is his masterpiece—lay in his clever manipulation of other men's ideas rather than in his personal vision and voice.

The term "Decadence" is commonly associated with the 1890's, but it is an error to assume that the decade was "yellow"; indeed, the color white—symbol of purity, which, despite their protestations, the Decadents yearned for—dominates the literature of the period. Though the English Aesthetes and Decadents were a relatively small group, they were vocal and colorful. Many of the Rhymers, for example, were reviewers for some of the leading periodicals and newspapers, in some cases capturing the literary pages of the publication for the purpose of logrolling.[21] Many Aesthetes and Decadents actively contributed to the numerous aesthetic or semi-aesthetic periodicals with such titles as *The Hobby Horse*, *The Rose Leaf*, *The Butterfly*, *The Dome*, *The Pageant*, and *The Chameleon*—the forerunners of our "little magazines" today—presenting for an interested public the new trends in art and literature.

Early in the Nineties, there developed simultaneously with the fad of Decadence a counter-decadent movement centered chiefly in the editorial offices of *The National Observer*, where Henley, its editor as well as Parnassian poet,[22] gathered about him a number of energetic young men whom Max Beerbohm dubbed "the Henley Regatta." The activist pose in turn became as frenetic as its decadent counterpart. Another counter-trend to the Decadence, though not conceived as such, was the Irish literary renaissance, given impetus by Yeats and his fellow Irishmen in the Rhymers' Club who emphasized the use of Irish myth and legend in litera-

---

[21] Debates over the practice of logrolling culminated in a series of articles which appeared in the *Westminster Gazette* at the end of 1894.

[22] Henley, like Robert Louis Stevenson, dabbled in French fixed forms but had only scorn for *l'art pour l'art*. His experimentation with new subject matter convinced Symons that he was part of the Decadence (see "The Decadent Movement in Literature"). Henley's Parnassianism and aggressively masculine pose are discussed in Hoxie Neal Fairchild's *Religious Trends in English Poetry*, v. 5 (1962), in a chapter wittily entitled "Chiefly Hearty, Slightly Arty."

ture to revivify Ireland's great heritage and divorce itself from English culture. Though Yeats, in the Nineties, urged his fellow Rhymers to write "pure poetry"—suggesting an adherence to *l'art pour l'art*—he himself wrote verse with strong political overtones and entered the Irish revival with the purpose of transforming existing poetic practice. Both Aesthete and Activist, Yeats tirelessly organized and reorganized Irish literary societies in both London and Dublin to advance the national cause.[23]

The publishing house which achieved fame in the decade as the publisher of *The Yellow Book*, the anthologies of the Rhymers' Club, the works of Le Gallienne, Wilde, and John Gray was the Bodley Head, founded by the enterprising John Lane and Elkin Mathews. Named after Sir Thomas Bodley, the famed founder of the library at Oxford University, whose head appeared on the sign over the entrance of the shop in Vigo Street, the Bodley Head published its first book—Le Gallienne's *Volumes in Folio*—in 1889. Lane and Mathews found that by purchasing "remainders" of fine paper and printing small editions they could make profits out of poetry. The slender, elongated shape of John Gray's *Silverpoints* (1893) with its exquisite cover design, was a typical example of the economical use of available paper for which the Bodley Head was noted. As the leading publisher of well-known Aesthetes and Decadents, it figured prominently in the satires of the period, and indeed the Bodley Head wisely drew attention to itself by publishing such volumes as Owen Seaman's *Battle of the Bays* (1896), a collection of satires and parodies of the Bodley Head poets. Though many respectable authors were also on the publisher's list, the Decadence and the Bodley Head were synonomous in the public mind. Thus, one satire began:

> *Tell me, where is Fancy bred?*
> *Certes, near the Bodley Head.*

[23] The apparent paradox of the Aesthete who is also an Activist is not uncommon in the period; though some wrote of ennui, lassitude, disillusionment, and disengagement, at the same time they might praise the virtue of energy, the glory of nationalism, or the mystique of manhood. Few writers committed themselves to only one cause.

> In the Vigo Street domain,
> In the shadow of the Lane.

And when The Yellow Book appeared, Punch, to the annoyance of some Bodley Head authors, scoffed, "Uncleanliness is next to Bodliness."

The Yellow Book, the inspiration of Henry Harland, its literary editor; Aubrey Beardsley, its art editor; and John Lane of the Bodley Head, is unquestionably the most famous of the aesthetic magazines of the Nineties, though not the best. Though Wilde was a "Bodley Head poet," Lane agreed with Harland and Beardsley, who grew to dislike Wilde intensely, that he should be excluded from participating in the venture. Rumors concerning his behavior had grown alarmingly, and Lane knew of one young boy in his own office who had become the object of Wilde's attentions. But Wilde, excluded from The Yellow Book, was ironically to be the cause of that journal's eventual death, for in 1895, when he became the object of prosecution after dropping his libel suit against Lord Alfred Douglas' father, the Marquis of Queensberry, who had called him a sodomist, he took with him to the arraignment a copy of a French novel in the traditionally suspect yellow paper cover. One newspaper ran the headline: "Arrest of Oscar Wilde: Yellow Book under his arm."

Katherine Mix, in her book A Study in Yellow: The Yellow Book and Its Contributors (1960), has told the story of the pressure on Lane to discharge Beardsley, who was, in the public mind, associated with Wilde, since he had done the shocking illustrations for Salomé. Concerned more with profits than with loyalty, Lane fired Beardsley. Harland, kept on, selected material calculated not to offend anyone. In April, 1897, exactly three years from the appearance of the first volume, The Yellow Book expired.

In London, during and after the Wilde debacle, the literary taverns where many Aesthetes and Decadents habitually met—the Café Royal and the Crown, where Dowson, Symons, Beardsley, Wilde, Lord Alfred Douglas, Beerbohm, Gray, and Wratislaw might be seen almost nightly—were now under the cloud of suspicion. It was said that "every suitcase in London was packed for instant flight." Many who knew Wilde went to Dieppe, a popular resort in the Nineties, to escape the unpleasantness of the entire proceeding.

In the summer of 1895 in Dieppe, Leonard Smithers, a former solicitor who had acquired a reputation as a publisher of erotica and who had had the courage to publish Arthur Symons' *London Nights* when no other publisher would touch it,[24] proposed to Symons that he edit a magazine that would be the rival of *The Yellow Book,* which, as Symons has written, "had by that time ceased to mark a movement and had come to be little more than a publisher's house magazine." Smithers, who had a keen eye for sensationalism, persuaded Symons, widely known as a spokesman for the Decadent Movement, to become literary editor; in turn, Symons suggested that Beardsley, in low spirits since his dismissal from *The Yellow Book,* be its art editor. The new magazine, named by Beardsley, was to be *The Savoy.* The title, accepted after considerable discussion, was a daring one, since the fashionable hotel of that name in London had been prominently mentioned in some of the most damaging testimony against Wilde in his trial for homosexuality.[25]

Symons managed to solicit contributions from such writers as Bernard Shaw (whose essay "On Going to Church" appeared in the first number), Joseph Conrad, and Ford Madox Hueffer,[26] while persuading many *Yellow Book* authors, such as Dowson, Yeats, Moore, and Crackanthorpe, to contribute to *The Savoy.* In the first number, which appeared in January, 1896, Symons, determined not to have the magazine, despite its title, associated in the public mind with Wilde, stated in the opening editorial comment:

[24] Symons referred to him as "my cynical publisher with the diabolical monocle."

[25] In 1897, after both *The Yellow Book* and *The Savoy* had ceased publication, Leonard Smithers, publisher of the latter journal, approached Beardsley with a proposal that he participate in a new journal to be called *The Peacock.* Beardsley wrote in December: "By all means bring forth the *Peacock.* I will contribute cover and what you will, and also be editor, that is if it is *quite agreed that Oscar Wilde contributes nothing to the magazine, anonymously, pseudonymously or otherwise."*

[26] Hueffer later changed his name to Ford Madox Ford.

> *We have no formulas and we desire no false unity of form*
> *or matter. We have not invented a new point of view. We*
> *are not Realists or Romanticists or Decadents. For us, all art*
> *is good which is good art. We hope to appeal to the tastes*
> *of the intelligent by not being original for originality's sake,*
> *or audacious for the sake of advertisement, or timid for the*
> *convenience of the elderly minded.*

The Savoy, which had a far less sensational debut than *The Yellow Book,* was received by the press with generally favorable notices.[27] (The *Sunday Times,* for example, called it a *Yellow Book* "redeemed of its puerilities.") Its success seemed assured: Beardsley was contributing his most striking and mature illustrations, and the literary contributions were consistently high. (From Pont Avon, France, Dowson wrote to Smithers: "It is a great and admirable institution the 'Savoy' and held in high esteem here and elsewhere. . . . May the hair of John Lane grow green with Envy!") Smithers decided to publish monthly instead of quarterly.

The death of *The Savoy,* however, came rapidly, the result of late Victorian prudery and the lack of adequate public support. Smith and Son, the company which controlled distribution of most magazines in railway book stalls, objected to an illustration, previously unpublished, by William Blake, *Antaeus Setting Virgil and Dante upon the Verge of Cocytus,* which appeared in an article by Yeats. Largely because the company banned the magazine, Smithers found himself cut off from a major outlet. The concluding number of *The Savoy*—its most famous, perhaps—appeared in December, 1896, entirely written by Symons and illustrated by Beardsley. In "By Way of Epilogue," Symons concluded the magazine's career:

[27] *Punch,* as might be expected, parodied *The Savoy,* referring to it as *The Savoloy* (a kind of sausage) and introducing such contributors as Simple Symons, Mr. Weirdsley, and Max Mereboom: "There is not an article in the volume that one can put down without feeling the better and purer for it." And elsewhere in the parody: ". . . every mother should present it to her daughter, for it is bound to have an ennobling and purifying influence."

On the other hand, Richard Ellmann has recently written: "[*The Savoy*] was the first and only English magazine to expound and illustrate [the Symbolist] movement."

> *We are obliged to retire from existence on account of the too*
> *meagre support of our friends. Our first mistake was in giv-*
> *ing so much for so little money; our second, in abandoning*
> *a quarterly for a monthly issue. The action of Messrs. Smith*
> *and Son in refusing to place "The Savoy" on their bookstalls*
> *. . . was another misfortune. And then, worst of all, we as-*
> *sumed that there were many people in the world who really*
> *cared for art, and really for art's sake.*

The American *Chap-Book,* noting its end, referred to Symons as "playing the Hindoo widow and entombing himself
with the sad remains."

In the advertisements at the back of the final issue of *The*
Savoy, there appeared an announcement of a forthcoming
book to be published by Smithers, *The Decadent Movement*
in Literature, by Arthur Symons, who was in the process of
expanding his 1893 essay into book form. When the book
finally appeared in 1899, its title was changed to *The Sym-*
bolist Movement in Literature. In the latter part of the decade, Symons had been clarifying his thinking on Symbolism
and Decadence, perhaps under the influence of Yeats, who
had been his close friend since 1895. In the introduction
to *The Symbolist Movement,* which is dedicated to Yeats,
Symons attempted to rescue the term "Decadence" from the
journalists and satirists who had used and abused it to refer
to a way of life rather than to a style of literature:

> *It pleased some young men in various countries to call them-*
> *selves Decadents, with all the thrill of unsatisfied virtue mas-*
> *querading as uncomprehended vice. As a matter of fact, the*
> *term is in its place only when applied to style, to that in-*
> *genious deformation of the language, in Mallarmé, for in-*
> *stance. . . . No doubt perversity of form and perversity of*
> *matter are often found together, and, among the lesser men*
> *especially, experiment was carried far, not only in the direc-*
> *tion of style. But a movement which in this sense might be*
> *called Decadence could but have been straying aside from*
> *the main road of literature. Nothing, not even conventional*
> *virtue, is so provincial as conventional vice; and the desire*
> *to "bewilder the middle classes" is itself middle class. The*
> *interlude, half a mock-interlude, of Decadence, diverted the*
> *attention of the critics while something more serious was in*
> *preparation.*

This attitude had appeared earlier in an essay on George Meredith (1897), in which Symons wrote: "What Decadence, in literature, really means is that learned corruption of language by which style ceases to be organic, and becomes, in the pursuit of some new expressiveness or beauty, deliberately abnormal." But the confusion between the use of the term decadence to refer either to an artist's behavior or to his art persisted throughout the decade. In 1900, Andrew Lang, with some levity, described the typical Decadent:

> By kicking holes in his boots, crushing in his hat and avoiding soap, any young man may achieve a comfortable degree of sordidness, and then, if his verses are immaterial, and his life suicidal, he may regard himself as a Decadent indeed.

The blurring of the term was, to some extent, part of Symons' own doing, for he used it for both literary characters and authors: in his essay on the Decadent Movement, he describes Des Esseintes, hero of *A Rebours*, as "a typical Decadent." In another essay, Symons somewhat erroneously refers to Dowson as one who "without a certain sordidness in his surroundings was never quite comfortable, never quite himself," adding that the "curious love of the sordid" was a "common affectation of the modern decadent."

Yeats, however, looking back to his youth and recalling the unfortunate ends to which some of his friends came (early death, madness, and suicide), preferred to designate them as the "Tragic Generation." Le Gallienne, also recording his memories, called the decade "romantic." Both views account for the legendary quality of the period, for in the midst of the posing,[28] the epigrams, and the calculated shock, the dark shadow of self-destruction moves across the decade to claim a number of lives. Though Wilde impresses us not only as a symbol but also a cipher by which the Nineties may be read, to Yeats the youthful Dowson and Johnson, in their splendid, terrible isolation, most vividly characterized

---

[28] Towards the end of the Nineties, W. P. Ryan, in *Literary London*, wrote: "One grows tired of their pipings about mean sins and timid indecencies. We agree with Max [Beerbohm] that they are not strong enough to be wicked."

the "Tragic Generation." They lingered in his memory, indeed haunted him and enriched his life, for they described the trajectory of a tragic but stunning waste of talent. In the pantheon of Yeats's poetic imagination, they took their place in his hieratic mysteries as his saint-poets. It is in telling a story of the two poets from hearsay that Yeats reveals—as late as 1936 in a broadcast over the B.B.C.—the strange effect that these two minor figures had on his life:

> *Some friends of mine saw them one moonlight night returning from The Crown public house which had just closed, their zigzagging feet requiring the whole width of Oxford Street, Lionel Johnson talking. My friend stood still eavesdropping; Lionel Johnson was expounding a Father of the Church. Their piety, in Dowson a penitential sadness, in Lionel Johnson more often a notable ecstasy, was as, I think, illuminated and intensified by their contrasting puppet shows, those elegant, tragic penitents, those great men in their triumph.*

Yet most of the Aesthetes and Decadents survived the Nineties, leaving behind them the protests against a society reluctant to grant importance to the artist but seeing in the following century the development of a more mature Aestheticism—though the term would fall into disrepute—aware that the Nineties were not so much a climax as a transition.[29] One critic has remarked that while the French Aesthetes and Decadents were explorers of the human spirit, the English were merely tourists. Like most epigrams, this has partial truth. But the English Aesthetes and Decadents command our attention by their determination to transform their lives into works of art, to center the meaning of life in private vision in order to resist a civilization intent on debasing the imagination and thus making man less human. The courage to do this was considerable—then, as it is now—and the danger of failure made life a perilous, though extraordinary, adventure.

[29] The Imagist Movement (launched before World War I by T. E. Hulme, Ezra Pound, Richard Aldington, and others), the work of James Joyce and T. S. Eliot, and the development of the New Criticism have all felt the influence of late nineteenth-century Aestheticism.

Aesthetes and Decadents OF THE 1890's

AN ANTHOLOGY OF BRITISH POETRY AND PROSE

John Barlas

[1860–1914]

OBLIVION

Oblivion! is it not one name of death?
  Nay, is not Lethe death's most dismal name,
  Death growing hour by hour within our frame,
Death settling slowly in our brain, the breath
Of the soul ebbing, so that he who saith,
  I am to-day as yesterday the same,
  Lies, for his thoughts are fled like smoke from flame,
And like the dew his sorrow vanisheth.
Changed is the river, though the waves remain,
  Which rocks of slowlier-changing circumstance
    Plough up in every day of chafing foam.
Changed is the river, gone, gone to the main,
  Yesterday's dream and last year's happy chance,
    And the heart's thoughts again return not home.

THE MEMPHIAN TEMPLE

By the yellow Nile a temple of black marble,
  Swart colossal columns on the fulvous Nile!
In the precinct palm-trees grow, and wild birds warble;
  'Neath the gate-way basks the crocodile;

In the vista stalks the ibis flaunting
　　Feathers black and white;
From the shrine come songs of wild priests haunting
　　　All the night.
Mystery, Memphian gloom. The vast hawk-sphinxes slumber
　　Either side the portal, where, white-robed, the dark
Votaries, in procession, endless, without number,
　　Bear the sacred beetle in the ark,
To the waters of the sacred river,
　　Chanting in a row,
In the hoof-prints of the gold-horned heifer
　　　As they go.

THE DANCING GIRL

Gaudy painted hangings, fringed by many a tatter,
　　Daubed with bird or beast! Pipe, whistle and scream,
Flute and clarion, trump and drum, and clatter
　　Of the doll-musicians, blown by steam!
There before the screen a damsel tinkling
　　With a timbrel, timed by bell and gong,
Sashed with scarlet, blue, and tinsel twinkling,
　　　　　　Danced and leapt along.

With her shadow on the painted canvas dancing
　　Fitful cast by the jet's flickering glare,
Sinuous limbs, arms waving, quick feet glancing,
　　True to cymbal's clash and clarion's blare!
How the pure grace of her girlish motion
　　Made the vulgar show seem half divine,
Steeped my breast as with an opiate potion
　　Of enchanted wine!

But the shadow on the waving back-ground thrilled me,
　　For it seemed a skeleton on springs,
And its jerky leaps and gestures filled me
　　With a dream of hollow eyeless rings,

Bony shanks, and blackened teeth a-grinning,
  Lurid damp-fires of sepulchral dew,—
Till my dizzy brain, betwixt them, spinning,
           Wondered which was true.

BEAUTY'S ANADEMS[1]

A dagger-hilt crusted with flaming gems:
A queen's rich girdle clasped with tiger's claws;
A lady's glove or a cat's velvet paws;
The whisper of a judge when he condemns;
Fierce night-shade berries purple on their stems
Among the rose's healthsome scarlet haws;
A rainbow-sheathed snake with jagged jaws:
Such are queen Beauty's sovran anadems.
For she caresses with a poisoned hand,
And venom hangs about her moistened lips,
And plots of murder lurk with her eyes
She loves lewd girls dancing a saraband
The murderer stabbing till all his body drips,
And thee, my gentle lady, and thy soft sighs.

THE CAT-LADY

Her hair is yellow as sulphur, and her gaze
As brimstone burning blue and odorous:
I know not how her eyes came to be thus
But I do think her soul must be ablaze:
Their pupils wane or wax to blame or praise;
As a cat watches mice, she watches us;
And I am sure her claws are murderous,
So feline are her velvet coaxing ways.
She purrs like a young leopard soothed and pleased
At flattery; so too turns and snarls when teased,

---

[1] An anadem is a garland.

And pats her love like a beast of prey.
I fancy too that over wine and food
Her saffron hair turns tawny and grand her mood—
She broods like a young lioness of play.

TERRIBLE LOVE

The marriage of two murderers in the gloom
Of a dark fane to hymns of blackest night;
Before a priest who keeps his hands from sight
Hidden away beneath his robe of doom,
Lest any see the flowers of blood that bloom
For gems upon the fingers, red on white;
The while far up in domes of dizzy height
The trumpets of the organ peal and boom:
Such is our love. Oh sweet delicious lips
From which I fancy all the world's blood drips!
Oh supple waist, pale cheek, and eyes of fire,
Hard little breasts and white gigantic hips,
And blue-black hair with serpent coils that slips
Out of my hand in hours of red desire.

MY LADY'S BATH

See where the silver walls enclose
    The rippling lake her song-bird sips!
The powdery fume the fountain throws,
    The jet the dolphin spouts from his lips,
    Whose neck Arion closely clips;
And the polished pebbles and gems, that pave,
    As the sea-floor deep down under the ships,
The silver bath of the perfumed wave.

And now the maid a drapet strows,
    And next a fragrant cream she whips;

Then napkins come like warmed snows;
  And hither my lady lightly trips,
  And dabbles her dainty finger-tips;
For my lady is fair, but is not brave,
  And loves not water that burns or nips
In the silver bath of the perfumed wave.

Hark! she is coming my beautiful rose!
  Hush! we are hidden, and she! she strips:
The petals fall, and the white skin shows,
  The marble breasts, and the polished hips.
  Then one foot in the tide she dips;
Then over her body the waters lave;
  And then she rises and warmly drips
In the silver bath of the perfumed wave.

Into my arms the dear form slips.
  I dare not think of it, lest I rave;
The naked body's pale eclipse
  In the silver bath of the perfumed wave.

Aubrey Beardsley

[1 8 7 2 – 1 8 9 8]

THE BALLAD OF A BARBER

When Beardsley submitted "The Ballad of a Barber" for publication in *The Savoy*, Arthur Symons told Smithers that it would not do. In a letter to Smithers, Beardsley wrote in April, 1896:

> I am horrified at what you tell me about "The Ballad." I had no idea it was "poor." For goodness sake print the poem under a pseudonym and separately from Under the Hill. What do you think of "Symons" as a nom de plume? Seriously the thing must not be printed under my name.

However, Beardsley revised the poem, which appeared in the July number under his own name. Jerome H. Buckley, in *The Victorian Temper*, has written that it was "surely intended to convey a complete allegory of Decadence itself." The idea of the demon barber may have come from John Gray's "The Barber," a sexual fantasy which had appeared in *Silverpoints* (1893).

Beardsley worked on a sequel, but it was never published. In a letter to Smithers in July, 1896, he wrote:

> The first ten verses give a very spirited description of the post-mortem examination of the princess.

Here is the tale of Carrousel,
The barber of Meridian Street,
He cut, and coiffed, and shaved so well,
That all the world was at his feet.

The King, the Queen, and all the Court,
To no one else would trust their hair,
And reigning belles of every sort
Owed their successes to his care.

With carriage and with cabriolet
Daily Meridian Street was blocked,
Like bees about a bright bouquet
The beaux about his doorway flocked.

Such was his art he could with ease
Curl wit into the dullest face;
Or to a goddess of old Greece
Add a new wonder and a grace.

All powders, paints, and subtle dyes,
And costliest scents that men distil,
And rare pomades, forgot their price
And marvelled at his splendid skill.

The curling irons in his hand
Almost grew quick enough to speak,
The razor was a magic wand
That understood the softest cheek.

Yet with no pride his heart was moved;
He was so modest in his ways!
His daily task was all he loved,
And now and then a little praise.

An equal care he would bestow
On problems simple or complex;
And nobody had seen him show
A preference for either sex.

How came it then one summer day,
Coiffing the daughter of the King,
He lengthened out the least delay
And loitered in his hairdressing?

The Princess was a pretty child,
Thirteen years old, or thereabout.
She was as joyous and as wild
As spring flowers when the sun is out.

Her gold hair fell down to her feet
And hung about her pretty eyes;
She was as lyrical and sweet
As one of Schubert's melodies.

Three times the barber curled a lock,
And thrice he straightened it again;
And twice the irons scorched her frock,
And twice he stumbled in her train.

His fingers lost their cunning quite,
His ivory combs obeyed no more;
Something or other dimmed his sight,
And moved mysteriously the floor.

He leant upon the toilet table,
His fingers fumbled in his breast;
He felt as foolish as a fable,
And feeble as a pointless jest.

He snatched a bottle of Cologne,
And broke the neck between his hands;
He felt as if he was alone,
And mighty as a king's commands.

The Princess gave a little scream,
Carrousel's cut was sharp and deep;
He left her softly as a dream
That leaves a sleeper to his sleep.

He left the room on pointed feet;
Smiling that things had gone so well.
They hanged him in Meridian Street.
You pray in vain for Carrousel.

THE STORY OF VENUS AND TANNHÄUSER

in which is set forth an exact account of the manner of State held by Madam Venus, Goddess and Meretrix, under the famous Hörselberg, and containing the Adventures of Tannhäuser in that Place, his Repentance, his Journeying to Rome and Return to the Loving Mountain.

A ROMANTIC NOVEL

In 1894, Beardsley was at work on a book which the publisher John Lane listed as *Venus and Tannhäuser* (to include twenty-four full-page illustrations). The first three chapters —with a new title, *Under the Hill*—appeared with several Beardsley illustrations in the first number of *The Savoy* in January, 1896; a fourth chapter appeared in April. *Under the Hill*—a drastically bowdlerized version—removed much of the wit and daring of the original.

In 1907—nine years after Beardsley's death—Leonard Smithers, the publisher of *The Savoy*, issued privately the original *Venus and Tannhäuser*, adding in a "Foreword" that it was "the whole of the manuscript as originally projected by Beardsley." The tale had never been completed, but its design may be surmised from the elaborate title.

The legend of Venus and Tannhäuser—employed by Wagner in his opera, which Beardsley greatly admired; by Swinburne in his poem "Laus Veneris" ("Praise of Venus"); and by William Morris in his poem "The Hill of Venus"— is based upon the wanderings of a thirteenth-century German troubadour. Beardsley's brilliant parody of the legend with its elaborately artificial style, its obvious desire to shock, and its fascination with bizarre sexuality are here superbly illustrative of the Decadence. (Wrote Arthur Symons: "I think Beardsley would rather have been a great writer than a great artist . . .")

The tale is filled with private jokes, such as the mock solemnity of the dedication and the elaborately humble epistle to the non-existent Cardinal Pezzoli. In 1895, Beardsley wrote to Smithers:

> *I don't want the dedication to be pictured after all. It would be underlining the joke too much. To say nothing of the fact that I am not very successful with cardinals' hats.*

Beardsley's illustrations for the tale—with their elaborate artifice and wit—are brilliant visualizations of what Smithers referred to as Beardsley's "wayward genius."

TO

THE MOST EMINENT AND REVEREND PRINCE

GIULIO POLDO PEZZOLI

CARDINAL OF THE HOLY ROMAN CHURCH

TITULAR BISHOP OF S. MARIA IN TRASTAVERE

ARCHBISHOP OF OSTIA AND VELLETRI

NUNCIO TO THE HOLY SEE

IN

NICARAGUA AND PATAGONIA

A FATHER TO THE POOR

A REFORMER OF ECCLESIASTICAL DISCIPLINE

A PATTERN OF LEARNING

WISDOM AND HOLINESS OF LIFE

THIS BOOK IS DEDICATED WITH DUE REVERENCE

BY HIS HUMBLE SERVITOR

A SCRIVENER AND LIMNER OF WORLDLY THINGS

WHO MADE THIS BOOK

AUBREY BEARDSLEY

TO
THE MOST EMINENT AND REVEREND PRINCE

GIULIO POLDO PEZZOLI

Most Eminent Prince,

I know not by what mischance the writing of epistles dedicatory has fallen into disuse, whether through the vanity of authors or the humility of patrons. But the practice seems to me so very beautiful and becoming that I have ventured to make an essay in the modest art, and lay with formalities my first book at your feet. I have, it must be confessed, many fears lest I shall be arraigned of presumption in choosing so exalted a name as your own to place at the beginning of these histories; but I hope that such a censure will not be too lightly passed upon me, for, if I am guilty, 'tis but of a most natural pride that the accidents of my life should allow me to sail the little pinnace of my wit under your protection.

But though I can clear myself of such a charge, I am still minded to use the tongue of apology, for with what face can I offer you a book treating of so vain and fantastical a thing as Love? I know that in the judgment of many the amorous passion is accounted a shameful thing and ridiculous; indeed, it must be confessed that more blushes have risen for Love's sake than for any other cause, and that lovers are an eternal laughing-stock. Still, as the book will be found to contain matter of deeper import than mere venery, inasmuch as it treats of the great contrition of its chiefest character, and of canonical things in its chapters, I am not without hopes that your Eminence will pardon my writing of the Hill of Venus, for which exposition let my youth excuse me.

Then I must crave your forgiveness for addressing you in a language other than the Roman, but my small freedom in Latinity forbids me to wander beyond the idiom of my vernacular. I would not for the world that your delicate Southern ear should be offended by a barbarous assault of rude and Gothic words: but methinks no language is rude that can boast polite writers, and not a few have flourished in this country in times past, bringing our common speech to very great perfection. In the present age, alas! our pens are ravished by unlettered authors and unmannered critics, that make a havoc rather than a building, a wilderness rather than a garden. But, alack! what boots it to drop tears upon the preterit?

'Tis not of our own shortcomings, though, but of your own great merits that I should speak, else I should be forgetful of the duties I have drawn upon myself in electing to address you in a dedication. 'Tis of your noble virtues (though all the world know of 'em), your taste and wit, your care for letters, and very real regard for the arts, that I must be the proclaimer.

Though it be true that all men have sufficient wit to pass a judgment on this or that, and not a few sufficient impudence to print the same (these last being commonly accounted critics), I have ever held that the critical faculty is more rare than the inventive. 'Tis a faculty your Eminence possesses in so great a degree that your praise or blame is something oracular, your utterance infallible as great genius or as a beautiful woman. Your mind, I know, rejoicing in fine distinctions and subtle procedures of thought, beautifully discursive rather than hastily conclusive, has found in criticism its happiest exercise. 'Tis pity that so perfect a Mecænas[1] should have no Horace to befriend, no Georgics to accept; for the offices and function of patron or critic must of necessity be lessened in an age of little men and little work. In times past 'twas nothing derogatory for great princes and men of State to extend their loves and favour to poets, for thereby they received as much honour as they conferred. Did not Prince Festus with pride take the master-work of Julian into his protection, and was not the Æneis a pretty thing to offer Cæsar?[2]

Learning without appreciation is a thing of nought, but I know not which is greatest in you, your love of the arts or

[1] Roman patron of literature and diplomat under the Emperor Augustus, Mecænas (d. 8 B.C.) was the friend and benefactor of Horace. Vergil wrote the Georgics at his suggestion.

[2] Emperor Julian (332–363 A.D.), known as "the Apostate," was an author of considerable distinction. No biography of Julian mentions Prince Festus, who may be Beardsley's invention. The Aeneis may be an error for Vergil's Aeneid, the national epic emphasizing the divine origins of the Romans.

your knowledge of 'em. What wonder, then, that I am studious to please you, and desirous of your protection? How deeply thankful I am for your past affections, you know well, your great kindness and liberality having far outgone my slight merits and small accomplishment that seemed scarce to warrant any favour. Alas! 'tis a slight offering I make you now, but, if after glancing into its pages (say of an evening upon your terrace), you should deem it worthy of the most remote place in your princely library, the knowledge that it rested there would be reward sufficient for my labours, and a crowning happiness to my pleasure in the writing of this slender book.

The humble and obedient servant of your Eminence,

AUBREY BEARDSLEY

Chapter 1

HOW THE CHEVALIER TANNHÄUSER ENTERED INTO THE HILL OF VENUS

The Chevalier Tannhäuser,[3] having lighted off his horse, stood doubtfully for a moment beneath the ombre gateway of the Venusberg, troubled with an exquisite fear lest a day's travel should have too cruelly undone the laboured niceness of his dress. His hand, slim and gracious as La Marquise du Deffand's in the drawing by [Louis C. de] Carmontelle [1717–1806], played nervously about the gold hair that fell upon his shoulders like a finely curled peruke, and from point to point of a precise toilet, the fingers wandered, quelling the little mutinies of cravat and ruffle.

It was taper-time; when the tired earth puts on its cloak of mists and shadows, when the enchanted woods are stirred with light footfalls and slender voices of the fairies, when all the air is full of delicate influences, and even the beaux, seated at their dressing-tables, dream a little.

A delicious moment, thought Tannhäuser, to slip into exile. The place where he stood waved drowsily with strange

[3] In *Under the Hill*, Venus is named "Helen"; Tannhäuser is the "Abbé Fanfreluche." In the manuscript, Beardsley whimsically named him "Abbé Aubrey."

THE CHEVALIER TANNHÄUSER

flowers, heavy with perfume, dripping with odours. Gloomy and nameless weeds not to be found in Mentzelius. Huge moths so richly winged they must have banqueted upon tapestries and royal stuffs, slept on the pillars that flanked either side of the gateway, and the eyes of all the moths remained open, and were burning and bursting with a mesh of veins. The pillars were fashioned in some pale stone, and rose up like hymns in the praise of Venus, for, from cap to base, each one was carved with loving sculptures, showing such a cunning invention and such a curious knowledge that Tannhäuser lingered not a little in reviewing them. They surpassed all that Japan has ever pictured from her *maisons vertes* ["green houses"], all that was ever painted on the pretty bathrooms of Cardinal La Motte, and even outdid the astonishing illustrations to Jones' *"Nursery Numbers."*

"A pretty portal," murmured the Chevalier, correcting his sash.

As he spake, a faint sound of singing was breathed out from the mountain, faint music as strange and distant as sea-legends that are heard in shells.

"The Vespers of Venus, I take it," said Tannhäuser and struck a few chords of accompaniment ever so lightly upon his little lute. Softly across the spell-bound threshold the song floated and wreathed itself about the subtle columns till the moths were touched with passion, and moved quaintly in their sleep. One of them was awakened by the intenser notes of the Chevalier's lute-strings, and fluttered into his cave. Tannhäuser felt it was his cue for entry.

"Adieu," he exclaimed, with an inclusive gesture, and "Good-bye, Madonna," as the cold circle of the moon began to show, beautiful and full of enchantments. There was a shadow of sentiment in his voice as he spake the words.

"Would to heaven," he sighed, "I might receive the assurance of a looking-glass before I make my début! However, as she is a goddess, I doubt not her eyes are a little sated with perfection, and may not be displeased to see it crowned with a tiny fault."

A wild rose had caught upon the trimmings of his muff, and in the first flush of displeasure he would have struck it brusquely away, and most severely punished the offending flower. But the ruffled mood lasted only a moment, for there was something so deliciously incongruous in the hardy petal's invasion of so delicate a thing, that Tannhäuser withheld the finger of resentment, and vowed that the wild rose should stay where it had clung—a passport, as it were, from the upper to the underworld.

"The very excess and violence of the fault," he said, "will be its excuse;" and, undoing a tangle in the tassel of his stick, stepped into the shadowy corridor that ran into the bosom of the wan hill, stepped with the admirable aplomb and unwrinkled suavity of Don John.

Chapter 2

OF THE MANNER IN WHICH VENUS WAS COIFFED AND PREPARED FOR SUPPER

Before a toilet that shone like the altar of Nôtre Dame des Victoires, Venus was seated in a little dressing-gown of black and heliotrope. The coiffeur Cosmé was caring for her scented chevelure, and with tiny silver tongs, warm from the caresses of the flame, made delicious intelligent curls that fell as lightly as a breath about her forehead and over her eyebrows, and clustered like tendrils about her neck. Her three favourite girls, Pappelarde, Blanchemains, and Loreyne, waited immediately upon her with perfume and powder in delicate flaçons and frail cassolettes, and held in porcelain jars the ravishing paints prepared by Chateline for those cheeks and lips that had grown a little pale with anguish of exile. Her three favourite boys, Claude, Clair, and Sarrasine, stood amorously about with salver, fan and napkin. Millamant held a slight tray of slippers, Minette some tender gloves, La Popelinière, mistress of the robes, was ready with a frock of yellow and yellow. La Zambinella bore the jewels, Florizel some flowers, Amadour a box of various pins, and Vadius a box of sweets. Her doves, ever in attendance, walked about the room that was panelled with the gallant paintings of Jean Baptiste Dorat, and some dwarfs and doubtful creatures sat here and there, lolling out their tongues,

VENUS AT HER TOILET

pinching each other, and behaving oddly enough. Sometimes Venus gave them little smiles.

As the toilet was in progress, Priapusa,[4] the fat manicure and fardeuse, strode in and seated herself by the side of the dressing-table, greeting Venus with an intimate nod. She wore a gown of white watered silk with gold lace trimmings, and a velvet necklet of false vermilion. Her hair hung in bandeaux over her ears, passing into a huge chignon at the back of her head, and the hat, wide-brimmed and hung with a vallance of pink muslin, was floral with red roses.

Priapusa's voice was full of salacious unction; she had terrible little gestures with the hands, strange movements with the shoulders, a short respiration that made surprising wrinkles in her bodice, a corrupt skin, large horny eyes, a parrot's nose, a small loose mouth, great flaccid cheeks, and chin after chin. She was a wise person, and Venus loved her more than any of her other servants, and had a hundred pet names for her, such as, Dear Toad, Pretty Pol, Cock-robin, Dearest Lip, Touchstone, Little Cough-drop, Bijou, Buttons, Dear Heart, Dick-dock, Mrs Manly, Little Nipper, Cochon-de-lait ["sucking pig"], Naughty-naughty, Blessèd Thing, and Trump.

The talk that passed between Priapusa and her mistress was of that excellent kind that passes between old friends, a perfect understanding giving to scraps of phrases their full meaning, and to the merest reference, a point. Naturally Tannhäuser, the new comer, was discussed a little. Venus had not seen him yet, and asked a score of questions on his account that were delightfully to the point.

Priapusa told the story of his sudden arrival, his curious wandering in the gardens, and calm satisfaction with all he saw there, his impromptu affection for a slender girl upon the first terrace, of the crowd of frocks that gathered round and pelted him with roses, of the graceful way he defended himself with his mask, and of the queer reverence he made to the statue of the God of all gardens, kissing that deity

---

[4] Derived from Priapus, the ancient god of procreation, horticulture, and goat and sheep breeding. His emblem was the phallus. In *Under the Hill*, Priapusa is called "Mrs. Marsuple."

with a pilgrim's devotion. Just now Tannhäuser was at the baths, and was creating a most favourable impression.

The report and the coiffing were completed at the same moment.

"Cosmé," said Venus, "you have been quite sweet and quite brilliant, you have surpassed yourself to-night."

"Madam flatters me," replied the antique old thing, with a girlish giggle under his black satin mask. "Gad, Madam; sometimes I believe I have no talent in the world, but to-night I must confess to a touch of the vain mood."

It would pain me horribly to tell you about the painting of her face; suffice it that the sorrowful work was accomplished frankly, magnificently, and without a shadow of deception.

Venus slipped away the dressing-gown, and rose before the mirror in a flutter of frilled things. She was adorably tall and slender. Her neck and shoulders were so wonderfully drawn, and the little malicious breasts were full of the irritation of loveliness that can never be entirely comprehended, or ever enjoyed to the utmost. Her arms and hands were loosely but delicately articulated, and her legs were divinely long. From the hip to the knee, twenty-two inches; from the knee to the heel, twenty-two inches, as befitted a Goddess.

I should like to speak more particularly about her, for generalities are not of the slightest service in a description. But I am afraid that an enforced silence here and there would leave such numerous gaps in the picture that it had better not be begun at all than left unfinished.

Those who have only seen Venus in the Vatican, in the Louvre, in the Uffizi, or in the British Museum, can have no idea of how very beautiful and sweet she looked. Not at all like the lady in "Lemprière."

Priapusa grew quite lyric over the dear little person, and pecked at her arms with kisses.

"Dear Tongue, you must really behave yourself," said Venus, and called Millamant to bring her the slippers.

The tray was freighted with the most exquisite and shapely *pantoufles* ["house slippers"], sufficient to make Cluny a place of naught. There were shoes of grey and black and brown suéde, of white silk and rose satin, and velvet and sarcenet;

there were some of sea-green sewn with cherry blossoms, some of red with willow branches, and some of grey with bright-winged birds. There were heels of silver, of ivory, and of gilt; there were buckles of very precious stones set in most strange and esoteric devices; there were ribands tied and twisted into cunning forms; there were buttons so beautiful that the button-holes might have no pleasure till they closed upon them; there were soles of delicate leathers scented with maréchale, and linings of soft stuffs scented with the juice of July flowers. But Venus, finding none of them to her mind, called for a discarded pair of blood-red maroquin, diapered with pearls. These looked very distinguished over her white silk stockings.

As the tray was being carried away, the capricious Florizel snatched as usual a slipper from it, and fitted the foot over his penis, and made the necessary movements. That was Florizel's little caprice. Meantime, La Popelinière stepped forward with the frock.

"I shan't wear one to-night," said Venus. Then she slipped on her gloves.

When the toilet was at an end all her doves clustered round her feet, loving to *frôler* ["brush against"] her ankles with their plumes, and the dwarfs clapped their hands, and put their fingers between their lips and whistled. Never before had Venus been so radiant and compelling. Spiridion, in the corner, looked up from his game of Spellicans and trembled. Claude and Clair, pale with pleasure, stroked and touched her with their delicate hands, and wrinkled her stockings with their nervous lips, and smoothed them with their thin fingers; and Sarrasine undid her garters and kissed them inside and put them on again, pressing her thighs with his mouth. The dwarfs grew very daring, I can tell you. There was almost a mêlée. They illustrated pages 72 and 73 of Delvau's dictionary.[5]

In the middle of it all, Pranzmungel announced that sup-

---

[5] *Dictionnaire de la langue verte*, a dictionary of slang by Alfred Delvau (1825–67). Pages 72–73 are concerned with various expressions for such *vices abjects* as masturbation and the deflowering of maidens.

per was ready upon the fifth terrace. "Ah!" cried Venus,
"I'm famished!"

Chapter 3

HOW VENUS SUPPED AND THEREAFTER WAS MIGHTILY
AMUSED BY THE CURIOUS PRANKS OF HER ENTOURAGE

She was quite delighted with Tannhäuser, and, of course, he
sat next her at supper.

The terrace, made beautiful with a thousand vain and fantastical devices, and set with a hundred tables and four hundred couches, presented a truly splendid appearance. In the
middle was a huge bronze fountain with three basins. From
the first rose a many-breasted dragon, and four little Loves
mounted upon swans, and each Love was furnished with a
bow and arrow. Two of them that faced the monster seemed
to recoil in fear, two that were behind made bold enough to
aim their shafts at him. From the verge of the second sprang
a circle of slim golden columns that supported silver doves,
with tails and wings spread out. The third, held by a group
of grotesquely attenuated satyrs, was centred with a thin pipe
hung with masks and roses, and capped with children's heads.

From the mouths of the dragon and the Loves, from the
swans' eyes, from the breasts of the doves, from the satyrs'
horns and lips, from the masks at many points, and from the
children's curls, the water played profusely, cutting strange
arabesques and subtle figures.

The terrace was lit entirely by candles. There were four
thousand of them, not numbering those upon the tables. The
candlesticks were of a countless variety, and smiled with
moulded *cochônneries* ["filthy comments and tales"]. Some
were twenty feet high, and bore single candles that flared
like fragrant torches over the feast, and guttered till the wax
stood round the tops in tall lances. Some, hung with dainty
petticoats of shining lustres, had a whole bevy of tapers upon
them, devised in circles, in pyramids, in squares, in cunei-
forms, in single lines regimentally and in crescents.

Then on quaint pedestals and Terminal Gods and gracious

pilasters of every sort, were shell-like vases of excessive
fruits and flowers that hung about and burst over the edges
and could never be restrained. The orange-trees and myrtles,
looped with vermilion sashes, stood in frail porcelain pots,
and the rose-trees were wound and twisted with superb invention over trellis and standard. Upon one side of the terrace, a long gilded stage for the comedians was curtained off
with Pagonian tapestries, and in front of it the music-stands
were placed. The tables arranged between the fountain and
the flight of steps to the sixth terrace were all circular, covered with white damask, and strewn with irises, roses, king-
cups, columbines, daffodils, carnations and lilies; and the
couches, high with soft cushions and spread with more stuffs
than could be named, had fans thrown upon them, and little
amorous surprise packets.

Beyond the escalier stretched the gardens, which were
designed so elaborately and with so much splendour that the
architect of the Fêtes d'Armailhacq could have found in them
no matter for cavil, and the still lakes strewn with profuse
barges full of gay flowers and wax marionettes, the alleys of
tall trees, the arcades and cascades, the pavilions, the grot-
toes, and the garden-gods—all took a strange tinge of revelry
from the glare of the light that fell upon them from the feast.

The frockless Venus and Tannhäuser, with Priapusa and
Claude and Clair, and Farcy, the chief comedian, sat at the
same table. Tannhäuser, who had doffed his travelling suit,
wore long black silk stockings, a pair of pretty garters, a
very elegant ruffled shirt, slippers and a wonderful dressing-
gown. Claude and Clair wore nothing at all, delicious privilege of immaturity, and Farcy was in ordinary evening
clothes. As for the rest of the company, it boasted some very
noticeable dresses, and whole tables of quite delightful coiffures. There were spotted veils that seemed to stain the skin
with some exquisite and august disease, fans with eye-slits in
them through which their bearers peeped and peered; fans
painted with postures and covered with the sonnets of Sporion and the short stories of Scaramouche, and fans of big
living moths stuck upon mounts of silver sticks. There were
masks of green velvet that make the face look trebly powdered; masks of the heads of birds, of apes, of serpents, of

dolphins, of men and women, of little embryons and of cats; masks like the faces of gods; masks of coloured glass, and masks of thin talc and of india-rubber. There were wigs of black and scarlet wools, of peacocks' feathers, of gold and silver threads, of swansdown, of the tendrils of the vine, and of human hairs; huge collars of stiff muslin rising high above the head; whole dresses of ostrich feathers curling inwards; tunics of panthers' skins that looked beautiful over pink tights; capotes of crimson satin trimmed with the wings of owls; sleeves cut into the shapes of apocryphal animals; drawers flounced down to the ankles, and flecked with tiny, red roses; stockings clocked with fêtes galantes, and curious designs, and petticoats cut like artificial flowers. Some of the women had put on delightful little moustaches dyed in purples and bright greens, twisted and waxed with absolute skill; and some wore great white beards after the manner of Saint Wilgeforte. Then Dorat had painted extraordinary grotesques and vignettes over their bodies, here and there. Upon a cheek, an old man scratching his horned head; upon a forehead, an old woman teased by an impudent amor; upon a shoulder, an amorous singerie; round a breast, a circlet of satyrs; about a wrist, a wreath of pale, unconscious babes; upon an elbow, a bouquet of spring flowers; across a back, some surprising scenes of adventure; at the corners of a mouth, tiny red spots; and upon a neck, a flight of birds, a caged parrot, a branch of fruit, a butterfly, a spider, a drunken dwarf, or, simply, some initials. But most wonderful of all were the black silhouettes painted upon the legs, and which showed through a white silk stocking like a sumptuous bruise.

The supper provided by the ingenious Rambouillet was quite beyond parallel. Never had he created a more exquisite menu. The *consommé impromptu* alone would have been sufficient to establish the immortal reputation of any chef. What, then, can I say of the *Dorade bouillie sauce maréchale*, the *ragoût aux langues de carpes*, the *ramereaux à la charnière*, the *ciboulette de gibier à l'espagnole*, the *paté de cuisses d'oie aux pois de Monsalvie*, the *queues d'agneau au clair de lune*, the *artichauts à la Grecque*, the *charlotte de pommes à la Lucy Waters*, the *bombes à la marée*, and the *glaces aux*

THE FRUIT BEARERS

*rayons d'or?*⁶ A veritable *tour de cuisine* ["culinary feat"] that surpassed even the famous little suppers given by the Marquis de Réchale at Passy, and which the Abbé Mirliton pronounced "impeccable, and too good to be eaten."

Ah! Pierre Antoine Berquin de Rambouillet; you are worthy of your divine mistress!

Mere hunger quickly gave place to those finer instincts of the pure gourmet, and the strange wines, cooled in buckets of snow, unloosed all the *décolleté* ["licentious"] spirits of astonishing conversation and atrocious laughter.

Chapter 4

HOW THE COURT OF VENUS BEHAVED STRANGELY AT HER SUPPER

At first there was the fun with the surprise packets that contained myriads of amusing things, then a general criticism of the decorations, everyone finding a delightful meaning in the fall of festoon, turn of twig, and twist of branch. Pulex [Latin, "flea"], as usual, bore the palm for insight and invention, and to-night he was more brilliant than ever. He leant across the table and explained to the young page, Macfils de Martaga, what thing was intended by a certain arrangement of roses. The young page smiled and hummed the refrain of "La petite balette." Sporion, too, had delicate perceptions, and was vastly entertained by the disposition of the candelabra.

As the courses advanced, the conversation grew bustling and more personal. Pulex and Cyril and Marisca and Cathelin opened a fire of raillery. The infidelities of Cerise, the difficulties of Brancas, Sarmean's caprices that morning in the lily garden, Thorilliere's declining strength, Astarte's affection for Roseola, Felix's impossible member, Cathelin's passion for Sulpilia's poodle, Sola's passion for herself, the nasty bite that Marisca gave Chloe, the *épilatiere* ["removal of hair"] of Pulex, Cyril's diseases, Butor's illness, Maryx's

⁶ Some of the culinary delicacies listed are carps' tongues stew, pâté of goose thighs, lambs' tails in moonlight, and golden rays ices.

tiny cemetery, Lesbia's profound fourth letter, and a thousand amatory follies of the day were discussed.

From harsh and shrill and clamant, the voices grew blurred and inarticulate. Bad sentences were helped out by worse gestures, and at one table, Scabius could only express himself with his napkin, after the manner of Sir Jolly Jumble in the *Soldier's Fortune* of Otway.[7] Basalissa and Lysistrata tried to pronounce each other's names, and became very affectionate in the attempt, and Tala, the tragedian, robed in ample purple, and wearing plume and buskin, rose to his feet, and with swaying gestures began to recite one of his favourite parts. He got no further than the first line, but repeated it again and again, with fresh accents and intonations each time, and was only silenced by the approach of the asparagus that was being served by satyrs costumed in white muslin.

Clitor and Sodon had a violent struggle over the beautiful Pella, and nearly upset a chandelier. Sophie became very intimate with an empty champagne bottle, swore it had made her *enceinte* ["pregnant"], and ended by having a mock accouchement on the top of the table; and Belamour pretended to be a dog, and pranced from couch to couch on all fours, biting and barking and licking. Mellefont crept about dropping love philtres into glasses. Juventus and Ruella stripped and put on each other's things, Spelto offered a prize for whoever should come first, and Spelto won it! Tannhäuser, just a little *grisé* ["tipsy"], lay down on the cushions and let Julia do whatever she liked.

I wish I could be allowed to tell you what occurred round table 15, just at this moment. It would amuse you very much, and would give you a capital idea of the habits of Venus' retinue. Indeed, for deplorable reasons, by far the greater part of what was said and done at this supper must remain unrecorded and even unsuggested.

Venus allowed most of the dishes to pass untasted, she was so engaged with the beauty of Tannhäuser. She laid her

[7] The play by Thomas Otway (1652–85) does indeed have in it the old lecher Sir Jolly Jumble, but Beardsley may have been recalling a stage production he had seen, for in the text of the play, no such gestures are described.

head many times on his robe, kissing him passionately; and
his skin, at once firm and yielding, seemed to those exquisite
little teeth of hers, the most incomparable pasture. Her upper
lip curled and trembled with excitement, showing the gums.
Tannhäuser, on his side, was no less devoted. He adored her
all over and all the things she had on, and buried his face
in the folds and flounces of her linen, and ravished away a
score of frills in his excess. He found her exasperating, and
crushed her in his arms, and slaked his parched lips at her
mouth. He caressed her eyelids softly with his finger tips,
and pushed aside the curls from her forehead, and did a
thousand gracious things, tuning her body as a violinist tunes
his instrument before he plays upon it.

Priapusa snorted like an old war horse at the sniff of powder, and tickled Tannhäuser and Venus by turns, and slipped
her tongue down their throats, and refused to be quiet at all
until she had had a mouthful of the Chevalier. Claude, seizing his chance, dived under the table and came up the other
side just under the queen's couch, and before she could say
"One!" he was taking his coffee *aux deux colonnes* [literally,
"at the two columns," i.e. between her legs]. Clair was furious at his friend's success, and sulked for the rest of the
evening.

Chapter 5

OF THE BALLET DANCED BY THE SERVANTS OF VENUS

After the fruits and fresh wines had been brought in by a
troop of woodland creatures, decked with green leaves and
all sorts of Spring flowers, the candles in the orchestra were
lit, and in another moment the musicians bustled into their
places. The wonderful Titurel de Schentefleur was the *chef
d'orchestre* ["orchestra leader"], and the most insidious of
conductors. His bâton dived into a phrase and brought out
the most magical and magnificent things, and seemed rather
to play every instrument than to lead it. He could add a
grace even to Scarlatti and a wonder to Beethoven. A delicate, thin, little man with thick lips and a *nez retroussé*
["upturned nose"], with long black hair and curled mous-

tache, in the manner of Molière. What were his amatory tastes, no one in the Venusberg could tell. He generally passed for a virgin, and Cathos had nicknamed him "The Solitaire."

To-night he appeared in a court suit of white silk, brilliant with decorations. His hair was curled into resplendent ringlets that trembled like springs at the merest gesture of his arm, and in his ears swung the diamonds given him by Venus.

The orchestra was, as usual, in its uniform of red vest and breeches trimmed with gold lace, white stockings and red shoes. Titurel had written a ballet for the evening's divertissement, founded upon De Bergerac's comedy of "Les Bacchanales de Fanfreluche," [8] in which the action and dances were designed by him as well as the music.

i

The curtain rose upon a scene of rare beauty, a remote Arcadian valley, and watered with a dear river as fresh and pastoral as a perfect fifth of this scrap of Tempe. It was early morning, and the re-arisen sun, like the prince in the "Sleeping Beauty," woke all the earth with his lips. In that golden embrace the night dews were caught up and made splendid, the trees were awakened from their obscure dreams, the slumber of the birds was broken, and all the flowers of the valley rejoiced, forgetting their fear of the darkness.

Suddenly, to the music of pipe and horn, a troop of satyrs stepped out from the recesses of the woods, bearing in their hands nuts and green boughs and flowers and roots and whatsoever the forest yielded, to heap upon the altar of the mysterious Pan that stood in the middle of the stage; and from the hills came down the shepherds and shepherdesses, leading their flocks and carrying garlands upon their crooks. Then a rustic priest, white-robed and venerable, came slowly across the valley followed by a choir of radiant children.

The scene was admirably stage-managed, and nothing could have been more varied yet harmonious than this

[8] No such work is attributed to Cyrano de Bergerac. In a letter to Smithers in 1895, Beardsley wrote that in *Under the Hill*, the play would be called "The Bacchanals of Sporion."

Arcadian group. The service was quaint and simple, but with sufficient ritual to give the corps-de-ballet an opportunity of showing its dainty skill. The dancing of the satyrs was received with huge favour, and when the priest raised his hand in final blessing, the whole troop of worshippers made such an intricate and elegant exit that it was generally agreed that Titurel had never before shown so fine an invention.

Scarcely had the stage been empty for a moment, when Sporion entered, followed by a brilliant rout of dandies and smart women. Sporion was a tall, slim, depraved young man with a slight stoop, a troubled walk, an oval impassable face, with its olive skin drawn tightly over the bone, strong scarlet lips, long Japanese eyes, and a great gilt toupet. Round his shoulders hung a high-collared satin cape of salmon pink, with long black ribands untied and floating about his body. His coat of sea-green spotted muslin was caught in at the waist by a scarlet sash with scalloped edges, and frilled out over the hips for about six inches. His trousers, loose and wrinkled, reached to the end of the calf, and were brocaded down the sides, and ruched magnificently at the ankles. The stockings were of white kid, with stalls for the toes, and had delicate red sandals strapped over them. But his little hands, peeping out from their frills, seemed quite the most insinuating things, such supple fingers tapering to the point, with tiny nails stained pink, such unquenchable palms, lined and mounted like Lord Fanny's in "Love at all Hazards," and such blue-veined, hairless backs! In his left hand he carried a small lace handkerchief broidered with a coronet.

As for his friends and followers they made the most superb and insolent crowd imaginable, but to catalogue the clothes they had on would require a chapter as long as the famous tenth in Pénillière's history of underlinen. On the whole they looked a very distinguished chorus.

Sporion stepped forward and explained with swift and various gesture that he and his friends were tired of the amusements, wearied with the poor pleasures offered by the civil world, and had invaded the Arcadian valley hoping to experience a new *frisson* ["shudder"] in the destruction of some shepherd's or some satyr's naïveté, and the infusion of their venom among the dwellers of the woods.

The chorus assented with languid but expressive movements.

Curious, and not a little frightened, at the arrival of the worldly company, the sylvans began to peep nervously at those subtle souls through the branches of the trees, and one or two fauns and a shepherd or so crept out warily. Sporion and all the ladies and gentlemen made enticing sounds and invited the rustic creatures with all the grace in the world to come and join them. By little batches they came, lured by the strange looks, by the scents and the doings, and by the brilliant clothes, and some ventured quite near, timorously fingering the delicious textures of the stuffs. Then Sporion and each of his friends took a satyr or a shepherd or something by the hand, and made the preliminary steps of a courtly measure, for which the most admirable combinations had been invented, and the most charming music written.

The pastoral folk were entirely bewildered when they saw such restrained and graceful movements, and made the most grotesque and futile efforts to imitate them.

Dio mio, a pretty sight! A charming effect too was obtained by the intermixture of stockinged calf and hairy leg, of rich brocaded bodice and plain blouse, of tortured head-dress and loose untutored locks.

When the dance was ended, the servants of Sporion brought on champagne, and, with many pirouettes, poured it magnificently into slender glasses, and tripped about plying those Arcadian mouths that had never before tasted such a royal drink.

* * * * * * *

Then the curtain fell with a pudic rapidity.

ii

'Twas not long before the invaders began to enjoy the first fruits of their expedition, plucking them in the most seductive manner with their smooth fingers, and feasting lip and tongue and tooth, whilst the shepherds and satyrs and shepherdesses fairly gasped under the new joys, for the pleasure they experienced was almost too keen and too profound for their simple and untilled natures. Fanfreluche and the rest of the rips and ladies tingled with excitement and frolicked like young lambs in a fresh meadow. Again and again the wine was danced round, and the valley grew as busy as a market day. Attracted by the noise and merrymaking, all those sweet infants I told you of, skipped suddenly on to the stage, and began clapping their hands and laughing immoderately at the passion and the disorder and commotion, and mimicking the nervous staccato movements they saw in their pretty childish way.

In a flash, Fanfreluche disentangled himself and sprang to his feet, gesticulating as if he would say, "Ah, the little dears!" "Ah, the rorty little things!" "Ah, the little ducks!" for he was so fond of children. Scarcely had he caught one by the thigh than a quick rush was made by everybody for the succulent limbs; and how they tousled them and mousled them! The children cried out, I can tell you. Of course there were not enough for everybody, so some had to share, and some had simply to go on with what they were doing before.

I must not, by the way, forget to mention the independent attitude taken by six or seven of the party, who sat and stood about with half-closed eyes, inflated nostrils, clenched teeth, and painful, parted lips, behaving like the Duc de Broglio when he watched the amours of the Regent d'Orleans.

Now as Fanfreluche and his friends began to grow tired and exhausted with the new debauch, they cared no longer to take the initiative, but, relaxing every muscle, abandoned themselves to passive joys, yielding utterly to the ardent embraces of the intoxicated satyrs, who waxed fast and furious, and seemed as if they would never come to the end of their strength. Full of the new tricks they had learnt that morning, they played them passionately and roughly, making havoc of the cultured flesh, and tearing the splendid frocks and dresses into ribands. Duchesses and Maréchales, Marquises and Princesses, Dukes and Marshalls, Marquesses and Princes, were ravished and stretched and rumpled and crushed beneath the interminable vigour and hairy breasts of the inflamed woodlanders. They bit at the white thighs and nozzled wildly in the crevices. They sat astride the women's chests and consummated frantically with their bosoms; they caught their prey by the hips and held it over their heads, irrumating ["sucking a teat"] with prodigious gusto. It was the triumph of the valley.

High up in the heavens the sun had mounted and filled all the air with generous warmth, whilst shadows grew shorter and sharper. Little light-winged papillons flitted across the stage, the bees made music on their flowery way, the birds were very gay and kept up a jargoning and refraining, the lambs were bleating upon the hill side, and the orchestra kept playing, playing the uncanny tunes of Titurel.

Chapter 6

OF THE AMOROUS ENCOUNTER WHICH TOOK PLACE
BETWEEN VENUS AND TANNHÄUSER

Venus and Tannhäuser had retired to the exquisite little boudoir or pavilion Le Con [slang for vagina] had designed for the queen on the first terrace, and which commanded the most delicious view of the parks and gardens. It was a sweet little place, all silk curtains and soft cushions. There were eight sides to it, bright with mirrors and candelabra, and rich with pictured panels, and the ceiling, dome shaped and some thirty feet above the head, shone obscurely with gilt mouldings through the warm haze of candle light below. Tiny wax statuettes dressed theatrically and smiling with plump cheeks, quaint magots that looked as cruel as foreign gods, gilded monticules, pale celadon vases, clocks that said nothing, ivory boxes full of secrets, china figures playing whole scenes of plays, and a world of strange preciousness crowded the curious cabinets that stood against the walls. On one side of the room there were six perfect little card tables, with quite the daintiest and most elegant chairs set primly round them; so, after all, there may be some truth in that line of Mr. Theodore Watts [-Dunton, 1832–1914],—

I played at piquet with the Queen of Love

Nothing in the pavilion was more beautiful than the folding screens painted by De La Pine, with Claudian landscapes —the sort of things that fairly make one melt, things one can lie and look at for hours together, and forget the country can ever be dull and tiresome. There were four of them, delicate walls that hem in an amour so cosily, and make room within room.

The place was scented with huge branches of red roses, and with a faint amatory perfume breathed out from the couches and cushions—a perfume Chateline distilled in secret and called L' Eau Lavante ["washing water"].

Those who have only seen Venus at the Louvre or the British Museum, at Florence, at Naples, or at Rome, can have not the faintest idea how sweet and enticing and gracious, how really exquisitely beautiful she looked lying with Tannhäuser upon rose silk in that pretty boudoir.

Cosmé's precise curls and artful waves had been finally disarranged at supper, and strayed ringlets of the black hair fell loosely over her soft, delicious, tired, swollen eyelids. Her frail chemise and dear little drawers were torn and moist, and clung transparently about her, and all her body was nervous and responsive. Her closed thighs seemed like a vast replica of the little bijou she held between them; the beautiful *tétons du derrière* ["teats of the behind"] were as firm as a plump virgin's cheek, and promised a joy as profound as the mystery of the Rue Vendôme, and the minor *chevelure* ["*hair*"], just profuse enough, curled as prettily as the hair upon a cherub's head.

Tannhäuser, pale and speechless with excitement, passed his gem-girt fingers brutally over the divine limbs, tearing away smock and pantalon and stocking, and then, stripping himself of his own few things, fell upon the splendid lady with a deep-drawn breath!

It is, I know, the custom of all romancers to paint heroes who can give a lady proof of their dalliance at least twenty times a night. Now Tannhäuser had no such Gargantuan facility, and was rather relieved when, an hour later, Priapusa and Doricourt and some others burst drunkenly into the room and claimed Venus for themselves. The pavilion soon filled with a noisy crowd that could scarcely keep its feet. Several of the actors were there, and Lesfesses ["buttocks"], who had played Fanfreluche so brilliantly, and was still in his make-up, paid tremendous attention to Tannhäuser. But the Chevalier found him quite uninteresting off the stage, and rose and crossed the room to where Venus and the manicure were seated.

"How tired the dear baby looks," said Priapusa. "Shall I put him in his little cot?"

"Well, if he's as sleepy as I am," yawned Venus, "you can't do better."

Priapusa lifted her mistress off the pillows, and carried her in her arms in a nice, motherly way.

"Come along, children," said the fat old thing, "come along; it's time you were both in bed."

Chapter 7

HOW TANNHÄUSER AWAKENED AND TOOK HIS MORNING ABLUTIONS IN THE VENUSBERG

It is always delightful to wake up in a new bedroom. The fresh wall paper, the strange pictures, the positions of doors and windows—imperfectly grasped the night before—are revealed with all the charm of surprise when we open our eyes the next morning.

It was about eleven o'clock when Tannhäuser awoke and stretched himself deliciously in his great plumed four-post bed, and nursed his waking thoughts, and stared at the curious patterned canopy above him. He was very pleased with the room, which certainly was chic and fascinating, and recalled the voluptuous interiors of the elegant amorous Baudouin. Through the tiny parting of the long, flowered window curtains, the Chevalier caught a peep of the sun-lit lawns outside, the silver fountains, the bright flowers, and the gardeners at work.

"Quite sweet," he murmured, and turned round to freshen the frilled silk pillows behind him; "and what delightful pictures," he continued, wandering with his eyes from print to print that hung upon the rose-striped walls. Within the delicate, curved frames lived the corrupt and gracious creatures of Dorat and his school; slim children in masque and domino, smiling horribly, exquisite lechers leaning over the shoulders of smooth doll-like ladies, and doing nothing particular, terrible little pierrots posing as mulierasts, or pointing at something outside the picture, and unearthly fops and strange women mingling in some rococo room lighted mysteriously by the flicker of a dying fire that throws huge shadows upon wall and ceiling. One of the prints showing how an old marquis practised the five-finger exercise, while in front of him his mistress offered her warm *fesses* ["buttocks"] to a panting poodle, made the chevalier stroke himself a little.

After the chevalier got up, he slipped off his dainty nightdress, posturing elegantly before a long mirror, and made much of himself. Now he would bend forward, now lie upon the floor, now stand upright, and now rest upon one leg and let the other hang loosely till he looked as if he might have been drawn by some early Italian master. Anon he would lie upon the floor with his back to the glass, and glance amorously over his shoulder. Then with a white silk sash he draped himself in a hundred charming ways. So engrossed was he with his mirrored shape that he had not noticed the entrance of a troop of serving boys, who stood admiringly but respectfully at a distance, ready to receive his waking orders. As soon as the chevalier observed them he smiled sweetly, and bade them prepare his bath.

The bathroom was the largest and perhaps the most beautiful apartment in his splendid suite. The well-known engraving by Lorette that forms the frontispiece to Millevoye's "Architecture du XVIIIme siècle," will give you a better idea than any words of mine of the construction and decoration of the room. Only, in Lorette's engraving, the bath sunk into the middle of the floor is a little too small.

Tannhäuser stood for a moment, like Narcissus, gazing at his reflection in the still scented water, and then just ruffling its smooth surface with one foot, stepped elegantly into the cool basin, and swam round it twice, very gracefully.

"Won't you join me?" he said, turning to those beautiful boys who stood ready with warm towels and perfume. In a moment they were free of their light morning dress, and jumped into the water and joined hands, and surrounded the Chevalier with a laughing chain.

"Splash me a little," he cried, and the boys teased him with water and quite excited him. He chased the prettiest of them and bit his *fesses*, and kissed him upon the perineum till the dear fellow banded like a carmelite,[9] and its little bald top-knot looked like a great pink pearl under the water. As the boy seemed anxious to take up the active attitude, Tannhäuser graciously descended to the passive—a generous trait that won him the complete affections of his *valets de bain*, or pretty fish, as he called them, because they loved to swim between his legs.

However, it is not so much at the very bath itself, as in the drying and delicious frictions, that a bather finds his chiefest pleasures, and Tannhäuser was more than satisfied with the skill his attendants displayed in the performance of those quasi amorous functions. The delicate attention they paid his loving parts aroused feelings within him that almost amounted to gratitude; and when the rites were ended, any touch of home-sickness he might have felt before was utterly dispelled.

After he had rested a little, and sipped his chocolate, he wandered into the dressing-room. Daucourt, his *valet de chambre*, Chenille, the *perruquier* ["wig maker"] and barber, and two charming young dressers, were awaiting him and ready with suggestions for the morning toilet. The shaving over, Daucourt commanded his underlings to step forward with the suite of suits from which he proposed Tannhäuser should make a choice. The final selection was a happy one. A dear little coat of pigeon rose silk that hung loosely about his hips, and showed off the jut of his behind to perfection; trousers of black lace in flounces, falling—almost like a petticoat—as far as the knee; and a delicate chemise of white muslin, spangled with gold and profusely pleated.

The two dressers, under Daucourt's direction, did their work superbly, beautifully, leisurely, with an exquisite deference for the nude, and a really sensitive appreciation of Tannhäuser's scrumptious torso.

[9] "Banded" seems to mean "became marked with lines." A carmelite in the eighteenth century was a kind of pear. (A Carmelite is, of course, a member of the Roman Catholic order of mendicant friars. Beardsley no doubt delighted in the possibilities of the ambiguity.)

Chapter 8

OF THE ECSTASY OF ADOLPHE, AND THE REMARKABLE
MANIFESTATION THEREOF

When all was said and done, the Chevalier tripped off to bid
good morning to Venus. He found her wandering, in a sweet
white muslin frock, upon the lawn outside, plucking flowers
to deck her little *déjeuner* ["breakfast"]. He kissed her
lightly upon the neck.

"I'm just going to feed Adolphe," she said, pointing to a
little reticule of buns that hung from her arm. Adolphe was
her pet unicorn. "He is such a dear," she continued; "milk-
white all over excepting his black eyes, rose mouth and nostrils, and scarlet John."

The unicorn had a very pretty palace of its own, made of
green foliage and golden bars—a fitting home for such a delicate and dainty beast. Ah, it was indeed a splendid thing to
watch the white creature roaming in its artful cage, proud
and beautiful, and knowing no mate except the Queen herself.

As Venus and Tannhäuser approached the wicket,
Adolphe began prancing and curvetting, pawing the soft turf
with his ivory hoofs, and flaunting his tail like a gonfalon.[10]
Venus raised the latch and entered.

"You mustn't come in with me—Adolphe is so jealous,"
she said, turning to the Chevalier who was following her;
"but you can stand outside and look on; Adolphe likes an
audience." Then in her delicious fingers she broke the spicy
buns, and with affectionate niceness, breakfasted her ardent
pet. When the last crumbs had been scattered, Venus
brushed her hands together and pretended to leave the cage,
without taking any more notice of Adolphe. Every morning
she went through this piece of play, and every morning the
amorous unicorn was cheated into a distressing agony lest
that day should have proved the last of Venus's love. Not for
long, though, would she leave him in that doubtful, piteous

---

[10] A banner or ensign with streamers suspended from a cross-bar, frequently used in religious processions.

state, but running back passionately to where he stood, make adorable amends for her unkindness.

Poor Adolphe! How happy he was, touching the Queen's breasts with his quick tongue-tip. I have no doubt that the keener scent of animals must make women much more attractive to them than to men; for the gorgeous odour that but faintly fills our nostrils must be revealed to the brute creation in divine fulness. Anyhow, Adolphe sniffed as never a man did around the skirts of Venus. After the first charming interchange of affectionate delicacies was over, the unicorn lay down upon his side, and, closing his eyes, beat his stomach wildly with the mark of manhood!

Venus caught that stunning member in her hands and lay her cheek along it; but few touches were wanted to consummate the creature's pleasure. The Queen bared her left arm to the elbow, and with the soft underneath of it made amazing movements horizontally upon the tight-strung instrument. When the melody began to flow, the unicorn offered up an astonishing vocal accompaniment. Tannhäuser was amused to learn that the etiquette of the Venusberg compelled everybody to await the outburst of these venereal sounds before they could sit down to *déjeuner*.

Adolphe had been quite profuse that morning.

Venus knelt where it had fallen, and lapped her little aperitif!

Chapter 9

HOW VENUS AND TANNHÄUSER BREAKFASTED AND THEN DROVE THROUGH THE PALACE GARDENS

The breakfasters were scattered over the gardens in *têtes-à-têtes* and tiny parties. Venus and Tannhäuser sat together upon the lawn that lay in front of the Casino, and made havoc of a ravishing *déjeuner*. The Chevalier was feeling very happy. Everything around him seemed so white and light and matinal; the floating frocks of the ladies, the scarce robed boys and satyrs stepping hither and thither elegantly, with meats and wines and fruits; the damask tablecloths, the delicate talk and laughter that rose everywhere; the flowers' colour and the flowers' scent; the shady trees, the wind's cool voice, and the sky above that was as fresh and pastoral as a perfect fifth. And Venus looked so beautiful. Not at all like the lady in Lemprière.

"You're such a dear!" murmured Tannhäuser, holding her hand.

At the further end of the lawn, and a little hidden by a rose-tree, a young man was breakfasting alone. He toyed nervously with his food now and then, but for the most part leant back in his chair with unemployed hands, and gazed stupidly at Venus.

"That's Felix," said the Goddess, in answer to an enquiry from the Chevalier; and she went on to explain his attitude. Felix always attended Venus upon her little latrinal excursions, holding her, serving her, and making much of all she did. To undo her things, to lift her skirts, to wait and watch the coming, to dip a lip or finger in the royal output, to stain himself deliciously with it, to lie beneath her as the favours fell, to carry off the crumpled, crotted paper—these were the pleasures of that young man's life.

Truly there never was a queen so beloved by her subjects as Venus. Everything she wore had its lover. Heavens! how her handkerchiefs were filched, her stockings stolen! Daily, what intrigues, what countless ruses to possess her merest frippery! Every scrap of her body was adored. Never, for Savaral, could her ear yield sufficient wax! Never, for Pradon, could she spit prodigally enough! And Saphius found a month an interminable time.

After breakfast was over, and Felix's fears lest Tannhäuser should have robbed him of his capricious rights had been dispelled, Venus invited the Chevalier to take a more extensive view of the gardens, parks, pavilions, and ornamental waters. The carriage was ordered. It was a delicate, shell-like affair, with billowy cushions and a light canopy, and was drawn by ten satyrs, dressed as finely as the coachmen of the Empress Pauline the First.

The drive proved interesting and various, and Tannhäuser was quite delighted with almost everything he saw.

And who is not pleased when on either side of him rich lawns are spread with lovely frocks and white limbs,—and upon flower-beds the dearest ladies are implicated in a glory of underclothing,—when he can see in the deep cool shadows of the trees warm boys entwined, here at the base, there in the branch,—when in the fountain's wave Love holds his court, and the insistent water burrows in every delicious crease and crevice?

A pretty sight, too, was little Rosalie, perched like a postilion upon the painted phallus of the god of all gardens. Her eyes were closed and she was smiling as the carriage passed. Round her neck and slender girlish shoulders there was a cloud of complex dress, over which bulged her wig-like flaxen tresses. Her legs and feet were bare, and the toes twisted in an amorous style. At the foot of the statue lay her shoes and stockings and a few other things.

Tannhäuser was singularly moved at this spectacle, and rose out of all proportion. Venus slipped the fingers of comfort under the lace flounces of his trousers, saying, "Is it all mine? Is it all mine?" and doing fascinating things. In the end, the carriage was only prevented from being overturned by the happy interposition of Priapusa, who stepped out from somewhere or other just in time to preserve its balance.

How the old lady's eye glistened as Tannhäuser withdrew his panting blade! In her sincere admiration for fine things, she quite forgot and forgave the shock she had received from the falling of the gay equipage. Venus and Tannhäuser were profuse with apology and thanks, and quite a crowd of loving courtiers gathered round, consoling and congratulating in a breath.

The Chevalier vowed he would never go in the carriage again, and was really quite upset about it. However, after he had had a little support from the smelling-salts, he recovered his self possession, and consented to drive on further.

The landscape grew rather mysterious. The park, no longer troubled and adorned with figures, was full of grey echoes and mysterious sounds; the leaves whispered a little sadly, and there was a grotto that murmured like the voice that haunts the silence of a deserted oracle. Tannhäuser became a little triste. In the distance, through the trees, gleamed a still, argent lake—a reticent, romantic water that must have held the subtlest fish that ever were. Around its marge the trees and flags and fleurs de luce were unbreakably asleep.

The Chevalier fell into a strange mood, as he looked at the lake. It seemed to him that the thing would speak, reveal some curious secret, say some beautiful word, if he should dare wrinkle its pale face with a pebble.

"I should be frightened to do that, though," he said to himself. Then he wondered what there might be upon the other side; other gardens, other gods? A thousand drowsy fancies passed through his brain. Sometimes the lake took fantastic shapes, or grew to twenty times its size, or shrunk into a miniature of itself, without ever once losing its unruffled calm, its deathly reserve. When the water increased, the Chevalier was very frightened, for he thought how huge the frogs must have become. He thought of their big eyes and monstrous wet feet, but when the water lessened, he laughed to himself, whilst thinking how tiny the frogs must have grown. He thought of their legs that must look thinner than spiders', and of their dwindled croaking that never could be heard. Perhaps the lake was only painted, after all. He had seen things like it at the theatre. Anyhow, it was a wonderful lake, a beautiful lake, and he would love to bathe in it, but he was sure he would be drowned if he did.

Chapter 10

OF THE STABAT MATER, SPIRIDION, AND DE LA PINE

When he woke up from his day-dream, he noticed that the carriage was on its way back to the palace. They stopped at the Casino first, and stepped out to join the players at *petits chevaux* [literally, "little horses"]. Tannhäuser preferred to watch the game rather than play himself, and stood behind Venus, who slipped into a vacant chair and cast gold pieces upon lucky numbers. The first thing that Tannhäuser noticed was the grace and charm, the gaiety and beauty of the croupiers. They were quite adorable even when they raked in one's little losings. Dressed in black silk, and wearing white kid gloves, loose yellow wigs and feathered toques: with faces oval and young, bodies lithe and quick, voices silvery and affectionate, they made amends for all the hateful arrogance, disgusting aplomb, and shameful ugliness of the rest of their kind.

The dear fellow who proclaimed the winner was really quite delightful. He took a passionate interest in the horses, and had licked all the paint off their *petits couillons* ["little balls"]!

You will ask me, no doubt, "Is that all he did?" I will answer, "Not quite," as the merest glance at their *petits derrières* ["little behinds"] would prove.

In the afternoon light that came through the great silken-blinded windows of the Casino, all the gilded decorations, all the chandeliers, the mirrors, the polished floor, the painted ceiling, the horses galloping round their green meadow, the fat rouleaux of gold and silver, the ivory rakes, the fanned and strange frocked crowd of dandy gamesters looked magnificently rich and warm. Tea was being served. It was so pretty to see some plushed little lady sipping nervously, and keeping her eyes over the cup's edge intently upon the slackening horses. The more indifferent left the tables and took their tea in parties here and there.

Tannhäuser found a great deal to amuse him at the Casino. Ponchon was the manager, and a person of extraordinary invention. Never a day but he was ready with a new show—a novel attraction. A glance through the old Casino programmes would give you a very considerable idea of his talent. What countless ballets, comedies, comedy-ballets, concerts, masques, charades, proverbs, pantomimes, tableaux-magiques, and peep-shows eccentriques; what troupes of marionettes, what burlesques!

Ponchon had an astonishing flair for new talent, and many of the principal comedians and singers at the Queen's Theatre and Opera House had made their first appearance and reputation at the Casino.

This afternoon the *pièce de résistance* was a performance of Rossini's *Stabat Mater*,[11] an adorable masterpiece. It was given in the beautiful Salle des Printemps Parfumés. Ah!

---

[11] A musical setting of *Stabat Mater Dolorosa* (Latin, "the sorrowful mother was standing"), a thirteenth-century prayer on the Virgin's sorrows at the Cross.

what a stunning rendering of the delicious *démodé pièce de décadence* ["old-fashioned decadent work"]. There is a subtle quality about the music, like the unhealthy bloom upon wax fruit, that both orchestra and singer contrived to emphasize with consummate delicacy.

The Virgin was sung by Spiridion, that soft incomparable alto. A miraculous virgin, too, he made of her. To begin with, he dressed the rôle most effectively. His plump legs up to the feminine hips of him, were in very white stockings, clocked with a false pink. He wore brown kid boots, buttoned to mid-calf, and his whorish thighs had thin scarlet garters round them. His jacket was cut like a jockey's, only the sleeves ended in manifold frills, and round the neck, and just upon the shoulders, there was a black cape. His hair, dyed green, was curled into ringlets, such as the smooth Madonnas of Morales are made lovely with, and fell over his high egg-shaped creamy forehead, and about his ears and cheeks and back.

The alto's face was fearful and wonderful—a dream face. The eyes were full and black, with puffy blue rimmed hemispheres beneath them, the cheeks, inclining to fatness, were powdered and dimpled, the mouth was purple and curved painfully, the chin tiny, and exquisitely modelled, the expression cruel and womanish. Heavens! how splendid he looked and sounded.

An exquisite piece of phrasing was accompanied with some curly gesture of the hand, some delightful undulation of the stomach, some nervous movement of the thigh, or glorious rising of the bosom.

The performance provoked enthusiasm—thunders of applause. Claude and Clair pelted the thing with roses, and carried him off in triumph to the tables. His costume was declared ravishing. The men almost pulled him to bits, and mouthed at his great quivering bottom! The little horses were quite forgotten for the moment.

Sup, the penetrating, burst through his silk fleshings, and thrust in bravely up to the hilt, whilst the alto's legs were feasted upon by Pudex, Cyril, Anquetin, and some others. Ballice, Corvo, Quadra, Senillé, Mellefont, Theodore, Le Vit [slang for the phallus], and Matta, all of the egoistic cult, stood and crouched round, saturating the lovers with warm douches.

Later in the afternoon, Venus and Tannhäuser paid a little visit to De La Pine's studio, as the Chevalier was very anxious to have his portrait painted. De La Pine's glory as a painter was hugely increased by his reputation as a *fouteur* [slang for "fornicator"], for ladies that had pleasant memories of him looked with a biassed eye upon his *fêtes galantes merveilleuses* ["wondrous love festivities"], portraits and *folies bergeres*.

Yes, he was a bawdy creature, and his workshop a regular brothel. However, his great talent stood in no need of such meretricious and phallic support, and he was every whit as strong and facile with his brush as with his tool!

When Venus and the Chevalier entered his studio, he was standing amid a group of friends and connoisseurs who were liking his latest picture. It was a small canvas, one of his delightful morning pieces. Upon an Italian balcony stood a lady in a white frock, reading a letter. She wore brown stockings, straw-coloured petticoats, white shoes, and a Leghorn hat. Her hair was red and in a chignon. At her feet lay a tiny Japanese dog, painted from the Queen's favourite "Fanny," and upon the balustrade stood an open empty bird cage. The background was a stretch of Gallic country, clusters of trees cresting the ridges of low hills, a bit of river, a chateau, and the morning sky.

De La Pine hastened to kiss the moist and scented hand of Venus. Tannhäuser bowed profoundly and begged to have some pictures shown him. The gracious painter took him round his studio.

Cosmé was one of the party, for De La Pine just then was painting his portrait—a portrait, by the way, which promised to be a veritable *chef d'œuvre* ["masterpiece"], Cosmé was loved and admired by everybody. To begin with, he was pastmaster in his art, that fine, relevant art of coiffing; then he was really modest and obliging, and was only seen and heard when he was wanted. He was useful; he was decorative in his white apron, black mask, and silver suit; he was discreet.

The painter was giving Venus and Tannhäuser a little dinner that evening, and he insisted on Cosmé joining them. The barber vowed he would be *de trop* ["one too many"], and required a world of pressing before he would accept the invitation. Venus added her voice, and he consented.

Ah! what a delightful little *partie carré* [literally, "square party," i.e. a foursome] it turned out. The painter was in purple and full dress, all tassels and grand folds. His hair magnificently curled, his heavy eyelids painted, his gestures large and romantic, he reminded one a little of Maurel playing Wolfram in the second act of the opera [*Tannhäuser*] of Wagner.

Venus was in a ravishing toilet and confection of Camille's, and looked like K* * * *. Tannhäuser was dressed as a woman and looked like a Goddess. Cosmé sparkled with gold, bristled with ruffs, glittered with bright buttons, was painted, powdered, gorgeously bewigged, and looked like a marquis in a comic opera.

The *salle à manger* ["dining room"] at De La Pine's was quite the prettiest that ever was.

[HERE THE MANUSCRIPT ENDS.]

Max Beerbohm

[1 8 7 2 – 1 9 5 6]

A DEFENCE OF COSMETICS

[1894]

This remarkable essay—which appeared in the first number
of *The Yellow Book* when Beerbohm was still an undergraduate at Oxford—was originally written for the *Pall Mall Gazette* with the title "The Philosophy of Rouge," but it never
appeared there. When the journalistic storm broke over it
(see the Introduction to this volume), Beerbohm whimsically
wrote to his friend Reggie Turner: "Like Meredith or Keats
or any great striker of new notes, I am rejected at first. So
long as I attract notice I am happy—and so long as I can do
beautiful work and have a little following that calls me 'Master.'" Most critics thought, as did the reviewer on *The
World*, that the essay was "pure nonsense," failing to grasp
Beerbohm's ironic championing of the Decadents' cult of artifice in order to satirize it. In his letter to the editor of *The
Yellow Book*, which follows this selection, he attempts to explain the intent of his essay but with no success other than to
extend the irony further. With slight changes, "A Defence
of Cosmetics" was included in his *Works* (1896) with the
title "The Pervasion of Rouge."

Nay, but it is useless to protest. Artifice must queen it once more in the town, and so, if there be any whose hearts chafe at her return, let them not say, "We have come into evil times," and be all for resistance, reformation or angry cavilling. For did the king's sceptre send the sea retrograde, or the wand of the sorcerer avail to turn the sun from its old course? And what man or what number of men ever stayed that reiterated process by which the cities of this world grow, are very strong, fail and grow again? Indeed, indeed, there is charm in every period, and only fools and flutterpates do not seek reverently for what is charming in their own day. No martyrdom, however fine, nor satire, however splendidly bitter, has changed by a little tittle the known tendency of things. It is the times that can perfect us, not we the times, and so let all of us wisely acquiesce. Like the little wired marionettes, let us acquiesce in the dance.

For behold! The Victorian era comes to its end and the day of sancta simplicitas is quite ended. The old signs are here and the portents to warn the seer of life that we are ripe for a new epoch of artifice. Are not men rattling the dice-box and ladies dipping their fingers in the rouge-pots? At Rome, in the keenest time of her dégringolade [French, fig. "decadence"], when there was gambling even in the holy temples, great ladies (does not Lucian [c. 125–180 A.D., Greek writer] tell us?) did not scruple to squander all they had upon unguents from Arabia. Nero's mistress and unhappy wife, Poppæa, of shameful memory, had in her travelling retinue fifteen—or, as some say, fifty—she-asses, for the sake of their milk, that was thought an incomparable guard against cosmetics with poison in them. Last century, too, when life was lived by candle-light, and ethics was but etiquette, and even art a question of punctilio, women, we know, gave the best hours of the day to the crafty larding of their faces and the towering of their coiffures. And men, throwing passion into the wine-bowl to sink or swim, turned out thought to browse upon the green cloth. Cannot we even now in our fancy see them, those silent exquisites round the long table at Brooks' [a fashionable club], masked, all of them, "lest the countenance should betray feeling," in quinze masks, through whose eyelets they sat peeping, peep-

ing, while macao brought them riches or ruin? We can see
them, those silent rascals, sitting there with their cards and
their rouleaux and their wooden money-bowls, long after the
dawn had crept up St. James' [Park] and pressed its haggard
face against the window of the little club. Yes, we can raise
their ghosts—and, more, we can see manywhere a devotion
to hazard [a dice game] fully as meek as theirs. In England
there has been a wonderful revival of cards. Roulette may
rival dead faro [gambling game at cards] in the tale of her
devotees. Her wheel is spinning busily in every house and ere
long it may be that tender parents will be waiting to complain of the compulsory baccarat [a card game] in our public schools.

In fact, we are all gamblers once more, but our gambling is
on a finer scale than ever it was. We fly from the card-room
to the heath, and from the heath to the City, and from the
City to the coast of the Mediterranean. And just as no one
seriously encourages the clergy in its frantic efforts to lay the
spirit of chance, that has thus resurged among us, so no
longer are many faces set against that other great sign of a
more complicated life, the love for cosmetics. No longer is a
lady of fashion blamed if, to escape the outrageous persecu-
tion of time, she fly for sanctuary to the toilet-table; and if a
damosel, prying in her mirror, be sure that with brush and
pigment she can trick herself into more charm, we are not
angry. Indeed, why should we ever have been? Surely it is
laudable, this wish to make fair the ugly and overtop fairness, and no wonder that within the last five years the trade
of the makers of cosmetics has increased immoderately—
twenty-fold, so one of these makers has said to me. We need
but walk down any modish street and peer into the little
broughams that flit past, or (in Thackeray's phrase) under
the bonnet of any woman we meet, to see over how wide a
kingdom rouge reigns. We men, who, from Juvenal [Roman
satirist of 2nd cent., A.D.] down to that discourteous painter
of whom Lord Chesterfield tells us, have especially shown a
dislike of cosmetics, are quite yielding; and there are, I
fancy, many such husbands as he who, suddenly realising
that his wife was painted, bade her sternly, "Go up and take it

all off," and, on her reappearance, bade her with increasing
sternness, "Go up and put it all on again."

But now that the use of pigments is becoming general, and
most women are not so young as they are painted, it may be
asked curiously how the prejudice ever came into being. Indeed, it is hard to trace folly, for that it is inconsequent, to
its start; and perhaps it savours too much of reason to suggest that the prejudice was due to the tristful confusion man
has made of soul and surface. Through trusting so keenly to
the detection of the one by keeping watch upon the other,
and by force of the thousand errors following, he has come
to think of surface even as the reverse of soul. He supposes
that every clown beneath his paint and lip-salve is moribund
and knows it, (though in verity, I am told, clowns are as
cheerful a class of men as any other), that the fairer the
fruit's rind and the more delectable its bloom, the closer are
packed the ashes within it. The very jargon of the hunting-
field connects cunning with a mask. And so perhaps came
man's anger at the embellishment of women—that lovely
mask of enamel with its shadows of pink and tiny pencilled
veins, what must lurk behind it? Of what treacherous
mysteries may it not be the screen? Does not the heathen
lacquer her dark face, and the harlot paint her cheeks, because sorrow has made them pale?

After all, the old prejudice is a-dying. We need not pry
into the secret of its birth. Rather is this a time of jolliness
and glad indulgence. For the era of rouge is upon us, and as
only in an elaborate era can man by the tangled accrescency
of his own pleasures and emotions reach that refinement
which is his highest excellence, and by making himself, so to
say, independent of Nature, come nearest to God, so only in
an elaborate era is woman perfect. Artifice is the strength of
the world, and in that same mask of paint and powder,
shadowed with vermeil tint and most trimly pencilled, is
woman's strength.

For see! We need not look so far back to see woman
under the direct influence of Nature. Early in this century,
our grandmothers, sickening of the odour of faded exotics
and spilt wine, came out into the daylight once more and let
the breezes blow around their faces and enter, sharp and

welcome, into their lungs. Artifice they drove forth, and they set Martin Tupper[1] upon a throne of mahogany to rule over them. A very reign of terror set in. All things were sacrificed to the fetish Nature. Old ladies may still be heard to tell how, when they were girls, affectation was not; and, if we verify their assertion in the light of such literary authorities as Dickens, we find that it is absolutely true. Women appear to have been in those days utterly natural in their conduct— flighty, gushing, blushing, fainting, giggling and shaking their curls. They knew no reserve in the first days of the Victorian era. No thought was held too trivial, no emotion too silly, to express. To Nature everything was sacrificed. Great heavens! And in those barren days what influence was exerted by women? By men they seem not to have been feared nor loved, but regarded rather as "dear little creatures" or "wonderful little beings," and in their relation to life as foolish and ineffectual as the landscapes they did in water-colour. Yet, if the women of those years were of no great account, they had a certain charm and they at least had not begun to trespass upon men's ground; if they touched not thought, which is theirs by right, at any rate they refrained from action, which is ours. Far more serious was it when, in the natural trend of time, they became enamoured of rinking and archery and galloping along the Brighton Parade [fashionable sea-front boulevard at Brighton]. Swiftly they have sped on since then from horror to horror. The invasion of the tennis-courts and of the golf-links, the seizure of the tricycle and of the type-writer, were but steps preliminary in that campaign which is to end with the final victorious occupation of St. Stephen's [the House of Commons]. But stay! The horrific pioneers of womanhood who gad hither and thither and, confounding wisdom with the device on her shield, shriek for the unbecoming, are doomed. Though they spin their tricycle-treadles so amazingly fast, they are too late. Though they scream victory, none follow them. Artifice, that fair exile, has returned.

Yes, though the pioneers know it not, they are doomed

[1] 1810–89, English author who achieved fame during the Victorian period for his *Proverbial Philosophy* (1838–76), consisting of moralizations in blank verse.

already. For of the curiosities of history not the least strange is the manner in which two social movements may be seen to overlap, long after the second has, in truth, given its death-blow to the first. And, in like manner as one has seen the limbs of a murdered thing in lively movement, so we need not doubt that, though the voices of those who cry out for reform be very terribly shrill, they will soon be hushed. Dear Artifice is with us. It needed but that we should wait.

Surely, without any of my pleading, women will welcome their great and amiable protectrix, as by instinct. For (have I not said?) it is upon her that all their strength, their life almost, depends. Artifice's first command to them is that they should repose. With bodily activity their powder will fly, their enamel crack. They are butterflies who must not flit, if they love their bloom. Now, setting aside the point of view of passion, from which very many obvious things might be said, (and probably have been by the minor poets), it is, from the intellectual point of view, quite necessary that a woman should repose. Hers is the resupinate sex. On her couch she is a goddess, but so soon as ever she put her foot to the ground—lo, she is the veriest little sillypop and quite done for. She cannot rival us in action, but she is our mis-tress in the things of the mind. Let her not by second-rate athletics, nor indeed by any exercise soever of the limbs, spoil the pretty procedure of her reason. Let her be content to remain the guide, the subtle suggester of what *we* must do, the strategist whose soldiers we are, the little architect whose workmen.

"After all," as a pretty girl once said to me, "women are a sex by themselves, so to speak," and the sharper the line between their worldly functions and ours, the better. This greater swiftness and less erring subtlety of mind, their forte and privilege, justifies the painted mask that Artifice bids them wear. Behind it their minds can play without let. They gain the strength of reserve. They become important, as in the days of the Roman Empire were the Emperor's mistresses, as was the Pompadour at Versailles, as was our Elizabeth. Yet do not their faces become lined with thought; beautiful and without meaning are their faces.

And, truly, of all the good things that will happen with the full renascence of cosmetics, one of the best is that surface will finally be severed from soul. That damnable confusion will be solved by the extinguishing of a prejudice which, as I suggest, itself created. Too long has the face been degraded from its rank as a thing of beauty to a mere vulgar index of character or emotion. We had come to troubling ourselves, not with its charm of colour and line, but with such questions as whether the lips were sensuous, the eyes full of sadness, the nose indicative of determination. I have no quarrel with physiognomy. For my own part, I believe in it. But it has tended to degrade the face æsthetically, in such wise as the study of cheirosophy [study of hands] has tended to degrade the hand. And the use of cosmetics, the masking of the face, will change this. We shall gaze at a woman merely because she is beautiful, not stare into her face anxiously, as into the face of a barometer.

How fatal it has been, in how many ways, this confusion of soul and surface! Wise were the Greeks in making plain masks for their mummers to play in, and dunces we not to have done the same! Only the other day, an actress was saying that what she was most proud of in her art—next, of course, to having appeared in some provincial pantomime at the age of three—was the deftness with which she contrived, in parts demanding a rapid succession of emotions, to dab her cheeks quite quickly with rouge from the palm of her right hand, or powder from the palm of her left. Gracious goodness! why do not we have masks upon the stage? Drama is the presentment of the soul in action. The mirror of the soul is the voice. Let the young critics, who seek a cheap reputation for austerity, by cavilling at "incidental music," set their faces rather against the attempt to justify inferior dramatic art by the subvention of a quite alien art like painting, of any art, indeed, whose sphere is only surface. Let those, again, who sneer, so rightly, at the "painted anecdotes of the Academy," censure equally the writers who trespass on painter's ground. It is a proclaimed sin that a painter should concern himself with a good little girl's affection for a Scotch greyhound, or the keen enjoyment of their port by elderly gentlemen of the early 'forties. Yet, for a painter to prod the soul with his paint-brush is no worse than for a novelist to refuse to dip under the surface, and the fashion of avoiding a psychological study of grief by stating that the owner's hair turned white in a single night, or of shame by mentioning a sudden rush of scarlet to the cheeks, is as lamentable as may be. But! But with the universal use of cosmetics and the consequent secernment [separation] of soul and surface, which, at the risk of irritating a reader, I must again insist upon, all those old properties that went to bolster up the ordinary novel—the trembling lips, the flashing eyes, the determined curve of the chin, the nervous trick of biting the moustache—aye and the hectic spot of red on either cheek—will be made spiflicate, as the puppets were spiflicated [destroyed] by Don Quixote. Yes, even now Demos [personification of Greek word for "people"] begins to discern. The same spirit that has revived rouge, smote his mouth as it grinned at the wondrous painter of mist and river, and now sends him sprawling for the pearls that [George] Meredith [1828–1909, English poet and novelist] dived for in the deep waters of romance.

Indeed the revival of cosmetics must needs be so splendid an influence, conjuring boons innumerable, that one inclines almost to mutter against the inexorable law by which Artifice must perish from time to time. That such branches of painting as the staining of glass or the illuminating of manuscripts should fall into disuse seems, in comparison, so likely; these were esoteric arts; they died with the monastic spirit. But personal appearance is art's very basis. The painting of the face is the first kind of painting man can have known. To make beautiful things—is it not an impulse laid upon few? But to make oneself beautiful is an universal instinct. Strange that the resultant art could never perish! So fascinating an art too! So various in its materials from stimmis, psimythium and fuligo [rouge] to bismuth and arsenic, so simple in that its ground and its subject-matter are one, so marvellous in that its very subject-matter becomes lovely when an artist has selected it! For surely this is no idle nor fantastic saying. To deny that "make-up" is an art, on the pretext that the finished work of its exponents depends for beauty and excellence upon the ground chosen for the work, is absurd. At the touch of a true artist, the plainest face turns comely. As subject-matter the face is no more than suggestive, as ground, merely a loom round which the *beatus artifex* ["happy artist"] may spin the threads of any gold fabric:

> *Quae nunc nomen habent operosi signa Maronis*
> *Pondus iners quondam duraque massa fuit.*
> *Multa viros nescire decet, pars maxima rerum*
> *Offendat, si non interiora tegas,*[2]

and, as Ovid would seem to suggest, by pigments any tone may be set aglow on a woman's cheek, from enamel the features take any form. Insomuch that surely the advocates of soup-kitchens and free-libraries and other devices for giving people what providence did not mean them to receive, should send out pamphlets in the praise of self-embellishment. For it will place Beauty within easy reach of many who could not otherwise hope to attain it.

But of course Artifice is rather exacting. In return for the repose she forces—so wisely!—upon her followers when the sun is high or the moon is blown across heaven, she demands that they should pay her long homage at the sun's rising. The initiate may not enter lightly upon her mysteries. For, if a bad complexion be inexcusable, to be ill-painted is unforgiveable; and when the toilet is laden once more with the fulness of its elaboration, we shall hear no more of the proper occupation for women. And think, how sweet an energy, to sit at the mirror of coquetry! See the dear merits of the toilet as shown upon old vases, or upon the walls of Roman dwellings, or, rather still, read Böttiger's alluring, scholarly description of "Morgenscenen im Puttzimmer Einer Reichen Römerin."[3] Read of Sabina's face as she comes through the curtain of her bed-chamber to the chamber of her toilet. The slave-girls have long been chafing their white feet upon the marble floor. They stand, those timid Greek girls, marshalled in little battalions. Each has her ap-

---

[2] "That which is now called the statue of laborious Maro was once an inert mass and a hard rock. It is proper that men should remain ignorant of many things; most things would cause offense if one did not hide their interior."

[3] A reference to Böttiger's work translated into French in 1813 as *Sabine ou Matinée d'une Dame Romaine à sa Toilette.*

pointed task, and all kneel in welcome as Sabina stalks, ugly and frowning, to the toilet chair. Scaphion steps forth from among them, and, dipping a tiny sponge in a bowl of hot milk, passes it lightly, ever so lightly, over her mistress' face. The Poppæan pastes melt beneath it like snow. A cooling lotion is poured over her brow and is fanned with feathers. Phiale comes after, a clever girl, captured in some sea-skirmish in the Aegean. In her left hand she holds the ivory box wherein are the phucus and that white powder, psimythium; in her right a sheaf of slim brushes. With how sure a touch does she mingle the colours, and in what sweet proportion blushes and blanches her lady's upturned face. Phiale is the cleverest of all the slaves. Now Calamis dips her quill in a certain powder that floats, liquid and sable, in the hollow of her palm. Standing upon tip-toe and with lips parted, she traces the arch of the eyebrows. The slaves whisper loudly of their lady's beauty, and two of them hold up a mirror to her. Yes, the eyebrows are rightly arched. But why does Psecas abase herself? She is craving leave to powder Sabina's hair with a fine new powder. It is made of the grated rind of the cedar-tree, and a Gallic perfumer, whose stall is near the Circus, gave it to her for a kiss. No lady in Rome knows of it. And so, when four special slaves have piled up the head-dress, out of a perforated box this glistening powder is showered. Into every little brown ringlet it enters, till Sabina's hair seems like a pile of gold coins. Lest the breezes send it flying, the girls lay the powder with sprinkled attar. Soon Sabina will start for the Temple of Cybele.

Ah! Such are the lures of the toilet[4] that none will for long hold aloof from them. Cosmetics are not going to be a mere prosaic remedy for age or plainness, but all ladies and all young girls will come to love them. Does not a certain blithe Marquise, whose *lettres intimes* from the Court of Louis Seize are less read than their wit would merit, tell us how she was scandalised to see *"même les toutes jeunes demoiselles émaillées comme ma tabatière?"* ["even the very young ladies enameled like my tobacco case?"] So it shall be with us. Surely the common prejudice against painting the

---

[4] Alas, the word has, in current usage, lost the meaning it had for Beerbohm and the nineteenth century—the process of dressing.

lily can be based on mere ground of economy. That which is already fair is complete, it may be urged—urged implausibly, for there are not so many lovely things in this world that we can afford not to know each one of them by heart. There is only one white lily, and who that has ever seen—as I have —a lily really well painted could grudge the artist so fair a ground for his skill? Scarcely do you believe through how many nice metamorphoses a lily may be passed by him. In like manner, we all know the young girl, with her simpleness, her goodness, her wayward ignorance. And a very charming ideal for England must she have been, and a very natural one, when a young girl sat even on the throne. But no nation can keep its ideal for ever and it needed none of Mr. Gilbert's delicate satire in "Utopia" [with music by Mr. Sullivan] to remind us that she had passed out of our ken with the rest of the early Victorian era. What writer of plays, as lately asked some pressman, who had been told off to attend many first nights and knew what he was talking about, ever dreams of making the young girl the centre of his theme? Rather he seeks inspiration from the tried and tired woman of the world, in all her intricate maturity, whilst, by way of comic relief, he sends the young girl flitting in and out with a tennis-racket, the poor εἴδωλον ἀμανρόν["wasted image"] of her former self. The season of the unsophisticated is gone by, and the young girl's final extinction beneath the rising tides of cosmetics will leave no gap in life and will rob art of nothing.

"Tush," I can hear some damned flutterpate exclaim, "girlishness and innocence are as strong and as permanent as womanhood itself! Why, a few months past, the whole town went mad over Miss Cissie Loftus! Was not hers a success of girlish innocence and the absence of rouge? If such things as these be outmoded, why was she so wildly popular?" Indeed, the triumph of that clever girl, whose début made London nice even in August, is but another witness to the truth of my contention. In a very sophisticated time, simplicity has a new dulcedo. Hers was a success of contrast. Accustomed to clever malaperts like Miss Lloyd or Miss Reeve, whose experienced pouts and smiles under the sun-bonnet are a standing burlesque of innocence and girlishness, Demos was really de-

lighted, for once and away, to see the real presentment of
these things upon his stage. Coming after all those sly serios,
coming so young and mere with her pink frock and straightly
combed hair, Miss Cissie Loftus had the charm which things
of another period often do possess. Besides, just as we adored
her for the abrupt nod with which she was wont at first to
acknowledge the applause, so we were glad for her to come
upon the stage with nothing to tinge the ivory of her cheeks.
It seemed so strange, that neglect of convention. To be behind footlights and not rouged! Yes, hers was a success of
contrast. She was like a daisy in the window at Solomons'.
She was delightful. And yet, such is the force of convention,
that when last I saw her, playing in some burlesque at the
Gaiety, her fringe was curled and her pretty face rouged
with the best of them. And, if further need be to show the
absurdity of having called her performance "a triumph of
naturalness over the jaded spirit of modernity," let us reflect
that the little mimic was not a real old-fashioned girl after
all. She had none of that restless naturalness that would seem
to have characterised the girl of the early Victorian days.
She had no pretty ways—no smiles nor blushes nor tremors.
Possibly Demos could not have stood a presentment of girlishness unrestrained.

But with her grave insouciance, Miss Cissie Loftus had
much of the reserve that is one of the factors of feminine
perfection, and to most comes only, as I have said, with artifice. Her features played very, very slightly. And in truth,
this may have been one of the reasons of her great success.
For expression is but too often the ruin of a face; and, since
we cannot as yet so order the circumstances of life that
women shall never be betrayed into "an unbecoming emotion," when the brunette shall never have cause to blush, and
the lady who looks well with parted lips be kept in a permanent state of surprise, the safest way by far is to create, by
brush and pigments, artificial expressions for every face.

And this—say you?—will make monotony? You are mistaken, *toto cœlo* ["completely"] mistaken. When your mistress has wearied you with one expression, then it will need
but a few touches of that pencil, a backward sweep of that
brush, and lo, you will be revelling in another. For though,

of course, the painting of the face is, in manner, most like the painting of canvas, in outcome it is rather akin to the art of music—lasting, like music's echo, not for very long. So that, no doubt, of the many little appurtenances of the Reformed Toilet Table, not the least vital will be a list of the emotions that become its owner, with recipes for simulating them. According to the colour she wills her hair to be for the time—black or yellow or, peradventure, burnished red—she will blush for you, sneer for you, laugh or languish for you. The good combinations of line and colour are nearly numberless, and by their means poor restless woman will be able to realise her moods in all their shades and lights and dappledoms, to live many lives and masquerade through many moments of joy. No monotony will be. And for us men matrimony will have lost its sting.

But be it remembered! Though we men will garner these oblique boons, it is into the hands of women that Artifice gives her pigments. I know, I know that many men in a certain sect of society have shown a marked tendency to the use of cosmetics. I speak not of the countless gentlemen who walk about town in the time of its desertion from August to October, artificially bronzed, as though they were fresh from the moors or from the Solent [western part of the English Channel]. This, I conceive, is done for purely social reasons and need not concern me here. Rather do I speak of those who make themselves up, seemingly with an æsthetic purpose. Doubtless—I wish to be quite just—there are many who look the better for such embellishment; but, at the hazard of being thought old-fashioned and prejudiced, I cannot speak of the custom with anything but strong disapproval. If men are to lie among the rouge-pots, inevitably it will tend to promote that amalgamation of the sexes which is one of the chief planks in the decadent platform[5] and to obtund that piquant contrast between him and her, which is one of the redeeming features of creation. Besides, really, men have not the excuse of facial monotony, that holds in the case of women. Have we not hair upon our chins and upper lips? And can we not, by diverting the trend of our moustache or

[5] Here, Beerbohm scoffs at the French and English Decadents' interest in hermaphroditism.

by growing our beard in this way or that, avoid the boredom of looking the same for long? Let us beware. For if, in violation of unwritten sexual law, men take to trifling with the paints and brushes that are feminine heritage, it may be that our great ladies will don false imperials, and the little doner deck her pretty chin with a Newgate[6] fringe! After all, I think we need not fear that many men will thus trespass. Most of them are in the City nowadays, and the great wear and tear of that place would put their use of rouge—that demands bodily repose from its dependents—quite outside the range of practical æsthetics.

But that in the world of women they will not neglect this art, so ripping in itself, in its result so wonderfully beneficent, I am sure indeed. Much, I have said, is already done for its full renascence. The spirit of the age has made straight the path of its professors. Fashion has made Jezebel surrender her monopoly of the rouge-pot. As yet, the great art of self-embellishment is for us but in its infancy. But if English-women can bring it to the flower of an excellence so supreme as never yet has it known, then, though Old England may lose her martial and commercial supremacy, we patriots will have the satisfaction of knowing that she has been advanced at one bound to a place in the councils of æsthetic Europe. And, in sooth, is this hoping too high of my countrywomen? True that, as the art seems always to have appealed to the ladies of Athens, and it was not until the waning time of the Republic that Roman ladies learned to love the practice of it, so Paris, Athenian in this as in all other things, has been noted hitherto as a far more vivid centre of the art than London. But it was in Rome, under the Emperors, that un-guentaria [a perfumed ointment] reached its zenith, and shall it not be in London, soon, that unguentaria shall outstrip its Roman perfection? Surely there must be among us artists as cunning in the use of brush and puff as any who lived at Versailles. Surely the splendid, impalpable advance of good taste, as shown in dress and in the decoration of houses, may justify my hope of the preëminence of English-women in the cosmetic art. By their innate delicacy of touch

[6] A reference to the street in London where the "Old Bailey" criminal court stands and where the famous Newgate Prison once stood.

they will accomplish much, and much, of course, by their swift feminine perception. Yet it were well that they should know something also of the theoretical side of the craft. Modern authorities upon the mysteries of the toilet are, it is true, rather few; but among the ancients many a writer would seem to have been fascinated by them. Archigenes, a man of science at the Court of Cleopatra, and Criton at the Court of the Emperor Trajan, both wrote treatises upon cosmetics—doubtless most scholarly treatises that would have given many a precious hint. It is a pity they are not extant. From Lucian or from Juvenal, with his bitter picture of a Roman *levée* [ceremony attending the rising of a nobleman], much may be learnt; from the staid pages of Xenophon and Aristophanes' dear farces. But best of all is that fine book of the *Ars Amatoria* [*Art of Love*] that Ovid has set aside for the consideration of dyes, perfumes and pomades. Written by an artist who knew the allurements of the toilet and understood its philosophy, it remains without rival as a treatise upon Artifice. It is more than a poem, it is a manual; and if there be left in England any lady who cannot read Latin in the original, she will do well to procure a discreet translation. In the Bodleian Library [at Oxford University] there is treasured the only known copy of a very poignant and delightful rendering of this one book of Ovid's masterpiece. It was made by a certain Wye Waltonstall, who lived in the days of Elizabeth, and, seeing that he dedicated it to "the Vertuous Ladyes and Gentlewomen of Great Britain," I am sure that the gallant writer, could he know of our great renascence of cosmetics, would wish his little work to be placed once more within their reach. "Inasmuch as to you, ladyes and gentlewomen," so he writes in his queer little dedication, "my booke of pigments doth first addresse itself, that it may kisse your hands and afterward have the lines thereof in reading sweetened by the odour of your breath, while the dead letters formed into words by your divided lips may receive new life by your passionate expression, and the words marryed in that Ruby coloured temple may thus happily united, multiply your contentment." It is rather sad to think that, at this crisis in the history of pigments, the Vertuous Ladyes and Gentlewomen cannot read the *libellus*

[Latin, "little book"] of Wye Waltonstall, who did so dearly love pigments.

But since the days when these great critics wrote their treatises, with what gifts innumerable has Artifice been loaded by Science! Many little partitions must be added to the *narthecium* [Latin, "an ointment box"] before it can comprehend all the new cosmetics that have been quietly devised since classical days, and will make the modern toilet chalks away more splendid in its possibilities. A pity that no one has devoted himself to the compiling of a new list; but doubtless all the newest devices are known to the admirable unguentarians of Bond Street, who will impart them to their clients. Our thanks, too, should be given to Science for ridding us of the old danger that was latent in the use of cosmetics. Nowadays they cannot, being purged of any poisonous element, do harm to the skin that they make beautiful. There need be no more sowing the seeds of destruction in the furrows of time, no martyrs to the cause like Georgina Gunning, that fair dame but infelix, who died, so they relate, from the effect of a poisonous rouge upon her lips. No, we need have no fears now. Artifice will claim not another victim from among her worshippers.

Loveliness shall sit at the toilet, watching her oval face in the oval mirror. Her smooth fingers shall flit among the paints and powder, to tip and mingle them, catch up a pencil, clasp a phial, and what not and what *not*, until the mask of vermeil tinct has been laid aptly, the enamel quite hardened. And, heavens, how she will charm us and ensorcel our eyes! Positively rouge will rob us for a time of all our reason; we shall go mad over masks. Was it not at Capua [important Roman town on the Appian Way] that they had a whole street where nothing was sold but dyes and unguents? We must have such a street, and, to fill our new Seplasia [a street in Capua], our Arcade of the Unguents, all herbs and minerals and live creatures shall give of their substance. The white cliffs of Albion[7] shall be ground to powder for loveliness, and perfumed by the ghost of many a little violet. The fluffy eider-ducks, that are swimming round the pond, shall lose

[7] Ancient literary name for England, derived probably from the Latin word *albus*, "white," to refer to the chalk cliffs.

their feathers, that the powder-puff may be moonlike as it passes over loveliness's lovely face. Even the camels shall become ministers of delight, giving their hair in many tufts to be stained by the paints in her colour-box, and across her cheek the swift hare's foot shall fly as of old. The sea shall offer her the phucus, its scarlet weed. We shall spill the blood of mulberries at her bidding. And, as in another period of great ecstasy, a dancing wanton, la belle Aubrey, was crowned upon a church's lighted altar, to Arsenic, that "green-tress'd goddess," ashamed at length of skulking between the soup of the unpopular and the test-tubes of the Queen's analyst, shall be exalted to a place of highest honour upon loveliness's toilet-table.

All these things shall come to pass. Times of jolliness and glad indulgence! For Artifice, whom we drove forth, has returned among us, and, though her eyes are red with crying, she is smiling forgiveness. She is kind. Let us dance and be glad, and trip the cockawhoop! Artifice, sweetest exile, is come into her kingdom. Let us dance her a welcome!

A LETTER TO THE EDITOR

Dear Sir,—

When The Yellow Book appeared I was in Oxford. So literary a little town is Oxford that its undergraduates see a newspaper nearly as seldom as the Venetians see a horse, and until yesterday, when coming to London, I found in the album of a friend certain newspaper cuttings, I had not known how great was the wrath of the pressmen.

What in the whole volume seems to have provoked the most ungovernable fury is, I am sorry to say, an essay about Cosmetics that I myself wrote. Of this it was impossible for any one to speak calmly. The mob lost its head, and, so far as any one in literature can be lynched, I was. In speaking of me, one paper dropped the usual prefix of "Mr." as though I were a well-known criminal, and referred to me shortly as "Beerbohm"; a second allowed me the "Mr." but urged that "a short Act of Parliament should be passed to make this

kind of thing illegal"; a third suggested, rather tamely, that I
should read one of Mr. William Watson's sonnets.[1] More
than one comic paper had a very serious poem about me, and
a known adherent to the humour which, forest-like, is called
new, declared my essay to be "the rankest and most nau-
seous thing in all literature." It was a bomb thrown by a
cowardly decadent, another outrage by one of that desperate
and dangerous band of madmen who must be mercilessly
stamped out by a comity of editors. May I, Sir, in justice to
myself and to you, who were gravely censured for harbour-
ing me, step forward, and assure the affrighted mob that it is
the victim of a hoax? May I also assure it that I had no
notion that it would be taken in? Indeed, it seems incredible
to me that any one on the face of the earth could fail to see
that my essay, so grotesque in subject, in opinion so flippant
in style so wildly affected, was meant for a burlesque upon
the "precious" school of writers. If I had only signed myself
D. Cadent or Parrar Docks, or appended a note to say that
the MS. had been picked up not a hundred miles from Tite
Street,[2] all the pressmen would have said that I had given
them a very delicate bit of satire. But I did not. And *hinc*, as
they themselves love to say, *illœ lacrimœ*.[3]

After all, I think it is a sound rule that a writer should not
kick his critics. I simply wish to make them a friendly philosophical suggestion. It seems to be thought that criticism
holds in the artistic world much the same place as, in the
moral world, is held by punishment—"the vengeance taken
by the majority upon such as exceed the limits of conduct
imposed by that majority." As in the case of punishment,
then, we must consider the effect produced by criticism upon
its object, how far is it reformatory? Personally I cannot
conceive how any artist can be hurt by remarks dropped
from a garret into a gutter. Yet it is incontestable that many
an illustrious artist has so been hurt. And these very remarks,
so far from making him change or temper his method, have

---

[1] William Watson (1858–1935), poet and critic who was partly responsible for Beardsley's removal as art editor of *The Yellow Book* in
1895.

[2] Where Oscar Wilde lived.

[3] *Hinc illœ lacrimœ*, "hence those tears."

rather made that method intenser, have driven him to retire further within his own soul, by shewing him how little he may hope for from the world but insult and ingratitude.

In fact, the police-constable mode of criticism is a failure. True that, here and there, much beautiful work of the kind has been done. In the old, old Quarterlies is many a slashing review, that, however absurd it be as criticism, we can hardly wish unwritten. In the *National Observer*,[4] before its reformation, were countless fine examples of the cavilling method. The paper was rowdy, venomous and insincere. There was libel in every line of it. It roared with the lambs and bleated with the lions. It was a disgrace to journalism and a glory to literature. I think of it often with tears and desiderium. But the men who wrote these things stand upon a very different plane to the men employed as critics by the press of Great Britain. These must be judged, not by their workmanship, which is naught, but by the spirit that animates them and the consequence of their efforts. If only they could learn that it is for the critic to seek after beauty and to try to interpret it to others, if only they would give over their eternal fault-finding and not presume to interfere with the artist at his work, then with an equally small amount of ability our pressmen might do nearly as much good as they have hitherto done harm. Why should they regard writers with such enmity? The average pressman, reviewing a book of stories or of poems by an unknown writer, seems not to think "where are the beauties of this work that I may praise them, and by my praise quicken the sense of beauty in others?" He steadily applies himself to the ignoble task of plucking out and gloating over its defects. It is a pity that critics should show so little sympathy with writers, and curious when we consider that most of them tried to be writers themselves, once. Every new school that has come into the world, every new writer who has brought with him a new mode, they have rudely persecuted. The dullness of Ibsen, the obscurity of Meredith, the horrors of Zola—all these are household words. It is not until the pack has yelled itself hoarse that the level voice of justice is heard in praise. To pretend that no

[4] Edited by W. E. Henley, who vigorously opposed the Decadents.

generation is capable of gauging the greatness of its own artists is the merest bauble-tit. Were it not for the accursed
abuse of their function by the great body of critics, no poet
need "live uncrown'd, apart." Many and irreparable are the
wrongs that our critics have done. At length let them repent
with ashes upon their heads. Where they see not beauty, let
them be silent, reverently feeling that it may yet be there,
and train their dull senses in quest of it.

Now is a good time for such penance. There are signs that
our English literature has reached that point, when, like the
literatures of all the nations that have been, it must fall at
length into the hands of the decadents. The qualities that I
tried in my essay to travesty—paradox and marivaudage, lassitude, a love of horror and all unusual things, a love of argot
and archaism and the mysteries of style—are not all these
displayed, some by one, some by another of *les jeunes
écrivains* ["the young writers"]? Who knows but that Artifice is in truth at our gates and that soon she may pass
through our streets? Already the windows of Grub Street[5]
are crowded with watchful, evil faces. They are ready, the
men of Grub Street, to pelt her, as they have pelted all that
came before her. Let them come down while there is still
time, and hang their houses with colours, and strew the road
with flowers. Will they not, for once, do homage to a new
queen? By the time this letter appears, it *may* be too late!

Meanwhile, Sir, I am, your obedient servant,

MAX BEERBOHM.

Oxford, May '94.

DIMINUENDO

First published in *The Pageant* in 1896 as "Be It Cosiness,"
"Diminuendo" was reprinted in *The Collected Works of
Max Beerbohm* (1896), a mock farewell (Beerbohm was
only twenty-four) to the literary life. With characteristic
whimsy, Beerbohm declares that his salvation lies not in

[5] Once the street in London where many hack writers lived.

Pater's faith in intense experiences but in withdrawal from them.

In the year of grace 1890, and in the beautiful autumn of that year, I was a freshman at Oxford. I remember how my tutor asked me what lectures I wished to attend, and how he laughed when I said that I wished to attend the lectures of Mr. Walter Pater. Also I remember how, one morning soon after, I went into Ryman's to order some foolish engraving for my room, and there saw, peering into a portfolio, a small, thick, rock-faced man, whose top-hat and gloves of *bright* dog-skin struck one of the many discords in that little city of learning or laughter. The serried bristles of his moustachio made for him a false-military air. I think I nearly went down when they told me that this was Pater.

Not that even in those more decadent days of my childhood did I admire the man as a stylist. Even then I was angry that he should treat English as a dead language, bored by that sedulous ritual wherewith he laid out every sentence as in a shroud—hanging, like a widower, long over its marmoreal beauty or ever he could lay it at length in his book, its sepulchre. From that laden air, the so cadaverous murmur of that sanctuary, I would hook it at the beck of any jade. The writing of Pater had never, indeed, appealed to me, ἀλλ' αἰεί ["but ever"], having regard to the couth solemnity of his mind, to his philosophy, his rare erudition, τινα φῶτα μέγαν χαὶ χαλὸν ἐδέγμην . . . ["I expected a great and noble man"]. And I suppose it was when at length I saw him that I first knew him to be fallible.

At school I had read *Marius the Epicurean* in bed and with a dark lantern. Indeed, I regarded it mainly as a tale of adventure, quite as fascinating as *Midshipman Easy* [1836, by Frederick Marryat], and far less hard to understand, because there were no nautical terms in it. Marryat, moreover, never made me wish to run away to sea, whilst certainly Pater did make me wish for more 'colour' in the curriculum, for a renaissance of the Farrar period, when there was always 'a sullen spirit of revolt against the authorities'; when lockers were always being broken into and marks falsified, and small boys prevented from saying their prayers, insomuch that they vowed they would no longer buy brandy for their seniors. In some schools, I am told, the pretty old custom of roasting a fourth-form boy, whole, upon Founder's Day still survives. But in my school there was less sentiment. I ended by acquiescing in the slow revolution of its wheel of work and play. I felt that at Oxford, when I should be of age to matriculate, a 'variegated dramatic life' was waiting for me. I was not a little too sanguine, alas!

How sad was my coming to the university! Where were those sweet conditions I had pictured in my boyhood? Those antique contrasts? Did I ride, one sunset, through fens on a palfrey, watching the gold reflections on Magdalen Tower? Did I ride over Magdalen Bridge and hear the consonance of evening-bells and cries from the river below? Did I rein in to wonder at the raised gates of Queen's, the twisted pillars of St. Mary's, the little shops, lighted with tapers? Did bull-pups snarl at me, or dons, with bent backs, acknowledge my salute? Anyone who knows the place as it is, must see that such questions are purely rhetorical. To him I need not explain the disappointment that beset me when, after being whirled in a cab from the station to a big hotel, I wandered out into the streets. *On aurait dit* ["One would have said"] a bit of Manchester through which Apollo had once passed; for here, among the hideous trams and the brand-new bricks— here, glared at by the electric-lights that hung from poles, screamed at by boys with the *Echo* and the *Star*—here, in a riot of vulgarity, were remnants of beauty, as I discerned. There were only remnants.

Soon also I found that the life of the place, like the place, had lost its charm and its tradition. Gone were the contrasts that made it wonderful. That feud between undergraduates and dons—latent, in the old days, only at times when it behoved the two academic grades to unite against the townspeople—was one of the absurdities of the past. The townspeople now looked just like undergraduates and the dons just like townspeople. So splendid was the train-service between Oxford and London that, with hundreds of passengers daily, the one had become little better than a suburb of the other.

What more could extensionists demand? As for me, I was disheartened. Bitter were the comparisons I drew between my coming to Oxford and the coming of Marius to Rome. Could it be that there was at length no beautiful environment wherein a man might sound the harmonies of his soul? Had civilization made beauty, besides adventure, so rare? I wondered what counsel Pater, insistent always upon contact with comely things, would offer to one who could nowhere find them. I had been wondering that very day when I went into Ryman's and saw him there.

When the tumult of my disillusioning was past, my mind grew clearer. I discerned that the scope of my quest for emotion must be narrowed. That abandonment of one's self to life, that merging of one's soul in bright waters, so often suggested in Pater's writing, were a counsel impossible for to-day. The quest of emotions must be no less keen, certainly, but the manner of it must be changed forthwith. To unswitch myself from my surroundings, to guard my soul from contact with the unlovely things that compassed it about, therein lay my hope. I must approach the Benign Mother with great caution. And so, while most of the freshman were doing her honour with wine and song and wreaths of smoke, I stood aside, pondered. In such seclusion I passed my first term— ah, how often did I wonder whether I was not wasting my days, and, wondering, abandon my meditations upon the right ordering of the future! Thanks be to Athene, who threw her shadow over me in those moments of weak folly!

At the end of term I came to London. Around me seethed swirls, eddies, torrents, violent cross-currents of human activity. What uproar! Surely I could have no part in modern life. Yet, yet for a while it was fascinating to watch the ways of its children. The prodigious life of the Prince of Wales fascinated me above all; indeed, it still fascinates me. What experience has been withheld from His Royal Highness? Was ever so supernal a type, as he, of mere Pleasure? How often he has watched, at Newmarket, the scud-a-run of quivering homuncules over the vert on horses, or, from some night-boat, the holocaust of great wharves by the side of the Thames; raced through the blue Solent [western part of the English Channel]; threaded *les coulisses* [the "wings" in a theatre]! He has danced in every palace of every capital, played in every club. He has hunted elephants through the jungles of India, boar through the forests of Austria, pigs over the plains of Massachusetts. From the Castle of Abergeldie he has led his Princess into the frosty night, Highlanders lighting with torches the path to the deer-larder, where lay the wild things that had fallen to him on the crags. He has marched the Grenadiers to chapel through the white streets of Windsor. He has ridden through Moscow, in strange apparel, to kiss the catafalque of more than one Tzar. For him the Rajahs of India have spoiled their temples, and Blondin has crossed Niagara along the tight-rope, and the Giant Guard done drill beneath the chandeliers of the Neue Schloss. Incline he to scandal, lawyers are proud to whisper their secrets in his ear. Be he gallant, the ladies are at his feet. *Ennuyé* ["bored"], all the wits from Bernal Osborne to Arthur Roberts have jested for him. He has been 'present always at the focus where the greatest number of forces unite in their purest energy,' for it is his presence that makes those forces unite.

'*Ennuyé?*' I asked. Indeed he never is. How could he be when Pleasure hangs constantly upon his arm! It is those others, overtaking her only after arduous chase, breathless and footsore, who quickly sicken of her company, and fall fainting at her feet. And for me, shod neither with rank nor riches, what folly to join the chase! I began to see how small a thing it were to sacrifice those external 'experiences,' so dear to the heart of Pater, by a rigid, complex civilization made so hard to gain. They gave nothing but lassitude to those who had gained them through suffering. Even to the kings and princes, who so easily gained them, what did they yield besides themselves? I do not suppose that, if we were invited to give authenticated instances of intelligence on the part of our royal pets, we could fill half a column of the *Spectator*. In fact, their lives are so full they have no time for thought, the highest energy of man. Now, it was to thought that *my* life should be dedicated. Action, apart from its absorption of time, would war otherwise against the pleasures of intellect, which, for me, meant mainly the pleasures of imagination. It is only (this is a platitude) the things one has not done, the faces or places one has not seen, or seen but darkly, that have charm. It is only mystery—such mystery as besets the eyes of children—that makes things superb. I thought of the voluptuaries I had known—they seemed so sad, so ascetic almost, like poor pilgrims, raising their eyes never or ever gazing at the moon of tarnished endeavour. I thought of the round, insouciant faces of the monks at whose monastery I once broke bread, and how their eyes sparkled when they asked me of the France that lay around their walls. I thought, *pardie* ["to be sure"], of the lurid verses written by young men who, in real life, know no haunt more lurid than a literary public-house. It was, for me, merely a problem how I could best avoid 'sensations,' 'pulsations,' and 'exquisite moments' that were not purely intellectual. I would not attempt to combine both kinds, as Pater seemed to fancy a man might. I would make myself master of some small area of physical life, a life of quiet, monotonous simplicity, exempt from all outer disturbance. I would shield my body from the world that my mind might range over it, not hurt nor fettered. As yet, however, I was in my first year at Oxford. There were many reasons that I should stay there and take my degree, reasons that I did not combat. Indeed, I was content to wait for my life.

And now that I have made my adieux to the Benign Mother, I need wait no longer. I have been casting my eye over the suburbs of London. I have taken a most pleasant little villa in ——ham, and here I shall make my home. Here there is no traffic, no harvest. Those of the inhabitants who do anything go away each morning and do it elsewhere. Here no vital forces unite. Nothing happens here. The days and the months will pass by me, bringing their sure recurrence of quiet events. In the spring-time I shall look out from my window and see the laburnum flowering in the little front garden. In summer cool syrups will come for me from the grocer's shop. Autumn will make the boughs of my mountain-ash scarlet, and, later, the asbestos in my grate will put forth its blossoms of flame. The infrequent cart of Buszard or Mudie will pass my window at all seasons. Nor will this be all. I shall have friends. Next door, there is a retired military man who has offered, in a most neighbourly way, to lend me his copy of *The Times*. On the other side of my house lives a charming family, who perhaps will call on me, now and again. I have seen them sally forth, at sundown, to catch the theatre-train; among them walked a young lady, the charm of whose figure was ill concealed by the neat waterproof that overspread her evening-dress. Some day it may be . . . but I anticipate. These things will be but the cosy accompaniment of my days. For I shall contemplate the world.

I shall look forth from my window, the laburnum and the mountain-ash becoming mere silhouettes in the foreground of my vision. I shall look forth and, in my remoteness, appreciate the distant pageant of the world. Humanity will range itself in the columns of my morning paper. No pulse of life will escape me. The strife of politics, the intriguing of courts, the wreck of great vessels, wars, dramas, earthquakes, national griefs or joys; the strange sequels to divorces, even, and the mysterious suicides of land-agents at Ipswich—in all such phenomena I shall steep my exhaurient mind. *Delicias quoque bibliothecae experiar* ["I shall also experience the delights of a library."]. Tragedy, comedy, chivalry, philosophy will be mine. I shall listen to their music perpetually and their colours will dance before my eyes. I shall soar from terraces of stone upon dragons with shining wings and make war upon Olympus. From the peaks of hills I shall swoop into recondite valleys and drive the pigmies, shrieking little curses, to their caverns. It may be my whim to wander through infinite parks where the deer lie under the clustering shadow of their antlers and flee lightly over the grass; to whisper with white prophets under the elms or bind a child with a daisy-chain or, with a lady, thread my way through the acacias. I shall swim down rivers into the sea and outstrip all ships. Unhindered I shall penetrate all sanctuaries and snatch the secrets of every dim confessional.[1]

Yes! among books that charm, and give wings to the mind, will my days be spent. I shall be ever absorbing the things great men have written; with such experience I will charge my mind to the full. Nor will I try to give anything in return.

[1] An echo of Pater's famous description of La Gioconda in *The Renaissance*: "[She] has been a diver in deep seas . . . and has learned the secrets of the grave . . ."

Once, in the delusion that Art, loving the recluse, would make his life happy, I wrote a little for a yellow quarterly [*The Yellow Book*, of course] and had that *succès de fiasco* which is always given to a young writer of talent. But the stress of creation soon overwhelmed me. Only Art with a capital H gives any consolations to her henchmen. And I, who crave no knighthood,[2] shall write no more. Already I feel myself to be a trifle outmoded. I belong to the Beardsley period. Younger men, with months of activity before them, with fresher schemes and notions, with newer enthusiasm, have pressed forward since then. *Credo junioribus* ["I believe in younger people"]. Indeed, I stand aside with no regret. For to be outmoded is to be a classic, if one has written well. I have acceded to the hierarchy of good scribes and rather like my niche.

[2] Beerbohm was, in fact, knighted in 1939.

Olive Custance
(Lady Alfred Douglas)

[1 8 7 4 — 1 9 4 4]

PEACOCKS: A MOOD

In gorgeous plumage, azure, gold and green,
They trample the pale flowers, and their shrill cry
Troubles the garden's bright tranquillity!
Proud birds of Beauty, splendid and serene,
Spreading their brilliant fans, screen after screen
Of burnished sapphire, gemmed with mimic suns—
Strange magic eyes that, so the legend runs,
Will bring misfortune to this fair demesne . . .

And my gay youth, that, vain and debonair,
Sits in the sunshine—tired at last of play
(A child, that finds the morning all too long),
Tempts with its beauty that disastrous day
When in the gathering darkness of despair
Death shall strike dumb the laughing mouth of song.

THE MASQUERADE

Masked dancers in the Dance of life
We move sedately . . . wearily together,
Afraid to show a sign of inward strife,
We hold our souls in tether.

We dance with proud and smiling lips,
With frank appealing eyes, with shy hands clinging.
We sing, and few will question if there slips
A sob into our singing.

Each has a certain step to learn,
Our prisoned feet move staidly in set paces,
And to and fro we pass, since life is stern,
Patiently, with masked faces.

Yet some there are who will not dance,
They sit apart most sorrowful and splendid,
But all the rest trip on as in a trance,
Until the Dance is ended.

HYACINTHUS

Fair boy, how gay the morning must have seemed
Before the fatal game that murdered thee!
Of such a dawn my wistful heart has dreamed:
Surely I too have lived in Arcady
When Spring, lap-full of roses, ran to meet
White Aphrodite risen from the sea . . .

Perchance I saw thee then, so glad and fleet,
Hasten to greet Apollo,[1] stoop to bind
The gold and jewelled sandals on his feet,
While he so radiant, so divinely kind,

[1] See Lord Alfred Douglas' "Rejected."

Lured thee with honeyed words to be his friend,
All heedless of thy fate, for Love is blind.

For Love is blind and cruel, and the end
Of every joy is sorrow and distress.
And when immortal creatures lightly bend
To kiss the lips of simple loveliness,
Swords are unsheathed in silence, and clouds rise,
Some God is jealous of the mute caress . . .

But who shall mourn thy death—ah, not the wise?
Better to perish in thy happiest hour,
To close in sight of beauty thy dark eyes,
And, dying so, be changed into a flower,
Than that the stealthy and relentless years
Should steal that grace which was thy only dower.

And bring thee in return dull cares and tears,
And difficult days and sickness and despair . . .
Oh, not for thee the griefs and sordid fears
That, like a burden, trembling age must bear;
Slain in thy youth, by the sweet hands of Love,
Thou shalt remain for ever young and fair . . .

THE WHITE STATUE

I love you, silent statue: for your sake
My songs in prayer up-reach
Frail hands of flame-like speech,
That some mauve-silver twilight you make wake!

I love you more than swallows love the south.
As sunflowers turn and turn
Towards the sun, I yearn
To press warm lips against your cold white mouth.

I love you more than scarlet-skirted dawn,
At sight of whose spread wings

The great world wakes and sings,
Forgetful of the long vague dark withdrawn.

*   *   *   *   *   *   *

I love you most at purple sunsetting,
When night with feverish eyes
Comes up the fading skies. . . .
I love you with a passion past forgetting!

STATUES

I have loved statues . . . spangled dawns have seen
Me bowed before their beauty . . . when the green
And silver world of Spring wears radiantly
The morning rainbows of an opal sky . . .
And I have chanted curious madrigals
To charm their coldness, twined for coronals
Blossoming branches, thinking thus to change
Their still contempt for mortal love, their bright
Proud scorn to something delicate and strange,
More sweet, more marvellous, than mere delight!

I have loved statues—passionately prone
My body worshipped the white form of stone!
And like a flower that lifts its chalice up
Towards the light—my soul became a cup
That over-brimming with enchanted wine
Of ecstasy—was raised to the divine
Indifferent lips of some young silent God
Standing aloof from all our tears and strife,
Tranced in the paradise of dreams, he trod
In the untroubled summer of his life!
I have loved statues . . . and at night the cold
Mysterious moon behind a mask of gold—
Or veiled in silver veils—has seen my pride
Utterly broken—seen the dream denied
For which I pleaded—heedless that for me

The miracle of joy could never be . . .
As in old legends beautiful and strange,
When bright gods loved fair mortals born to die,
And the frail daughters of despair and change
Became the brides of immortality?

CANDLE-LIGHT

Frail golden flowers that perish at a breath,
Flickering points of honey-coloured flame,
From sunset gardens of the moon you came,
Pale flowers of passion . . . delicate flowers of death . . .

Blossoms of opal fire that raised on high
Upon a hundred silver stems are seen
Above the brilliant dance, or set between
The brimming wine-cups . . . flowers of revelry!

Roses with amber petals that arise
Out of the purple darkness of the night
To deck the darkened house of Love, to light
The laughing lips, the beautiful glad eyes.

Lilies with violet-coloured hearts that break
In shining clusters round the silent dead,
A diadem of stars at feet and head,
The glory dazzles . . . but they do not wake . . .

O golden flowers the moon goes gathering
In magic gardens of her fairy-land,
While splendid angels of the sunset stand
Watching in flaming circles wing to wing . . .

Frail golden flowers that perish at a breath,
That wither in the hands of light, and die
When bright dawn wakens in a silver sky.
Pale flowers of passion . . . delicate flowers of death.

Lord Alfred Douglas

[1870–1945]

APOLOGIA[1]

Tell me not of Philosophies,
   Of morals, ethics, laws of life;
Give me no subtle theories,
   No instruments of wordy strife.
I will not forge laborious chains
   Link after link, till seven times seven,
I need no ponderous iron cranes
   To haul my soul from earth to heaven.
But with a burnished wing,
   Rainbow-hued in the sun,
   I will dive and leap and run
In the air, and I will bring
Back to the earth a heavenly thing,
   I will dance through the stars
   And pass the blue bars
Of heaven. I will catch hands with God
   And speak with Him,
   I will kiss the lips of the seraphim

[1] In a note appended to his *Collected Poems* (1919), Douglas commented: "For the childish egoism and the dubious morality of such pieces as 'Apologia' and 'Ode to my Soul,' and one or two of the earlier sonnets I hold no kind of brief . . . it would be foolish to change the essential character of pieces which are representative of various stages of my development as a man and as a poet."

And the deep-eyed cherubim;
I will pluck of the flowers that nod
   Row upon row upon row,
In the infinite gardens of God,
To the breath of the wind of the sweep of the lyres,
    And the cry of the strings
    And the golden wires,
    And the mystical musical things
That the world may not know.

[Oxford, 1892]

TWO LOVES

I dreamed I stood upon a little hill,
And at my feet there lay a ground, that seemed
Like a waste garden, flowering at its will
With buds and blossoms. There were pools that dreamed
Black and unruffled; there were white lilies
A few, and crocuses, and violets
Purple or pale, snake-like fritillaries
Scarce seen for the rank grass, and through green nets
Blue eyes of shy pervenche winked in the sun.
And there were curious flowers, before unknown,
Flowers that were stained with moonlight, or with shades
Of Nature's wilful moods; and here a one
That had drunk in the transitory tone
Of one brief moment in a sunset; blades
Of grass that in an hundred springs had been
Slowly but exquisitely nurtured by the stars,
And watered with the scented dew long cupped
In lilies, that for rays of sun had seen
Only God's glory, for never a sunrise mars
The luminous air of Heaven. Beyond, abrupt,
A gray stone wall, o'ergrown with velvet moss
Uprose; and gazing I stood long, all mazed
To see a place so strange, so sweet, so fair.
And as I stood and marvelled, lo! across

The garden came a youth; one hand he raised
To shield him from the sun, his wind-tossed hair
Was twined with flowers, and in his hand he bore
A purple bunch of bursting grapes, his eyes
Were clear as crystal, naked all was he,
White as the snow on pathless mountains frore,
Red were his lips as red wine-spilth that dyes
A marble floor, his brow chalccdony.
And he came near me, with his lips uncurled
And kind, and caught my hand and kissed my mouth,
And gave me grapes to eat, and said, "Sweet friend,
Come I will show thee shadows of the world
And images of life. See from the South
Comes the pale pageant that hath never an end."
And lo! within the garden of my dream
I saw two walking on a shining plain
Of golden light. The one did joyous seem
And fair and blooming, and a sweet refrain
Came from his lips; he sang of pretty maids
And joyous love of comely girl and boy,
His eyes were bright, and 'mid the dancing blades
Of golden grass his feet did trip for joy;
And in his hand he held an ivory lute
With strings of gold that were as maidens' hair,
And sang with voice as tuneful as a flute,
And round his neck three chains of roses were.
But he that was his comrade walked aside;
He was full sad and sweet, and his large eyes
Were strange with wondrous brightness, staring wide
With gazing; and he sighed with many sighs
That moved me, and his cheeks were wan and white
Like pallid lilies, and his lips were red
Like poppies, and his hands he clenched tight,
And yet again unclenched, and his head
Was wreathed with moon-flowers pale as lips of death.
A purple robe he wore, o'erwrought in gold
With the device of a great snake, whose breath
Was fiery flame: which when I did behold
I fell a-weeping, and I cried, "Sweet youth,
Tell me why, sad and sighing, thou dost rove

These pleasant realms? I pray thee speak me sooth
What is thy name?" He said, "My name is Love."
Then straight the first did turn himself to me
And cried, "He lieth, for his name is Shame,
But I am Love, and I was wont to be
Alone in this fair garden, till he came
Unasked by night; I am true Love, I fill
The hearts of boy and girl with mutual flame."
Then sighing, said the other, "Have thy will,
I am the love that dare not speak its name." [1]

IMPRESSION DE NUIT

LONDON

See what a mass of gems the city wears
Upon her broad live bosom! row on row
Rubies and emeralds and amethysts glow.
See! that huge circle like a necklace, stares
With thousands of bold eyes to heaven, and dares
The golden stars to dim the lamps below,
And in the mirror of the mire I know
The moon has left her image unawares.

[1] The final lines were read in court at the first trial of Oscar Wilde by
the prosecutor for the Crown. Asked whether the love described was
natural or unnatural, Wilde replied that "the love that dare not
speak its name" was a "deep spiritual affection that is as pure as it
is perfect . . . the noblest form of affection. There is nothing unnatural about it. It is intellectual, and it repeatedly exists between
an elder and a younger man, when the elder has intellect, and the
younger man has all the joy, hope, and glamour of life before him.
. . . The world mocks at it and sometimes puts one in the pillory for
it." From the public gallery, there followed a burst of applause with
some hisses. In 1935, when Douglas printed the poem in *Lyrics* for
the first time since the Nineties, he added in a footnote that the poem
was "merely the outcome of a classical education and a passion for
the sonnets of Shakespeare. Its morality or immorality is in 'the eye
of the beholder' or, I should say, more properly, the mind of the
reader."

That's the great town at night: I see her breasts,
Pricked out with lamps they stand like huge black towers.
I think they move! I hear her panting breath.
And that's her head where the tiara rests.
And in her brain, through lanes as dark as death,
Men creep like thoughts . . . The lamps are like pale
    flowers.

[*London, 1894*]

REJECTED

Alas! I have lost my God,
    My beautiful God Apollo.
Wherever his footsteps trod
    My feet were wont to follow.

But Oh! it fell out one day
    My soul was so heavy with weeping,
That I laid me down by the way;
    And he left me while I was sleeping.

And my soul awoke in the night,
    And I bowed my ear for his fluting,
And I heard but the breath of the flight
    Of wings and the night-birds hooting.

And night drank all her cup,
    And I went to the shrine in the hollow,
And the voice of my cry went up:
    "Apollo! Apollo! Apollo!"

But he never came to the gate,
    And the sun was hid in a mist,
And there came one walking late,
    And I knew it was Christ.

He took my soul and bound it
   With cords of iron wire,
Seven times round He wound it
   With the cords of my desire.

The cords of my desire,
   While my desire slept,
Were seven bands of wire
   To bind my soul that wept.

And He hid my soul at last
   In a place of stones and fears,
Where the hours like days went past
   And the days went by like years.

And after many days
   That which had slept awoke,
And desire burnt in a blaze,
   And my soul went up in the smoke.

And we crept away from the place
   And would not look behind,
And the angel that hides his face
   Was crouched on the neck of the wind.

And I went to the shrine in the hollow
   Where the lutes and the flutes were playing,
And cried: "I am come, Apollo,
   Back to thy shrine, from my straying."

But he would have none of my soul
   That was stained with blood and with tears,
That had lain in the earth like a mole,
   In the place of great stones and fears.

And now I am lost in the mist
   Of the things that can never be,
For I will have none of Christ
   And Apollo will none of me.

[Paris, 1896]

ODE TO MY SOUL

Rise up my soul!
Shake thyself from the dust.
Lift up thy head that wears an aureole,
Fulfil thy trust.
Out of the mire where they would trample thee
Make images of clay,
Whereon having breathed from thy divinity
Let them take mighty wings and soar away right up to God.
Out of thy broken past
Where impious feet have trod,
Build thee a golden house august and vast,
Whereto these worms of earth may some day crawl.
Let there be nothing small
Henceforth with thee;
Take thou unbounded scorn of all their scorn, Eternity
Of high contempt: be thou no more forlorn
But proud in thy immortal loneliness,
And infinite distress:
And, being 'mid mortal things divinely born,
Rise up my soul!

[Paris, 1896]

THE DEAD POET[1]

I dreamed of him last night, I saw his face
All radiant and unshadowed of distress,
And as of old, in music measureless,
I heard his golden voice and marked him trace
Under the common thing the hidden grace,
And conjure wonder out of emptiness,
Till mean things put on beauty like a dress
And all the world was an enchanted place.

[1] Oscar Wilde, who had died the year before.

And then methought outside a fast locked gate
I mourned the loss of unrecorded words,
Forgotten tales and mysteries half said,
Wonders that might have been articulate,
And voiceless thoughts like murdered singing birds.
And so I woke and knew that he was dead.

[Paris, 1901]

Ernest Dowson

[1867–1900]

NUNS OF THE PERPETUAL ADORATION

Calm, sad, secure; behind high convent walls,
　These watch the sacred lamp, these watch and pray:
And it is one with them when evening falls,
　And one with them the cold return of day.

These heed not time; their nights and days they make
　Into a long, returning rosary,
Whereon their lives are threaded for Christ's sake:
　Meekness and vigilance and chastity.

A vowed patrol, in silent companies,
　Life-long they keep before the living Christ:
In the dim church, their prayers and penances
　Are fragrant incense to the Sacrificed.

Outside, the world is wild and passionate;
　Man's weary laughter and his sick despair
Entreat at their impenetrable gate:
　They heed no voices in their dream of prayer.

They saw the glory of the world displayed;
　They saw the bitter of it, and the sweet;

They knew the roses of the world should fade,
   And be trod under by the hurrying feet.

Therefore they rather put away desire,
   And crossed their hands and came to sanctuary;
And veiled their heads and put on coarse attire:
   Because their comeliness was vanity.

And there they rest; they have serene insight
   Of the illuminating dawn to be:
Mary's sweet Star dispels for them the night,
   The proper darkness of humanity.

Calm, sad, secure; with faces worn and mild:
   Surely their choice of vigil is the best?
Yea! for our roses fade, the world is wild;
   But there, beside the altar, there, is rest.

[1891]

NON SUM QUALIS ERAM BONAE SUB REGNO CYNARAE[1]

Last night, ah, yesternight, betwixt her lips and mine
There fell thy shadow, Cynara! thy breath was shed
Upon my soul between the kisses and the wine;
And I was desolate and sick of an old passion,
   Yea, I was desolate and bowed my head:
I have been faithful to thee, Cynara! in my fashion.

All night upon mine heart I felt her warm heart beat,
Night-long within mine arms in love and sleep she lay;

[1] The title—taken from Horace's *Odes*—means "I am not what once
I was in kind Cynara's day." Concerned about its daring subject,
Dowson wrote to a friend in March, 1891: "I have just seen the
proofs of my 'Cynara' poem for the April *Hobby* [*Horse*]. It looks
less indecent in print, but I am still nervous! though I admire [Her-
bert] Horne's audacity [in printing it]. I read it, or rather Lionel
[Johnson] did for me, at the last Rhymers' [Club meeting]. . . .

Surely the kisses of her bought red mouth were sweet;
But I was desolate and sick of an old passion,
   When I awoke and found the dawn was gray:
I have been faithful to thee, Cynara! in my fashion.

I have forgot much, Cynara! gone with the wind,
Flung roses, roses riotously with the throng,
Dancing, to put thy pale, lost lilies out of mind;
But I was desolate and sick of an old passion,
   Yea, all the time, because the dance was long:
I have been faithful to thee, Cynara! in my fashion.

I cried for madder music and for stronger wine,
But when the feast is finished and the lamps expire,
Then falls thy shadow, Cynara! the night is thine;
And I am desolate and sick of an old passion,
   Yea hungry for the lips of my desire:
I have been faithful to thee, Cynara! in my fashion.

[1891]

O MORS! QUAM AMARA EST MEMORIA TUA HOMINI PACEM HABENTI IN SUBSTANTIIS SUIS[1]

Exceeding sorrow
   Consumeth my sad heart!
Because to-morrow
   We must depart,

---

[1] "O Death! How bitter is thy memory to the man who has peace in the marrow of his being." In his autobiography, Yeats wrote: "I only knew Dowson's 'O Mors' to quote but the first words of its long title, and his 'Villanelle of Sunset' from his reading, and it was because of the desire to hold them in my hand that I suggested the first *Book of the Rhymers' Club* [published in 1892]."

Now is exceeding sorrow
   All my part!

Give over playing,
   Cast thy viol away:
Merely laying
   Thine head my way:
Prithee, give over playing,
   Grave or gay.

Be no word spoken;
   Weep nothing: let a pale
Silence, unbroken
   Silence prevail!
Prithee, be no word spoken,
   Lest I fail!

[1892]

VILLANELLE OF SUNSET

Come hither, Child! and rest:
   This is the end of day,
Behold the weary West!

Sleep rounds with equal zest
   Man's toil and children's play:
Come hither, Child! and rest.

My white bird, seek thy nest,
   Thy drooping head down lay:
Behold the weary West!

Now are the flowers confest
   Of slumber: sleep, as they!
Come hither, Child! and rest.

Now eve is manifest,
    And homeward lies our way:
Behold the weary West!

Tired flower! upon my breast,
    I would wear thee alway:
Come hither, Child! and rest;
Behold, the weary West!

[1892]

EXTREME UNCTION[1]
For Lionel Johnson[2]

Upon the eyes, the lips, the feet,
    On all the passages of sense,
The atoning oil is spread with sweet
    Renewal of lost innocence.

The feet, that lately ran so fast
    To meet desire, are soothly sealed;

[1] In a letter to his friend Arthur Moore, dated around 1888, Dowson mentions a chapter from Zola's novel *Le Rêve* in which a priest gives extreme unction to a girl who is supposedly dying: "You must read the 'extreme unction' pages even if you can't stomach the whole. The purifying of the separate orifices of sensation with the consecrated oils strikes me as an excessively fine notion. I think if I have a deathbed (which I don't desire) I must be reconciled to Rome for the sake of that piece of ritual. It seems the most fitting exit for the epicurean—after all one is chiefly that—and one would procure it— (it seems essentially pagan) without undue compromise or affectation of a belief in 'a sort of a something somewhere,' simply as an exquisite sensation, and for the sensation's sake." (Quoted by permission of the Morgan Library.)
[2] Dowson, who regarded Johnson's conversion to Roman Catholicism as "an act of great courage," himself converted in the same year— 1891—as the result of Johnson's persuasion, though close friends said later that Dowson did not practice his faith seriously.

The eyes, that were so often cast
  On vanity, are touched and healed.

From troublous sights and sounds set free;
  In such a twilight hour of breath,
Shall one retrace his life, or see,
  Through shadows, the true face of death?

Vials of mercy! Sacring oils!
  I know not where nor when I come,
Nor through what wanderings and toils,
  To crave of you Viaticum.[3]

Yet, when the walls of flesh grow weak,
  In such an hour, it well may be,
Through mist and darkness, light will break,
  And each anointed sense will see.

[1894]

EXILE

By the sad waters of separation
  Where we have wandered by divers ways,
I have but the shadow and imitation
  Of the old memorial days.

In music I have no consolation,
  No roses are pale enough for me;
The sound of the waters of separation
  Surpasseth roses and melody.

By the sad waters of separation
  Dimly I hear from an hidden place
The sigh of mine ancient adoration:
  Hardly can I remember your face.

[3] Holy Communion, given to someone in danger of death.

If you be dead, no proclamation
    Sprang to me over the waste, gray sea:
Living, the waters of separation
    Sever for ever your soul from me.

No man knoweth our desolation;
    Memory pales of the old delight;
While the sad waters of separation
    Bear us on to the ultimate night.

                         [1896]

BENEDICTIO DOMINI[1]
For Selwyn Image[2]

Without, the sullen noises of the street!
    The voice of London, inarticulate,
Hoarse and blaspheming, surges in to meet
    The silent blessing of the Immaculate.

Dark is the church, and dim the worshippers,
    Hushed with bowed heads as though by some old spell,
While through the incense-laden air there stirs
    The admonition of a silver bell.

Dark is the church, save where the altar stands,
    Dressed like a bride, illustrious with light,
Where one old priest exalts with tremulous hands
    The one true solace of man's fallen plight.

Strange silence here: without, the sounding street
    Heralds the world's swift passage to the fire:

[1] "The Lord's Blessing."
[2] 1849–1930, poet, designer of stained glass, engraver, member of the Century Guild and editor of the *Hobby Horse*, to which Dowson contributed in the early Nineties. Later, Image was Slade Professor of Fine Arts at Oxford, 1910–16.

O Benediction, perfect and complete!
   When shall men cease to suffer and desire?

[1896]

SPLEEN
For Arthur Symons

I was not sorrowful, I could not weep,
And all my memories were put to sleep.

I watched the river grow more white and strange,
All day till evening I watched it change.

All day till evening I watched the rain
Beat wearily upon the window pane.

I was not sorrowful, but only tired
Of everything that ever I desired.

Her lips, her eyes, all day became to me
The shadow of a shadow utterly.

All day mine hunger for her heart became
Oblivion, until the evening came,

And left me sorrowful, inclined to weep,
With all my memories that could not sleep.

[1896]

A LAST WORD

Let us go hence: the night is now at hand;
The day is overworn, the birds all flown;
And we have reaped the crops the gods have sown;

Despair and death; deep darkness o'er the land,
Broods like an owl; we cannot understand
Laughter or tears, for we have only known
Surpassing vanity: vain things alone
Have driven our perverse and aimless band.
Let us go hence, somewhither strange and cold,
To Hollow Lands where just men and unjust
Find end of labour, where's rest for the old,
Freedom to all from love and fear and lust.
Twine our torn hands! O pray the earth enfold
Our life-sick hearts and turn them into dust.

[1896]

Michael Field

FROM BAUDELAIRE

There shall be beds full of light odours blent,
Divans, great couches, deep, profound as tombs,
And, frown for us, in light magnificent,
Over the flower-stand there shall droop strange blooms.

Careful of their last flame declining,
As two vast torches our two hearts shall flare,
And our two spirits in their double shining
Reflect the double lights enchanted there.

One night—a night of mystic blue, of rose,
A look will pass supreme from me, from you,
Like a long sob, laden with long adieux.

And, later on, an angel will unclose
The door, and, entering joyously, re-light
The tarnished mirrors and the flames blown to the night.

THE POET

Within his eyes are hung lamps of the sanctuary:
A wind, from whence none knows, can set in sway
And spill their light by fits; but yet their ray
Returns, deep-boled, to its obscurity.

The world as from a dullard turns annoyed
To stir the days with show or deeds or voices;
But if one spies him justly one rejoices,
With silence that the careful lips avoid.

He is a plan, a work of some strange passion
Life has conceived apart from Time's harsh drill,
A thing it hides and cherishes to fashion.

At odd bright moments to its secret will:
Holy and foolish, ever set apart,
He waits the leisure of his god's free heart.

A DANCE OF DEATH

How strange this ice, so motionless and still,
Yet calling as with music to our feet,
So that they chafe and dare
Their swiftest motion to repeat
These harmonies of challenge, sounds that fill
The floor of ice, as the crystalline sphere
Around the heavens is filled with such a song
That, when they hear,
The stars, each in their heaven, are drawn along!

Oh, see, a dancer! One whose feet
Move on unshod with steel!
She is not skating fleet
On toe and heel,
But only tip-toe dances in a whirl,
A lovely dancing-girl,
Upon the frozen surface of the stream,
Without a wonder, it would seem,
She could not keep her sway,
The balance of her limbs
Sure on the musical, iced river-way
That sparkling, dims

Her trinkets as they swing, so high its sparks
Tingle the sun and scatter song like larks.

She dances 'mid the sumptuous whiteness set
Of winter's sunniest noon;
She dances as the sun-rays that forget
In winter sunset falleth soon
To sheer sunset:
She dances with a languor through the frost
As she never had lost,
In lands where there is snow,
The Orient's immeasurable glow.

Who is this dancer white?
A creature slight,
Weaving the East upon a stream of ice,
That in a trice
Might trip the dance and fling the dancer down?
Does she not know deeps under ice can drown?

This is Salome, in a western land,
An exile with Herodias, her mother,
With Herod and Herodias:
And she has sought the river's icy mass,
Companioned by no other,
To dance upon the ice—each hand
Held, as a snow-bird's wings,
In heavy poise.
Ecstatic, with no noise,
Athwart the ice her dream, her spell she flings;
And Winter in a rapture of delight
Flings up and down the spangles of her light.

Oh, hearken, hearken! . . . Ice and frost,
From these cajoling motions freed,
Have straight given heed
To Will more firm: In their obedience
Their masses dense
Are riven as by a sword. . . .
Where is the Vision by the snow adored?

The Vision is no more
Seen from the noontide shore.

Oh, fearful crash of thunder from the stream,
As there were thunder-clouds upon its wave!
Could nothing save
The dancer in the noontide beam?
She is engulphed and all the dance is done.
Bright leaps the noontide sun—
But stay, what leaps beneath it? A gold head,
That twinkles with its jewels bright
As water-drops. . . .
O murdered Baptist of the severed head,
Her head was caught and girded tight,
And severed by the ice-brook sword, and sped
In dance that never stops.
It skims and hops
Across the ice that rasped it. Smooth and gay,
And void of care,
It takes its sunny way:
But underneath the golden hair,
And underneath those jewel-sparks,
Keen noontide marks
A little face as gray as evening ice;
Lips, open in a scream no soul may hear,
Eyes fixed as they beheld the silver plate
That they at Macherontis once beheld;
While the hair trails, although so fleet and nice
The motion of the head is subjugate
To its own law: yet in the face what fear,
To what excess compelled!

Salome's head is dancing on the bright
And silver ice. O holy John, how still
Was laid thy head upon the salver white,
When thou hadst done God's will!

LA GIOCONDA[1]

Leonardo Da Vinci
THE LOUVRE

Historic, side-long, implicating eyes;
A smile of velvet's lustre on the cheek;
Calm lips the smile leads upward; hand that lies
Glowing and soft, the patience in its rest
Of cruelty that waits and doth not seek
For prey; a dusky forehead and a breast
Where twilight touches ripeness amorously:
Behind her, crystal rocks, a sea and skies
Of evanescent blue on cloud and creek;
Landscape that shines suppressive of its zest
For those vicissitudes by which men die.

A DYING VIPER

The lethargy of evil in her eyes—
As blue snow is the substance of a mere
Where the dead waters of a glacier drear
Stand open and behold—a viper lies.

Brooding upon her hatreds: dying thus
Wounded and broken, helpless with her fangs,
She dies of her sealed curse, yea, of her pangs
At God's first ban that made her infamous.

Yet, by that old curse frozen in her wreath,
She, like a star, hath central gravity
That draws and fascinates the soul to death;

While round her stark and terrible repose,
Vaults for its hour a glittering sapphire fly,
Mocking the charm of death. O God, it knows!

[1] See Pater's description of La Gioconda in the Appendix.

John Gray

[1866–1934]

From SILVERPOINTS [1893]

In design and shape, *Silverpoints*, published by the Bodley Head, is one of the famous products of the Nineties. Tall and narrow, with a flame motif (designed by the well-known artist Charles Ricketts) stamped in gold on the cover and printed on expensive handmade paper, the volume, consisting of only thirty-five pages (half of which are devoted to translations of Baudelaire, Mallarmé, Verlaine, and Rimbaud) is printed entirely in small, almost unreadable italics on wide margins. According to Rupert Hart-Davis, the edition (consisting of only 275 copies) was entirely paid for by Wilde as a gesture of friendship.

Recalling the taste for exquisite little volumes during the period, the novelist Ada Leverson wrote in the preface to *Letters to the Sphinx from Oscar Wilde*:

> . . . *There was more margin; margin in every sense of the word was in demand, and I remember, looking at the poems of John Gray (then considered the incomparable poet of the age), when I saw the tiniest rivulet of text meandering through the very largest meadow of margin, I suggested to Oscar Wilde that he should go a step further than these minor poets; that he should publish a book all margin; full of beautiful unwritten thoughts, and have this blank volume bound in some Nile-green skin powdered with gilt nenuphars and smoothed with hard ivory, decorated*

*with gold by Ricketts and printed on Japanese paper, each
volume must be a collector's piece, a numbered one of a
limited "first" (and last) edition: "very rare."*

    He approved.

    *"It shall be dedicated to you, and the unwritten text illus-
trated by Aubrey Beardsley. There must be five hundred
signed copies for particular friends, six for the general public, and one for America."*

═══════════════════════════════════

ON A PICTURE
To Pierre Louÿs[1]

Not pale, as one in sleep or holier death,
Nor illcontent the lady seems, nor loth
To lie in shadow of shrill river growth,
So steadfast are the river's arms beneath.

Pale petals follow her in very faith,
Unmixed with pleasure or regret, and both
Her maidly hands look up, in noble sloth
To take the blossoms of her scattered wreath.

No weakest ripple lives to kiss her throat,
Nor dies in meshes of untangled hair;
No movement stirs the floor of river moss.

Until some furtive glimmer gleam across
Voluptuous mouth, where even teeth are bare,
And gild the broidery of her petticoat. . . .

POEM

Geranium, houseleek, laid in oblong beds
On the trim grass. The daisies' leprous stain

[1] French poet and novelist (1870–1925) to whom Wilde sent his
French version of *Salomé* for correction.

Is fresh. Each night the daisies burst again,
Though every day the gardener crops their heads.

A wistful child, in foul unwholesome shreds,
Recalls some legend of a daisy chain
That makes a pretty necklace. She would fain
Make one, and wear it, if she had some threads.

Sun, leprous flowers, foul child. The asphalt burns.
The garrulous sparrows perch on metal Burns.
Sing! Sing! they say, and flutter with their wings.
He does not sing, he only wonders why
He is sitting there. The sparrows sing. And I
Yield to the strait allure of simple things.

A CRUCIFIX
To Ernest Dowson

A gothic church. At one end of an aisle,
Against a wall where mystic sunbeams smile
Through painted windows, orange, blue, and gold,
The Christ's unutterable charm behold.
Upon the cross, adorned with gold and green,
Long fluted golden tongues of sombre sheen,
Like four flames joined in one, around the head
And by the outstretched arms, their glory spread.
The statue is of wood; of natural size;
Tinted; one almost sees before one's eyes
The last convulsion of the lingering breath.
"Behold the man!" Robust and frail. Beneath
That breast indeed might throb the Sacred Heart.
And from the lips, so holily dispart,
The dying murmur breathes "Forgive! Forgive!"
O wide-stretched arms! "I perish, let them live."
Under the torture of the thorny crown,
The loving pallor of the brow looks down.
On human blindness, on the toiler's woes;
The while, to overturn Despair's repose,
And urge to Hope and Love, as Faith demands,

Bleed, bleed the feet, the broken side, the hands.
A poet, painter, Christian,—it was a friend
Of mine—his attributes most fitly blend—
Who saw this marvel, and made an exquisite
Copy; and, knowing how I worshipped it,
Forgot it, in my room, by accident.
I write these verses in acknowledgment.

PARSIFAL IMITATED FROM THE FRENCH OF PAUL VERLAINE

Conquered the flower-maidens, and the wide embrace
Of their round proffered arms, that tempt the virgin boy;
Conquered the trickling of their babbling tongues; the coy
Back glances, and the mobile breasts of subtle grace;

Conquered the Woman Beautiful, the fatal charm
Of her hot breast, the music of her babbling tongue;
Conquered the gate of Hell, into the gate the young
Man passes, with the heavy trophy at his arm,

The holy Javelin that pierced the Heart of God.
He heals the dying king, he sits upon the throne,
King, and high priest of that great gift, the living Blood.

In robe of gold the youth adores the glorious Sign
Of the green goblet, worships the mysterious Wine.
And oh! the chime of children's voices in the dome.

FEMMES DAMNÉES

Like moody beasts they lie along the sands;
Look where the sky against the sea-rim clings:
Foot stretches out to foot, and groping hands
Have languors soft and bitter shudderings.

Some, smitten hearts with the long secrecies,
On velvet moss, deep in their bower's ease,

Prattling the love of timid infancies,
Are tearing the green bark from the young trees.

Others, like sisters, slowly walk and grave;
By rocks that swarm with ghostly legions,
Where Anthony saw surging on the waves
The purple breasts of his temptations.

Some, by the light of crumbling, resinous gums,
In the still hollows of old pagan dens,
Call thee in aid to their deliriums
O Bacchus! cajoler of ancient pains.

And those whose breasts for scapulars are fain
Nurse under their long robes the cruel thong.
These, in dim woods, where huddling shadows throng,
Mix with the foam of pleasure tears of pain.

THE BARBER [1]

i

I dreamed I was a barber; and there went
Beneath my hand, oh! manes extravagant.
Beneath my trembling fingers, many a mask
Of many a pleasant girl. It was my task
To gild their hair, carefully, strand by strand;
To paint their eyebrows with a timid hand;
To draw a bodkin, from a vase of kohl,
Through the closed lashes; pencils from a bowl
Of sepia to paint them underneath;
To blow upon their eyes with a soft breath.
They lay them back and watched the leaping bands.

ii

The dream grew vague. I moulded with my hands
The mobile breasts, the valley; and the waist
I touched; and pigments reverently placed

[1] See Beardsley's "Ballad of a Barber."

Upon their thighs in sapient spots and stains,
Beryls and crysolites and diaphanes,
And gems whose hot harsh names are never said.
I was a masseur; and my fingers bled
With wonder as I touched their awful limbs.

iii

Suddenly, in the marble trough, there seems
O, last of my pale mistresses, Sweetness!
A twylipped scarlet pansie. My caress
Tinges thy steelgray eyes to violet.
Adown thy body skips the pit-a-pat
Of treatment once heard in a hospital
For plagues that fascinate, but half appal.

iv

So, at the sound, the blood of me stood cold.
Thy chaste hair ripened into sullen gold.
The throat, the shoulders, swelled and were uncouth.
The breasts rose up and offered each a mouth.
And on the belly pallid blushes crept,
That maddened me, until I laughed and wept.

LE VOYAGE À CYTHÈRE[1]

Bird-like, my heart was glad to soar and vault;
Fluttering among the cordages; and on
The vessel flew, under an empty vault:
An angel drunken of a radiant sun.

Tell me, what is that gray, that sombre isle?
'Tis Cythera, famed on many a poet string;
A name that has not lacked the slavering smile;
But now, you see, it is not much to sing.

Isle of soft whispers, tremours of the heart!
The splendid phantom of thy rude goddess

[1] Another name for Aphrodite, or Venus, after the island Kythera, near which she rose from the sea.

Floats on thy seas like breath of spikenard,
Charging men's souls with love and lusciousness.

Sweet isle of myrtles, once of open blooms:
Now only of lean lands most lean: it seems
A flinty desert bitter with shrill screams:
But one strange object on its horror looms.

Not a fair temple, foiled with coppiced trees,
Where the young priestess, mistress of the flowers,
Goes opening her gown to the cool breeze,
To still the fire, the torment that devours.

But as along the shore we skirted, near
Enough to scare the birds with our white sails,
We saw a three-limbed gibbet rising sheer,
Detached against the sky in spare details.

Perched on their pasturage, ferocious fowl
Riddled with rage a more than putrid roast;
Each of them stabbing, like a tool, his foul
Beak in the oozing members of his host.

Below, a troop of jealous quadrupeds,
Looking aloft with eye and steadfast snout;
A larger beast above the others' heads,
A hangman with his porters round about.

The eyes, two caves; and from the rotten paunch,
Its freight, too heavy, streamed along the haunch.
Hang for these harpies' hideous delight,
Poor rag of flesh, torn of thy sex and sight!

Cythera's child, child of so sweet a sky!
Silent thou bearest insult—as we must—
In expiation of what faults deny
Thee even a shallow shelter in the dust.

Ludicrous sufferer! thy woes are mine.
There came, at seeing of thy dangling limbs,

Up to my lips, like vomiting, the streams
Of ancient miseries, of gall and brine.

Before thee, brother in my memory fresh!
I felt the mangling of the appetites
Of the black panthers, of the savage kites,
That were so fain to rend and pick my flesh.

The sea was sleeping. Blue and beautiful
The sky. Henceforth I saw but murk and blood.
Alas! and as it had been in a shroud,
My heart lay buried in that parable.

All thine isle showed me, Venus! was upthrust,
A symbol calvary where my image hung.
Give me, Lord God, to look upon that dung,
My body and my heart, without disgust.

MISHKA

Mishka is poet among the beasts.
When roots are rotten, and rivers weep,
The bear is at play in the land of sleep.
Though his head be heavy between his fists.
The bear is poet among the beasts.

THE DREAM:

Wide and large are the monster's eyes,
Nought saying, save one word alone:
Mishka! Mishka, as turned to stone,
Hears no word else, nor in anywise
Can see aught save the monster's eyes.

Honey is under the monster's lips;
And Mishka follows into her lair,
Dragged in the net of her yellow hair,
Knowing all things when honey drips
On his tongue like rain, the song of the hips

Of the honey-child, and of each twin mound.
Mishka! there screamed a far bird-note,
Deep in the sky, when round his throat
The triple coil of her hair she wound.
And stroked his limbs with a humming sound.

Mishka is white like a hunter's son;
For he knows no more of the ancient south
When the honey-child's lips are on his mouth,
When all her kisses are joined in one,
And his body is bathed in grass and sun.

Lionel Johnson

[1867–1902]

THE CULTURED FAUN [1891]

Published anonymously in the *Anti-Jacobin*, "The Cultured
Faun" ridicules the aesthetic shams of the day. Johnson,
whose own aestheticism was strong, nevertheless regarded
the doctrine of *l'art pour l'art* as absurd. True to his disciple-
ship to Pater, he rejects dilettantism in religion and art as
well as the pretentiousness of those who pretend to feel.

He, or shall we say it? is a curious creature; tedious after a
time, when you have got its habits by heart, but certainly
curious on first acquaintance. You breed it in this way:

Take a young man, who had brains as a boy, and teach
him to disbelieve everything that his elders believe in matters
of thought, and to reject everything that seems true to himself in matters of sentiment. He need not be at all revolutionary; most clever youths for mere experience's sake will dis-
card their natural or acquired convictions. He will then,
since he is intelligent and bright, want something to replace
his early notions. If Aristotle's *Poetics* are absurd, and Pope
is no poet, and politics are vulgar, and Carlyle is played out,
and Mr. Ruskin is tiresome, and so forth, according to the
circumstances of the case, our youth will be bored to death
by the nothingness of everything. You must supply him with

the choicest delicacies, and feed him upon the finest rarities. And what so choice as a graceful affectation, or so fine as a surprising paradox? So you cast about for these two, and at once you see that many excellent affectations and paradoxes have had their day. A treasured melancholy of the German moonlight sort, a rapt enthusiasm in the Byronic style, a romantic eccentricity after the French fashion of 1830, a "frank, fierce," sensuousness *à la jeunesse Swinburnienne*[1], our youth might flourish them in the face of society all at once, without receiving a single invitation to private views or suppers of the elect. And, in truth, it requires a positive genius for the absurd to discover a really promising affectation, a thoroughly fascinating paradox. But the last ten years have done it. And a remarkable achievement it is.

Externally, our hero should cultivate a reassuring sobriety of habit, with just a dash of the dandy. None of the wandering looks, the elaborate disorder, the sublime lunacy of his predecessor, the "apostle of culture." Externally, then, a precise appearance; internally, a catholic sympathy with all that exists, and "therefore" suffers, for art's sake. Now art, at present, is not a question of the senses so much as of the nerves. Botticelli, indeed, was very precious, but Baudelaire is very nervous. Gautier was adorably sensuous, but M. Verlaine is pathetically sensitive. That is the point: exquisite appreciation of pain, exquisite thrills of anguish, exquisite adoration of suffering. Here comes in a tender patronage of Catholicism: white tapers upon the high altar, an ascetic and beautiful young priest, the great gilt monstrance, the subtle-scented and mystical incense, the old world accents of the Vulgate, of the Holy Offices; the splendor of the sacred vestments.[2] We kneel at some hour, not too early for our convenience, repeating that solemn Latin, drinking in those Gregorian tones, with plenty of modern French sonnets in memory, should the sermon be dull. But to join the Church! Ah, no! better to dally with the enchanting mysteries, to pass from our dreams of delirium to our dreams of sanctity with no

[1] "in the manner of the youthful Swinburne."

[2] Though Johnson was himself attracted to the ritualism of the Church (see, for example, his "Church of a Dream"), he did not regard it—as did Wilde—as merely an intense aesthetic experience.

coarse facts to jar upon us. And so these refined persons cherish a double "passion," the sentiment of repentant yearning and the sentiment of rebellious sin.

To play the part properly a flavor of cynicism is recommended: a scientific profession of materialist dogmas, coupled—for you should forswear consistency—with gloomy chatter about "The Will to Live." If you can say it in German, so much the better; a gross tongue, partially redeemed by Heine, but an infallible oracle of scepticism. Jumble all these "impressions" together, your sympathies and your sorrows, your devotion and your despair; carry them about with you in a state of fermentation, and finally conclude that life is loathsome yet that beauty is beatific. And beauty—ah, beauty is everything beautiful! Isn't that a trifle obvious, you say? That is the charm of it, it shows your perfect simplicity, your chaste and catholic innocence. Innocence of course: beauty is always innocent, ultimately. No doubt there are "monstrous" things, terrible pains, the haggard eyes of an *absintheur*, the pallid faces of "neurotic" sinners; but all that is the portion of our Parisian friends, such and such a "group of artists," who meet at the Café So-and-So. We like people to think we are much the same, but it isn't true. We are quite harmless, we only concoct strange and subtle verse about it. And, anyway, beauty includes everything; there's another sweet saying for you from our "impressionist" copy-books. Impressions! that is all. Life is mean and vulgar, Members of Parliament are odious, the critics are commercial pedants: we alone know Beauty, and Art, and Sorrow, and Sin. Impressions! exquisite, dainty fantasies; fiery-colored visions; and impertinence straggling into epigram, for "the true" criticism; *c'est adorable!* And since we are scholars and none of your penny-a-line Bohemians, we throw in occasional doses of "Hellenism": by which we mean the Ideal of the Cultured Faun. That is to say, a flowery Paganism, such as no "Pagan" ever had; a mixture of "beautiful woodland natures," and "the perfect comeliness of the Parthenon frieze," together with the elegant languors and favorite vices of (let us parade our "decadent" learning) the *Stratonis Epigrammata*.[a] At

[a] Epigrams of Straton, numbering close to 100, which appeared in the *Greek Anthology*. Most deal with homosexual love.

this time of day we need not dilate upon the equivocal charm of everything Lesbian. And who shall assail us?—what stupid and uncultured critic, what coarse and narrow Philistine? We are the Elect of Beauty: saints and sinners, devils and devotees, Athenians and Parisians, Romans of the Empire and Italians of the Renaissance. *Fin de siècle! Fin de siècle!* Literature is a thing of beauty, blood, and nerves.

Let the Philistine critic have the last word; let him choose his words with all care, and define in his rough fashion. How would it do to call the Cultured Faun a feeble and a foolish beast?

THE CHURCH OF A DREAM
To Bernhard Berenson[1]

Sadly the dead leaves rustle in the whistling wind,
Around the weather-worn, gray church, low down the vale:
The Saints in golden vesture shake before the gale;
The glorious windows shake, where still they dwell enshrined;

Old Saints by long dead, shrivelled hands, long since designed;
There still, although the world autumnal be, and pale,
Still in their golden vesture the old saints prevail;
Alone with Christ, desolate else, left by mankind.

Only one ancient Priest offers the Sacrifice,
Murmuring holy Latin immemorial:
Swaying with tremulous hands the old censer full of spice,
In gray, sweet incense clouds; blue, sweet clouds mystical:
To him, in place of men, for he is old, suffice
Melancholy remembrances and vesperal.

[1890]

[1] 1865–1959, American art historian.

MYSTIC AND CAVALIER
To Herbert Percy Horne[1]

Go from me: I am one of those, who fall.
What! hath no cold wind swept your heart at all,
In my sad company? Before the end,
   Go from me, dear my friend!

Yours are the victories of light: your feet
Rest from good toil, where rest is brave and sweet.
But after warfare in a mourning gloom,
   I rest in clouds of doom.

Have you not read so, looking in these eyes?
Is it the common light of the pure skies,
Lights up their shadowy depths? The end is set:
   Though the end be not yet.

When gracious music stirs, and all is bright,
And beauty triumphs through a courtly night;
When I too joy, a man like other men:
   Yet, am I like them, then?

And in the battle, when the horsemen sweep
Against a thousand deaths, and fall on sleep:
Who ever sought that sudden calm, if I
   Sought not? Yet, could not die.

Seek with thine eyes to pierce this crystal sphere:
Canst read a fate there, prosperous and clear?
Only the mists, only the weeping clouds:
   Dimness, and airy shrouds.

Beneath, what angels are at work? What powers
Prepare the secret of the fatal hours?

[1] 1864–1916, poet, architect, art historian, and member of the Century Guild, which published *The Century Guild Hobby Horse*. In the early 1890's Johnson lived in rooms at the top of the house where the Century Guild had offices and studios.

See! the mists tremble, and the clouds are stirred:
   When comes the calling word?

The clouds are breaking from the crystal ball,
Breaking and clearing: and I look to fall.
When the cold winds and airs of portent sweep,
   My spirit may have sleep.

O rich and sounding voices of the air!
Interpreters and prophets of despair:
Priests of a fearful sacrament! I come,
   To make with you mine home.

                    [1894]

TO A PASSIONIST[1]

Clad in a vestment wrought with passion-flowers;
Celebrant of one Passion; called by name
Passionist: is thy world, one world with ours?
Thine, a like heart? Thy very soul, the same?

Thou pleadest an eternal sorrow: we
Praise the still changing beauty of this earth.
Passionate good and evil, thou dost see:
Our eyes behold the dreams of death and birth.

We love the joys of men: we love the dawn,
Red with the sun, and with the pure dew pearled.
Thy stern soul feels, after the sun withdrawn,
How much pain goes to perfecting the world.

[1] Of the genesis of this poem, Johnson wrote to Louise Imogen Guiney on July 8, 1897, ". . . quaint Wareham. . . . Were you there of a Sunday, I wonder, and heard Mass at the little Passionist chapel? It was after Mass there that I wrote the lines in my book, called 'To a Passionist.' The celebrant had a face of beautiful austerity, and was vested in a wondrous white chasuble broidered with purple passion-flowers."

Canst thou be right? Is thine the very truth?
Stands then our life in so forlorn a state?
Nay, but thou wrongest us: thou wrong'st our youth,
Who dost our happiness compassionate.

And yet! and yet! O royal Calvary!
Whence divine sorrow triumphed through years past:
Could ages bow before mere memory?
Those passion-flowers must blossom, to the last.

Purple they bloom, the splendour of a King:
Crimson they bleed, the sacrament of Death:
About our thrones and pleasaunces they cling,
Where guilty eyes read, what each blossom saith.

[1892]

IN HONOREM DORIANI CREATORISQUE EIUS

Benedictus sis, Oscare! [1]
Qui me libro hoc dignare
  Propter amicitias:
Modo modulans Romano
Laudes dignas Doriano,
  Ago tibi gratias.

Juventutis hic formosa
Floret inter rosas rosa
  Subito dum venit mors:
Ecce Homo! ecce Deus!

[1] Wilde, on a visit to Oxford in February, 1890, met Johnson, who, in a letter to a friend, described Wilde as "delightful . . . He discoursed, with infinite flippancy, of everyone . . . laughed at Pater: and consumed all my cigarettes. I am in love with him. He was come to visit Pater . . ." When Wilde's *Picture of Dorian Gray* was published, Johnson wrote these commendatory verses, which were not published in his lifetime. The translation which follows is by Ian Fletcher.

Si sic modo esset meus
  Genius misericors!

Amat avidus amores
Miros, miros carpit flores
  Saevus pulchritudine:
Quanto anima nigrescit,
Tanto facies splendescit,
  Mendax, sed quam splendide!

Hic sunt poma Sodomorum;
Hic sunt corda vitiorum;
  Et peccata dulcia.
In excelis et infernis,
Tibi sit, qui tanta cernis,
  Gloriaum gloria.

IN HONOUR OF DORIAN AND HIS CREATOR

Blessed be you, Oscar! Who deem me worthy of this book
For friendship's sake: Modulating in the Roman mode
Praises to the Dorian owed, I give you thanks./Here the
lovely rose Flourishes amid the roses When suddenly comes
death: Behold the Man! Behold the God! O that this mode of
pitying Genius were but mine!/Avidly he loves strange loves,
Savage with beauty Plucks strange flowers: The more his
soul is darkened, His face displays its brightness more, False,
but how radiantly so!/Here are apples of Sodom; Here the
hearts of vices; And sweet sins. In the heavens and in the
depths, Be to you, who perceive so much, Glory of all glo-
ries.

THE DESTROYER OF A SOUL

To — —.[1]

I hate you with a necessary hate.
First, I sought patience: passionate was she:
My patience turned in very scorn of me,
That I should dare forgive a sin so great,
As this, through which I sit disconsolate;
Mourning for that live soul, I used to see;
Soul of a saint, whose friend I used to be:
Till you came by! a cold, corrupting, fate.

Why come you now? You, whom I cannot cease
With pure and perfect hate to hate? Go, ring
The death-bell with a deep, triumphant toll!
Say you, my friend sits by me still? Ah, peace!
Call you this thing my friend? this nameless thing?
This living body, hiding its dead soul?

[1892]

THE DARK ANGEL

Dark Angel, with thine aching lust
To rid the world of penitence:
Malicious Angel, who still dost
My soul such subtile violence!

Because of thee, no thought, no thing,
Abides for me undesecrate:
Dark Angel, ever on the wing,
Who never reachest me too late!

When music sounds, then changest thou
Its silvery to a sultry fire:

[1] It is generally believed that this sonnet is addressed to Wilde; the soul is that of Lord Alfred Douglas, whom Johnson introduced to Wilde in 1891.

Nor will thine envious heart allow
Delight untortured by desire.

Through thee, the gracious Muses turn
To Furies, O mine Enemy!
And all the things of beauty burn
With flames of evil ecstasy.

Because of thee, the land of dreams
Becomes a gathering place of fears:
Until tormented slumber seems
One vehemence of useless tears.

When sunlight glows upon the flowers,
Or ripples down the dancing sea:
Thou, with thy troop of passionate powers,
Beleaguerest, bewilderest, me.

Within the breath of autumn woods,
Within the winter silences:
Thy venomous spirit stirs and broods,
O Master of impieties!

The ardour of red flame is thine,
And thine the steely soul of ice:
Thou poisonest the fair design
Of nature, with unfair device.

Apples of ashes, golden bright;
Waters of bitterness, how sweet!
O banquet of a foul delight,
Prepared by thee, dark Paraclete![1]

Thou art the whisper in the gloom,
The hinting tone, the haunting laugh:
Thou art the adorner of my tomb,
The minstrel of mine epitaph.

[1] "Advocate," used by St. John to characterize Christ as Divine Comforter and Intercessor. The "dark Paraclete" is Johnson's vision of the Dark Angel who opposes the holy Paraclete.

I fight thee, in the Holy Name!
Yet, what thou dost, is what God saith:
Tempter! should I escape thy flame,
Thou wilt have helped my soul from Death:

The second Death, that never dies,
That cannot die, when time is dead:
Live Death, wherein the lost soul cries,
Eternally uncomforted.

Dark Angel, with thine aching lust!
Of two defeats, of two despairs:
Less dread, a change to drifting dust,
Than thine eternity of cares.

Do what thou wilt, thou shalt not so,
Dark Angel! triumph over me:
Lonely, unto the Lone I go,
Divine, to the Divinity.

[1894]

NIHILISM

Among immortal things not made with hands;
Among immortal things, dead hands have made:
Under the Heavens, upon the Earth, there stands
Man's life, my life: of life I am afraid.

Where silent things, and unimpassioned things,
Where things of nought, and things decaying, are:
I shall be calm soon, with the calm, death brings.
The skies are gray there, without any star.

Only the rest! the rest! Only the gloom,
Soft and long gloom! The pausing from all thought!
My life, I cannot taste: the eternal tomb
Brings me the peace, which life has never brought

For all the things I do, and do not well;
All the forced drawings of a mortal breath:
Are as the hollow music of a bell,
That times the slow approach of perfect death.

[1888]

A DECADENT'S LYRIC [1]

Sometimes, in very joy of shame,
Our flesh becomes one living flame:
And she and I
Are no more separate, but the same.

Ardour and agony unite;
Desire, delirium, delight:
And I and she
Faint in the fierce and fevered night.

Her body music is: and ah,
The accords of lute and viola!
When she and I
Play on live limbs love's opera!

[1897]

[1] As Ian Fletcher, in his edition of Johnson's poems, has suggested,
this is a parody of "Symons' less wholesome love lyrics."

Richard Le Gallienne

[1866–1947]

From ENGLISH POEMS [1892]

The following poems reveal Le Gallienne's intense dislike of certain excesses of the Decadents, though he himself was attracted to the cult of artifice (see, for example, his "Ballad of London"). For Le Gallienne's definition of Decadence, see the headnote to Arthur Symons' "Decadent Movement in Literature."

TO THE READER

Art was a palace once, things great and fair,
And strong and holy, found a temple there:
Now 'tis a lazar-house of leprous men.
O shall we hear an English song again!
Still English larks mount in the merry morn,
An English May still brings an English thorn,
Still English daisies up and down the grass,
Still English love for English lad and lass—
Yet youngsters blush to sing an English song!

Thou nightingale that for six hundred years
Sang to the world—O art thou husht at last!

For, not of thee this new voice in our ears,
Music of France that once was of the spheres;
And not of thee these strange green flowers[1] that spring
From daisy roots and seemed to bear a sting.

Thou Helicon of numbers 'undefiled,'
Forgive that 'neath the shadow of thy name,
England, I bring a song of little fame;
Not as one worthy but as loving thee,
Not as a singer, only as a child.

THE DÉCADENT TO HIS SOUL

The Décadent was speaking to his soul—
Poor useless thing, he said,
Why did God burden me with such as thou?
The body were enough,
The body gives me all.

The soul's a sort of sentimental wife
That prays and whimpers of the higher life,
Objects to latch-keys, and bewails the old,
The dear old days, of passion and of dream,
When life was a blank canvas, yet untouched
Of the great painter Sin.

Yet, little soul, thou hast fine eyes,
And knowest fine airy motions,
Hast a voice—
Why wilt thou so devote them to the church?

His face grew strangely sweet—
As when a toad smiles.
He dreamed of a new sin:
An incest 'twixt the body and the soul.

[1] A reference to Oscar Wilde's green carnation. See Le Gallienne's
"The Boom in Yellow."

He drugged his soul, and in a house of sin
She played all she remembered out of heaven
For him to kiss and clip by.
He took a little harlot in his hands,
And she made all his veins like boiling oil,
Then that grave organ made them cool again.

Then from that day, he used his soul
As bitters to the over dulcet sins,
As olives to the fatness of the feast—
She made those dear heart-breaking ecstasies
Of minor chords amid the Phrygian flutes,
She sauced his sins with splendid memories,
Starry regrets and infinite hopes and fears;
His holy youth and his first love
Made pearly background to strange-coloured vice.

Sin is no sin when virtue is forgot.
It is so good in sin to keep in sight
The white hills whence we fell, to measure by—
To say I was so high, so white, so pure,
And am so low, so blood-stained and so base;
I revel here amid the sweet sweet mire
And yonder are the hills of morning flowers;
So high, so low; so lost and with me yet;
To stretch the octave 'twixt the dream and deed,
Ah, that's the thrill!
To dream so well, to do so ill,—
There comes the bitter-sweet that makes the sin.

First drink the stars, then grunt amid the mire,
So shall the mire have something of the stars,
And the high stars be fragrant of the mire.

The Décadent was speaking to his soul—
Dear witch, I said the body was enough.
How young, how simple as a suckling child!
And then I dreamed—'an incest 'twixt the body and the
    soul:'

Let's wed, I thought, the seraph with the dog,
And wait the purple thing that shall be born.

And now look round—seest thou this bloom?
Seven petals and each petal seven dyes,
The stem is gilded and the root in blood:
That came of thee.
Yea, all my flowers were single save for thee.
I pluck seven fruits from off a single tree,
I pluck seven flowers from off a single stem,
I light my palace with the seven stars,
And eat strange dishes to Gregorian chants:
All thanks to thee.

But the soul wept with hollow hectic face,
Captive in that lupanar of a man.
And I who passed by heard and wept for both,—
The man was once an apple-cheek dear lad,
The soul was once an angel up in heaven.

O let the body be a healthy beast,
And keep the soul a singing soaring bird;
But lure thou not the soul from out the sky
To pipe unto the body in the sty.

BEAUTY ACCURST

I am so fair that wheresoe'er I wend
    Men yearn with strange desire to kiss my face,
Stretch out their hands to touch me as I pass,
    And women follow me from place to place.

A poet writing honey of his dear
    Leaves the wet page,—ah! leaves it long to dry.
The bride forgets it is her marriage-morn,
    The bridegroom too forgets as I go by.

Within the street where my strange feet shall stray
    All markets hush and traffickers forget,

In my gold head forget their meaner gold,
 The poor man grows unmindful of his debt.

Two lovers kissing in a secret place,
 Should I draw nigh,—will never kiss again;
I come between the king and his desire,
 And where I am all loving else is vain.

Lo! when I walk along the woodland way
 Strange creatures leer at me with uncouth love
And from the grass reach upward to my breast,
 And to my mouth lean from the boughs above.

The sleepy kine move round me in desire
 And press their oozy lips upon my hair,
Toads kiss my feet and creatures of the mire,
 The snails will leave their shells to watch me there.

But all this worship, what is it to me?
 I smite the ox and crush the toad in death:
I only know I am so very fair,
 And that the world was made to give me breath.

I only wait the hour when God shall rise
 Up from the star where he so long hath sat,
And bow before the wonder of my eyes
 And set *me* there—I am so fair as that.

SUNSET IN THE CITY

Above the town a monstrous wheel is turning,
 With glowing spokes of red,
Low in the west its fiery axle burning;
 And, lost amid the spaces overhead,
A vague white moth, the moon, is fluttering.

Above the town an azure sea is flowing,
 'Mid long peninsulas of shining sand,

From opal unto pearl the moon is growing,
    Dropped like a shell upon the changing strand.

Within the town the streets grow strange and haunted,
    And, dark against the western lakes of green,
The buildings change to temples, and unwonted
    Shadows and sounds creep in where day has been.

Within the town, the lamps of sin are flaring,
    Poor foolish men that know not what ye are!
Tired traffic still upon his feet is faring—
    Two lovers meet and kiss and watch a star.

A BALLAD OF LONDON

Ah, London! London! our delight,
Great flower that opens but at night,
Great City of the midnight sun,
Whose day begins when day is done.

Lamp after lamp against the sky
Opens a sudden beaming eye,
Leaping alight on either hand,
The iron lilies of the Strand.

Like dragonflies, the hansoms hover,
With jewelled eyes, to catch the lover,
The streets are full of lights and loves,
Soft gowns, and flutter of soiled doves.

Upon thy petals butterflies,
But at thy root, some say, there lies
A world of weeping trodden things,
Poor worms that have not eyes or wings.

From out corruption of their woe
Springs this bright flower that charms us so,
Men die and rot deep out of sight
To keep this jungle-flower bright.

Paris and London, World-Flowers twain
Wherewith the World-Tree blooms again,
Since Time hath gathered Babylon
And withered Rome still withers on.

Sidon and Tyre were such as ye,
How bright they shone upon the tree!
But Time hath gathered, both are gone,
And no man sails to Babylon.

Ah, London! London! our delight,
For thee, too, the eternal night,
And Circe Paris hath no charm
To stay Time's unrelenting arm.

THE BOOM IN YELLOW

Green must always have a large following among artists and
art lovers; for, as has been pointed out, an appreciation of it
is a sure sign of a subtle artistic temperament. There is something not quite good, something almost sinister, about it—at
least, in its more complex forms, though in its simple form,
as we find it in outdoor nature, it is innocent enough; and,
indeed, is it not used in colloquial metaphor as an adjective
for innocence itself? Innocence has but two colours, white or
green. But Becky Sharp's[1] eyes also were green, and the
green of the æsthete does not suggest innocence. There will
always be wearers of the green carnation;[2] but the popular
vogue which green has enjoyed for the last ten or fifteen
years is probably passing. Even the æsthete himself would
seem to be growing a little weary of its indefinitely divided
tones, and to be anxious for a colour sensation somewhat
more positive than those to be gained from almost impercep-

[1] Becky Sharp, the notoriously immoral heroine of Thackeray's *Vanity
Fair.*
[2] Oscar Wilde, its most famous wearer, claimed to have invented it.
See the selection from Robert Hichens' satirical novel *The Green
Carnation* in Appendix.

tible *nuances* of green. Jaded with over-refinements and super-subtleties, we seem in many directions to be harking back to the primary colours of life. Blue, crude and unsoftened, and a form of magenta, have recently had a short innings; and now the triumph of yellow is imminent. Of course, a love for green implies some regard for yellow, and in our so-called æsthetic renaissance the sunflower[3] went before the green carnation—which is, indeed, the badge of but a small schism of æsthetes, and not worn by the great body of the more catholic lovers of beauty.

Yellow is becoming more and more dominant in decoration—in wall-papers, and flowers cultivated with decorative intention, such as chrysanthemums. And one can easily understand why: seeing that, after white, yellow reflects more light than any other colour, and thus ministers to the growing preference for light and joyous rooms. A few yellow chrysanthemums will make a small room look twice its size, and when the sun comes out upon a yellow wall-paper the whole room seems suddenly to expand, to open like a flower. When it falls upon the pot of yellow chrysanthemums, and sets them ablaze, it seems as though one had an angel in the room. Bill-posters are beginning to discover the attractive qualities of the colour. Who can ever forget meeting for the first time upon a boarding Mr. Dudley Hardy's wonderful Yellow Girl, the pretty advance-guard of *To-Day*? But I suppose the honour of the discovery of the colour for advertising purposes rests with Mr. Colman; though its recent boom comes from the publishers, and particularly from the Bodley Head. *The Yellow Book* with any other colour would hardly have sold as well—the first private edition of Mr. Arthur Benson's poems, by the way, came caparisoned in yellow, and with the identical name, *Le Cabier Jaune* [1892]; and no doubt it was largely its title that made the success of *The Yellow Aster*.[4] In literature, indeed, yellow has long been the colour of romance. The word 'yellow-back' witnesses its close association with fiction; and in France, as we know, it

[3] Favored by William Morris and by Wilde early in his æsthetic career.
[4] A novel published in 1894 by Kathleen Caffyn under the pseudonym "Iota."

is the all but universal custom to bind books in yellow paper.
Mr. Heinemann and Mr. Unwin [English publishers] have
endeavoured to naturalise the custom here; but, though in
cloth yellow has emphatically 'caught on,' in paper it still
hangs fire. The A B C Railway Guide is probably the only
exception, and that, it is to be hoped, is not fiction. Mr.
[Andrew] Lang has recently followed the fashion with his
Yellow Fairy Book; and, indeed, one of the best known figures in fairydom is yellow—namely, the Yellow Dwarf.[5]
Yellow, always a prominent Oriental colour, was but lately
of peculiar significance in the Far East; for were not the
sorrows of a certain high Chinese official intimately con-
nected with the fatal colour? The Yellow Book, the Yellow
Aster, the Yellow Jacket!—and the Yellow Fever, like
'Orion' Horne's sunshine, is always with us 'somewhere in
the world.' The same applies also, I suppose, to the Yellow
Sea.

Till one comes to think of it, one hardly realises how
many important and pleasant things in life are yellow. Blue
and green, no doubt, contract for the colouring of vast
departments of the physical world. 'Blue!' sings Keats, in a
fine but too little known sonnet—

> . . . 'Tis the life of heaven—the domain
> Of Cynthia—the wide palace of the sun—
> The tent of Hesperus, and all his train—
> The bosomer of clouds, gold, grey, and dun.
> Blue! 'Tis the life of waters . . .
> Blue! Gentle cousin of the forest green,
> Married to green in all the sweetest flowers.

Yellow might retort by quoting Mr. Grant Allen, in his
book on *The Colour Sense*, to the effect that the blueness of
sea and sky is mainly poetical illusion or inaccuracy, and
that sea and sky are found blue only in one experiment out

[5] A pseudonym used by Henry Harland, literary editor of *The Yellow Book*, who contributed occasional critical essays under that
name. In the eleventh volume (October, 1896), Beerbohm's famous
drawing depicts the Yellow Dwarf as a diminutive yellow creature
wearing a fringed black mask which conceals what appears to be an
enigmatic smile. In his hand are a bow and arrow; slung around his
back is a quiver of arrows.

of fourteen. At morning and evening they are usually in great part stained golden. Blue certainly has one advantage over yellow, in that it has the privilege of colouring some of the prettiest eyes in the world. Yellow has a chance only in cases of jaundice and liver complaint, and this colour scheme in such cases is seldom appreciated. Again, green has the contract for the greater bulk of the vegetable life of the globe; but his is a monotonous business, like the painting of miles and miles of palings: grass, grass, grass, trees, trees, trees, *ad infinitum*; whereas yellow leads a roving, versatile life, and is seldom called upon for such monotonous labour. The sands of Sahara are probably the only conspicuous instance of yellow thus working by the piece. It is in the quality, in the diversity of the things it colours, rather than in their mileage or tonnage, that yellow is distinguished; though, for that matter, we suppose, the sun is as big and heavy as most things, and that is yellow. Of course, when we say yellow we include golden, and all varieties of the colour —saffron, orange, flaxen, tawny, blonde, topaz, citron, etc.

If the sun may reasonably be described as the most important object in the world, surely money is the next. That, as we know, is, in its most potent metallic form, yellow also. The 'yellow gold' is a favourite phrase in certain forms of poetry; and 'yellow-boys' is a term of natural affection among sailors. Following the example of their lord the sun, most fires and lights are yellow or golden, and it is only in times of danger or superstition that they burn red or blue. And, if yellow be denied entrance to beautiful eyes, it enjoys a privilege which—except in the case of certain indigo-staining African tribes, who cannot be said to count—blue has never claimed: that of colouring perhaps the loveliest thing in the world, the hair of woman. Hair is naturally golden—unnaturally also. When Browning sings pathetically of 'dear dead women—with such hair too!' he continues [in "A Toccata of Galuppi's":]

> *What's become of all the gold*
> *Used to hang and brush their bosoms—*

not 'all the blue' or 'all the brown,' though some of us, it is true, are condemned to wear our hair brown or blue-black.

But such are only unhappy exceptions. Yellow or gold is the rule. The bravest men and the fairest women have had golden hair, and, we may add, in reference to another distinction of the colour we are celebrating, golden hearts. Hair at the present time is doing its best to conform to its normal conditions of colour. Numerous instances might be adduced of its changing from black to gold, in obedience to chemical law. 'Peroxide of hydrogen!' says the cynic. 'Beauty!' says the lover of art.

And it might be argued, in a world of inevitable compromise, that the damage done to the physical health and texture of the hair thus playing the chameleon may well be overbalanced by the happiness, and consequent increased effectiveness, of the person thus dyeing for the sake of beauty. Thaumaturgists lay much stress on the mystic influence of colours; and who knows but that, if we were only allowed to dye our hair what colour we chose, we might be different men and women? Strange things are told, of women who have dyed their hair the colour of blood or of wine, and we know from Christina Rossetti that golden hair is negotiable in fairyland—

> "*You have much gold upon your head,*"
> *They answered all together:*
>   "*Buy from us with a golden curl.*" [6]

Whether Laura could have done business with the goblin merchantmen with an oxidised curl is a difficult point, for fairies have sharp eyes; and, though it be impossible for a mortal to tell the real gold from the false gold hair, the fairies may be able to do so, and might reject the curl as counterfeit.

Again, if in the vegetable world green almost universally colours the leaves, yellow has more to do with the flowers. The flowers we love best are yellow: the cowslip, the daffodil, the crocus, the buttercup, half the daisy, the honeysuckle, and the loveliest rose. Yellow, too, has its turn even with the leaves; and what an artist he shows himself when, in autumn, he 'lays his fiery finger' upon them, lighting up the

[6] From "Goblin Market," a narrative poem in which the golden-haired Laura is a central character.

forlorn woodland with splashes—pure palette-colour of audacious gold! He hangs the mulberry with heart-shaped yellow shields—which reminds one of the heraldic importance of 'or,'—and he lines the banks of the Seine with phantasmal yellow poplars. And other leaves still dearer to the heart are yellow likewise; leaves of those sweet old poets whose thoughts seem to have turned the pages gold. Let us dream of this: a maid with yellow hair, clad in a yellow gown, seated in a yellow room, at the window a yellow sunset, in the grate a yellow fire, at her side a yellow lamplight, on her knee a Yellow Book. And the letters we love best to read—when we dare—are they not yellow too? No doubt some disagreeable things are reported of yellow. We have had the yellow-fever, and we have had pea-soup. The eyes of lions are said to be yellow, and the ugliest cats—the cats that infest one's garden—are always yellow. Some medicines are yellow, and no doubt there are many other yellow disagreeables; but we prefer to dwell upon the yellow blessings. I had almost forgotten that the gayest wines are yellow. Nor has religion forgotten yellow. It is to be hoped yellow will not forget religion. The sacred robe of the second greatest religion of the world is yellow, 'the yellow robe' of the Buddhist friar; and when the sacred harlots of Hindustan walk in lovely procession through the streets, they too, like the friars, are clad in yellow. Amber is yellow; so is the orange; and so were stage-coaches and many dashing things of the old time; and pink is yellow by lamplight. But gold-mines, it has been proved, are not so yellow as is popularly supposed. Hymen's robe is Miltonically 'saffron,' and the dearest petticoat in all literature—not forgetting the 'tempestuous' garment of Herrick's Julia[7]—was 'yaller.' Yes!—

> *Er petticoat was yaller an' 'er little cap was green,*
> *An'er name was Supi-yaw-lat, jes' the same as Theebaw's*
> *Queen.*[8]

Is it possible to say anything prettier for yellow than that?

[7] An allusion to the poem "Upon Julia's Clothes," by Robert Herrick.
[8] From "Mandalay" by Rudyard Kipling.

Arthur Symons

[1 8 6 5 – 1 9 4 5]

THE DECADENT MOVEMENT
IN LITERATURE

According to Roger Lhombreaud, Symons' biographer, "The Decadent Movement in Literature" (published in *Harper's New Monthly Magazine* in November, 1893) was designed as a reply to criticism and ridicule of the Decadence by Richard Le Gallienne, a fellow member of the Rhymers' Club. In 1892, in a review of *Illustrations of Tennyson* by Churton Collins (reprinted in *Retrospective Reviews*), Le Gallienne defined Decadence in literature as

> more than a question of style, nor is it, as some suppose, a question of theme. It is in the character of the treatment that we must seek it. In all great vital literature, the theme, great or small, is considered in all its relation to the sum-total of things, to the Infinite, as we phrase it; in decadent literature the relations, the due proportions, are ignored. One might say that literary decadence consists in the euphuistic expression of isolated observations. Thus disease, which is the favourite theme of décadents, does not in itself make for decadence: it is only when, as often, it is studied apart from its relations to health, to the great vital centre of things, that it does so. Any point of view, seriously taken, which ignores the complete view, approaches decadence.
>
> To notice only the picturesque effects of a begger's rags as Gautier; the colour-scheme of a tippler's nose, like M.

Huysmans, to consider one's mother merely prismatically,
like Mr. Whistler—these are examples of the decadent atti-
tude. At the bottom, decadence is merely limited thinking,
often insane thinking . . .

In *English Poems* (1892)—a volume which reveals, despite
denials, the influence of the Decadence—Le Gallienne com-
plained that the Decadents had made Art, which was "a
palace once," into a "lazar-house of leprous men." In "The
Décadent to his Soul," Le Gallienne satirized the characteristic verse of the Decadents and their quest for new and
strange sensations.

The latest movement in European literature has been called
by many names, none of them quite exact or comprehensive
—Decadence, Symbolism, Impressionism, for instance. It is
easy to dispute over words, and we shall find that Verlaine
objects to being called a Decadent, Maeterlinck to being
called a Symbolist, Huysmans to being called an Impressionist. These terms, as it happens, have been adopted as the
badge of little separate cliques, noisy, brainsick young people
who haunt the brasseries of the Boulevard Saint-Michel, and
exhaust their ingenuities in theorizing over the works they
cannot write. But, taken frankly as epithets which express
their own meaning, both Impressionism and Symbolism convey some notion of that new kind of literature which is perhaps more broadly characterized by the word Decadence
The most representative literature of the day—the writing
which appeals to, which has done so much to form, the
younger generation—is certainly not classic, nor has it any
relation with that old antithesis of the Classic, the Romantic.
After a fashion it is no doubt a decadence; it has all the
qualities that mark the end of great periods, the qualities that
we find in the Greek, the Latin, decadence: an intense self-
consciousness, a restless curiosity in research, an over-
subtilizing refinement upon refinement, a spiritual and moral
perversity. If what we call the classic is indeed the supreme
art—those qualities of perfect simplicity, perfect sanity, perfect proportion, the supreme qualities—then this representa-

tive literature of to-day, interesting, beautiful, novel as it is, is really a new and beautiful and interesting disease.

Healthy we cannot call it, and healthy it does not wish to be considered. The Goncourts, in their prefaces, in their *Journal*, are always insisting on their own pet malady, *la névrose* ["neurosis"]. It is in their work, too, that Huysmans notes with delight "le style tacheté et faisandé"—high-flavored and spotted with corruption—which he himself possesses in the highest degree. "Having desire without light, curiosity without wisdom, seeking God by strange ways, by ways traced by the hands of men; offering rash incense upon the high places to an unknown God, who is the God of darkness"—that is how Ernest Hello [French Catholic writer, 1828–85], in one of his apocalyptic moments, characterizes the nineteenth century. And this unreason of the soul—of which Hello himself is so curious a victim—this unstable equilibrium, which has overbalanced so many brilliant intelligences into one form or another of spiritual confusion, is but another form of the *maladie fin de siècle*. For its very disease of form, this literature is certainly typical of a civilization grown over-luxurious, over-inquiring, too languid for the relief of action, too uncertain for any emphasis in opinion or in conduct. It reflects all the moods, all the manners, of a sophisticated society; its very artificiality is a way of being true to nature: simplicity, sanity, proportion—the classic qualities—how much do we possess them in our life, our surroundings, that we should look to find them in our literature—so evidently the literature of a decadence?

Taking the word Decadence, then, as most precisely expressing the general sense of the newest movement in literature, we find that the terms Impressionism and Symbolism define correctly enough the two main branches of that movement. Now Impressionist and Symbolist have more in common than either supposes; both are really working on the same hypothesis, applied in different directions. What both seek is not general truth merely, but *la vérité vraie,* the very essence of truth—the truth of appearances to the senses, of the visible world to the eyes that see it; and the truth of spiritual things to the spiritual vision. The Impressionist, in literature as in painting, would flash upon you in a new, sudden way so exact an image of what you have just seen, just as you have seen it, that you may say, as a young American sculptor, a pupil of Rodin, said to me on seeing for the first time a picture of Whistler's, "Whistler seems to think his picture upon canvas—and there it is!" Or you may find, with Sainte-Beuve, writing of Goncourt, the "soul of the landscape"—the soul of whatever corner of the visible world has to be realized. The Symbolist, in this new, sudden way, would flash upon you the "soul" of that which can be apprehended only by the soul—the finer sense of things unseen, the deeper meaning of things evident. And naturally, necessarily, this endeavor after a perfect truth to one's impression, to one's intuition—perhaps an impossible endeavor—has brought with it, in its revolt from ready-made impressions and conclusions, a revolt from the ready-made of language, from the bondage of traditional form, of a form become rigid. In France, where this movement began and has mainly flourished, it is Goncourt who was the first to invent a style in prose really new, impressionistic, a style which was itself almost sensation. It is Verlaine who has invented such another new style in verse.

The work of the brothers De Goncourt—twelve novels, eleven or twelve studies in the history of the eighteenth century, six or seven books about art, the art mainly of the eighteenth century and of Japan, two plays, some volumes of letters and of fragments, and a *Journal* in six volumes—is perhaps, in its intention and its consequences, the most revolutionary of the century. No one has ever tried so deliberately to do something new as the Goncourts; and the final word in the summing up which the survivor has placed at the head of the *Préfaces et Manifestes* is a word which speaks of "tentatives, enfin, où les deux frères ont cherchés *à faire du neuf*, ont fait leurs efforts pour doter les diverses branches de la littérature de quelque chose que n'avaient point songé à trouver leurs prédécesseurs." [1] And in the preface to *Chérie*, in that pathetic passage which tells of the two brothers (one

[1] ". . . in short, attempts in which the two brothers sought *to do something new*, bent their efforts to endow the various branches of literature with something that their predecessors had not thought of finding."

mortally stricken, and within a few months of death) taking
their daily walk in the Bois de Boulogne, there is a definite
demand on posterity. "The search after *reality* in literature,
the resurrection of eighteenth-century art, the triumph of
Japonisme—are not these," said Jules, "the three great literary and artistic movements of the second half of the nineteenth century? And it is we who brought them about, these
three movements. Well, when one has done that, it is difficult
indeed not to be *somebody* in the future." Nor, even, is this
all. What the Goncourts have done is to specialize vision, so
to speak, and to subtilize language to the point of rendering
every detail in just the form and color of the actual impression. M. Edmond de Goncourt once said to me—varying, if I
remember rightly, an expression he had put into the *Journal*—"My brother and I invented an opera-glass: the young
people nowadays are taking it out of our hands."

An opera-glass—a special, unique way of seeing things—
that is what the Goncourts have brought to bear upon the
common things about us; and it is here that they have done
the "something new," here more than anywhere. They have
never sought "to see life steadily, and see it whole": their
vision has always been somewhat feverish, with the diseased
sharpness of over-excited nerves. "We do not hide from ourselves that we have been passionate, nervous creatures, un-
healthily impressionable," confesses the *Journal*. But it is this
morbid intensity in seeing and seizing things that has helped
to form that marvellous style—"a style perhaps too ambi-
tious of impossibilities," as they admit—a style which inher-
its some of its color from Gautier, some of its fine outline
from Flaubert, but which has brought light and shadow into
the color, which has softened outline in the magic of atmosphere. With them words are not merely color and sound,
they live. That search after "l'image peinte," "l'épithète
rare," ["the painted image, the rare epithet"] is not (as with
Flaubert) a search after harmony of phrase for its own sake;
it is a desperate endeavor to give sensation, to flash the impression of the moment, to preserve the very heat and motion
of life. And so, in analysis as in description, they have found
out a way of noting the fine shades; they have broken the
outline of the conventional novel in chapters, with its contin-

uous story, in order to indicate—sometimes in a chapter of half a page—this and that revealing moment, this or that significant attitude or accident or sensation. For the placid traditions of French prose they have had but little respect; their aim has been but one, that of having (as M. Edmond de Goncourt tells us in the preface to *Chérie*) "une langue rendant nos idées, nos sensations, nos figurations des hommes et des choses, d'une facon distincte de celui-ci ou de celui-là, un langue personnelle, une langue portant notre signature." [2]

What Goncourt has done in prose—inventing absolutely a new way of saying things, to correspond with that new way of seeing things which he has found—Verlaine has done in verse. In a famous poem, "Art Poétique," he has himself defined his own ideal of the poetic art:

> *Car nous voulons la Nuance encor,*
> *Pas la Couleur, rien que la Nuance!*
> *Oh! la Nuance seule fiance*
> *Le rêve au rêve et la flûte au cor!* [3]

Music first of all and before all, he insists; and then, not color, but *la nuance,* the last fine shade. Poetry is to be something vague, intangible, evanescent, a winged soul in flight "toward other skies and other loves." To express the inexpressible he speaks of beautiful eyes behind a veil, of the palpitating sunlight of noon, of the blue swarm of clear stars in a cool autumn sky; and the verse in which he makes this confession of faith has the exquisite troubled beauty—"sans rien en lui qui pèse ou qui pose" [4]—which he commends as the essential quality of verse. In a later poem of poetical counsel he tells us that art should, first of all, be absolutely clear, absolutely sincere: "L'art, mes enfants, c'est d'être

---

[2] "A language rendering our ideas, our sensations, our conceptions of men and things in a manner distinct from that of others, a personal language, a language bearing our signature."

[3] "For we still want Nuance,
   Not Color, only Nuance!
   Oh, Nuance alone links
   The dream to the dream and the flute to the horn!"

[4] "without anything in him which weighs or rests."

absolument soi-même." [5] The two poems, with their seven years' interval—an interval which means so much in the life of a man like Verlaine—give us all that there is of theory in the work of the least theoretical, the most really instinctive, of poetical innovators. Verlaine's poetry has varied with his life; always in excess—now furiously sensual, now feverishly devout—he has been constant only to himself, to his own self-contradictions. For, with all the violence, turmoil, and disorder of a life which is almost the life of a modern Villon, Paul Verlaine has always retained that childlike simplicity, and, in his verse, which has been his confessional, that fine sincerity, of which Villon may be thought to have set the example in literature.

Beginning his career as a Parnassian with the *Poèmes Saturniens,* Verlaine becomes himself, in his exquisite first manner, in the *Fêtes Galantes,* caprices after Watteau, followed, a year later, by *La Bonne Chanson,* a happy record of too confident a lover's happiness. *Romances sans Paroles,* in which the poetry of Impressionism reaches its very highest point, is more *tourmenté,* goes deeper, becomes more poignantly personal. It is the poetry of sensation, of evocation; poetry which paints as well as sings, and which paints as Whistler paints, seeming to think the colors and outlines upon the canvas, to think them only, and they are there. The mere magic of words—words which evoke pictures, which recall sensations—can go no further; and in his next book, *Sagesse,* published after seven years' wanderings and sufferings, there is a graver manner of more deeply personal confession—that "sincerity, and the impression of the moment followed to the letter," which he has defined in a prose criticism on himself as his main preference in regard to style. "Sincerity, and the impression of the moment followed to the letter," mark the rest of Verlaine's work, whether the sentiment be that of passionate friendship, as in *Amour;* of love, human and divine, as in *Bonheur;* of the mere lust of the flesh, as in *Parallèlement* and *Chansons pour Elle.* In his very latest verse the quality of simplicity has become exaggerated, has become, at times, childish; the once exquisite depravity

---

[5] "Art, my children, consists of being absolutely oneself."

of style has lost some of its distinction; there is no longer the same delicately vivid "impression of the moment" to render. Yet the very closeness with which it follows a lamentable career gives a curious interest to even the worst of Verlaine's work. And how unique, how unsurpassable in its kind, is the best! "Et tout le reste est littérature!" [6] was the cry, supreme and contemptuous, of that early "Art Poétique"; and, compared with Verlaine at his best, all other contemporary work in verse seems not yet disenfranchised from mere "literature." To fix the last fine shade, the quintessence of things; to fix it fleetingly; to be a disembodied voice, and yet the voice of a human soul: that is the ideal of Decadence, and it is what Paul Verlaine has achieved.

And certainly, so far as achievement goes, no other poet of the actual group in France can be named beside him or near him. But in Stéphane Mallarmé, with his supreme pose as the supreme poet, and his two or three pieces of exquisite verse and delicately artificial prose to show by way of result, we have the prophet and pontiff of the movement, the mystical and theoretical leader of the great emancipation. No one has ever dreamed such beautiful impossible dreams as Mallarmé; no one has ever so possessed his soul in the contemplation of masterpieces to come. All his life he has been haunted by the desire to create, not so much something new in literature, as a literature which should itself be a new art. He has dreamed of a work into which all the arts should enter, and achieve themselves by a mutual interdependence—a harmonizing of all the arts into one supreme art—and he has theorized with infinite subtlety over the possibilities of doing the impossible. Every Tuesday for the last twenty years he has talked more fascinatingly, more suggestively, than any one else has ever done, in that little room in the Rue de Rome, to that little group of eager young poets. "A seeker after something in the world, that is there in no satisfying measure, or not at all," he has carried his contempt for the usual, the conventional, beyond the point of literary expression, into the domain of practical affairs. Until the publication, quite recently, of a selection of *Vers et Prose*, it was

---

[6] "And all the rest is literature."

only possible to get his poems in a limited and expensive edition, lithographed in fac-simile of his own clear and elegant handwriting. An aristocrat of letters, Mallarmé has always looked with intense disdain on the indiscriminate accident of universal suffrage. He has wished neither to be read nor to be understood by the bourgeois intelligence, and it is with some deliberateness of intention that he has made both issues impossible. M. Catulle Mendès [1843–1909, poet and novelist] defines him admirably as "a difficult author," and in his latest period he has succeeded in becoming absolutely unintelligible. His early poems, "L'Après-midi d'un Faune," "Hérodiade," for example, and some exquisite sonnets, and one or two fragments of perfectly polished verse, are written in a language which has nothing in common with every-day language—symbol within symbol, image within image; but symbol and image achieve themselves in expression without seeming to call for the necessity of a key. The latest poems (in which punctuation is sometimes entirely suppressed, for our further bewilderment) consist merely of a sequence of symbols, in which every word must be taken in a sense with which its ordinary significance has nothing to do. Mallarmé's contortion of the French language, so far as mere style is concerned, is curiously similar to the kind of depravation which was undergone by the Latin language in its decadence. It is, indeed, in part a reversion to Latin phraseology, to the Latin construction, and it has made, of the clear and flowing French language, something irregular, unquiet, expressive, with sudden surprising felicities, with nervous starts and lapses, with new capacities for the exact noting of sensation. Alike to the ordinary and to the scholarly reader, it is painful, intolerable; a jargon, a massacre. Supremely self-confident, and backed, certainly, by an ardent following of the younger generation, Mallarmé goes on his way, experimenting more and more audaciously, having achieved by this time, at all events, a style wholly his own. Yet the "chef-d'œuvre inconnu" ["unknown masterpiece"] seems no nearer completion, the impossible seems no more likely to be done. The two or three beautiful fragments remain, and we still hear the voice in the Rue de Rome.

Probably it is as a voice, an influence, that Mallarmé will

be remembered. His personal magnetism has had a great deal to do with the making of the very newest French literature; few literary beginners in Paris have been able to escape the rewards and punishments of his contact, his suggestion. One of the young poets who form that delightful Tuesday evening coterie said to me the other day, "We owe much to Mallarmé, but he has kept us all back three years." That is where the danger of so inspiring, so helping a personality comes in. The work even of M. Henri de Regnier [1864–1936], who is the best of the disciples, has not entirely got clear from the influence that has shown his fine talent the way to develop. Perhaps it is in the verse of men who are not exactly following in the counsel of the master—who might disown him, whom he might disown—that one sees most clearly the outcome of his theories, the actual consequences of his practice. In regard to the construction of verse, Mallarmé has always remained faithful to the traditional syllabic measurement; but the freak or the discovery of "le vers libre" ["free verse"] is certainly the natural consequence of his experiments upon the elasticity of rhythm, upon the power of resistance of the cæsura [a natural pause in a line]. "Le vers libre" in the hands of most of the experimenters becomes merely rhymeless irregular prose; in the hands of Gustave Kahn [1859–1936] and Edouard Dujardin [1861–1949] it has, it must be admitted, attained a certain beauty of its own. I never really understood the charm that may be found in this apparently structureless rhythm until I heard, not long since, M. Dujardin read aloud the as yet unpublished conclusion of a dramatic poem in several parts. It was rhymed, but rhymed with some irregularity, and the rhythm was purely and simply a vocal effect. The rhythm came and went as the spirit moved. You might deny that it was rhythm at all; and yet, read as I heard it read, in a sort of slow chant, it produced on me the effect of really beautiful verse. But M. Dujardin is a poet: "vers libres" in the hands of a sciolist are the most intolerably easy and annoying of poetical exercises. Even in the case of *Le Pèlerin Passionné* I cannot see the justification of what is merely regular syllabic verse lengthened or shortened arbitrarily, with the Alexandrine [verse of twelve syllables] always evident in the background as the foot-rule

of the new metre. In this hazardous experiment M. Jean
Moréas, whose real talent lies in quite another direction, has
brought nothing into literature but an example of deliberate
singularity for singularity's sake. I seem to find the measure
of the man in a remark I once heard him make in a café,
where we were discussing the technique of metre: "You,
Verlaine!" he cried, leaning across the table, "have only
written lines of sixteen syllables; I have written lines of
twenty syllables!" And turning to me, he asked anxiously if
Swinburne had ever done that—had written a line of twenty
syllables.

That is indeed the measure of the man, and it points a
criticism upon not a few of the busy little *littérateurs* who
are founding new *revues* every other week in Paris. These
people have nothing to say, but they are resolved to say
something, and to say it in the newest mode. They are Impressionists because it is the fashion, Symbolists because it is
the vogue, Decadents because Decadence is in the very air of
the cafés. And so, in their manner, they are mile-posts on the
way of this new movement, telling how far it has gone. But
to find a new personality, a new way of seeing things, among
the young writers who are starting up on every hand, we
must turn from Paris to Brussels—to the so-called Belgian
Shakespeare, Maurice Maeterlinck. M. Maeterlinck was discovered to the general French public by M. Octave Mirbeau,
in an article in the *Figaro,* August 24, 1890, on the publication of *La Princesse Maleine.* "M. Maurice Maeterlinck nous
a donné l'œuvre la plus géniale de ce temps, et la plus ex-
traordinaire et la plus naïve aussi, comparable et—oserai-je le
dire?—supérieure en beauté à ce qui il y a de plus beau dans
Shakespeare. . . . plus tragique que *Macbeth,* plus extraor-
dinaire en pensée que *Hamlet.*" [7] That is how the enthusi-
ast announced his discovery. In truth, M. Maeterlinck is not
a Shakespeare, and the Elizabethan violence of his first play
is of the school of Webster and Tourneur rather than of

[7] "M. Maurice Maeterlinck has given us a work filled with the greatest genius of this age, and the most extraordinary and most artless
also, comparable and—dare I say it?—superior to the most beautiful
in Shakespeare . . . more tragic than *Macbeth,* more outstanding in
thought than *Hamlet.*"

Shakespeare. As a dramatist he has but one note, that of fear; he has but one method, that of repetition. In *La Prin-cesse Maleine* there is a certain amount of action—action which is certainly meant to reinvest the terrors of *Macbeth* and of *Lear*. In *L'Intruse* and *Les Aveugles* the scene is stationary, the action but reflected upon the stage, as if from another plane. In *Les Sept Princesses* the action, such as it is, is "such stuff as dreams are made of," and is literally, in great part, seen through a window.

This window, looking out upon the unseen—an open door, as in *L'Intruse,* through which Death, the intruder, may come invisibly—how typical of the new kind of symbolistic and impressionistic drama which M. Maeterlinck has invented! I say invented, a little rashly. The real discoverer of this new kind of drama was that strange, inspiring, incomplete man of genius whom M. Maeterlinck, above all others, delights to honor, Villiers de l'Isle-Adam. Imagine a combination of Swift, of Poe, and of Coleridge, and you will have some idea of the extraordinary, impossible poet and cynic who, after a life of brilliant failure, has left a series of unfinished works in every kind of literature; among the finished achievements one volume of short stories, *Contes Cruels,* which is an absolute masterpiece. Yet, apart from this, it was the misfortune of Villiers never to attain the height of his imaginings, and even *Axël,* the work of a lifetime, is an achievement only half achieved. Only half achieved, or achieved only in the work of others; for, in its mystical intention, its remoteness from any kind of outward reality, *Axël* is undoubtedly the origin of the symbolistic drama. This drama, in Villiers, is of pure symbol, of sheer poetry. It has an exalted eloquence which we find in none of his followers. As M. Maeterlinck has developed it, it is a drama which appeals directly to the sensations—sometimes crudely, sometimes subtly—playing its variations upon the very nerves themselves. The "vague spiritual fear" which it creates out of our nervous apprehension is unlike anything that has ever been done before, even by [E.T.A.] Hoffmann [German author, 1776–1822], even by Poe. It is an effect of atmosphere—an atmosphere in which outlines change and become mysterious, in which a word quietly uttered makes one start, in which all one's mental activity becomes concentrated on something, one knows not what, something slow, creeping, terrifying, which comes nearer and nearer, an impending nightmare.

La Princesse Maleine, it is said, was written for a theatre of marionettes, and it is certainly with the effect of marionettes that these sudden, exclamatory people come and go. Maleine, Hjalmar, Uglyane—these are no men and women, but a masque of shadows, a dance of silhouettes behind the white sheet of the "Chat Noir," and they have the fantastic charm of these enigmatical semblances, "luminous, gemlike, ghostlike," with, also, their somewhat mechanical eeriness. The personages of *L'Intruse*, of *Les Aveugles*—in which the spiritual terror and physical apprehension which are common to all M. Maeterlinck's work have become more interior —are mere abstractions, typifying age, infancy, disaster, but with scarcely a suggestion of individual character. And the style itself is a sort of abstraction, all the capacities of language being deliberately abandoned for a simplicity which, in its calculated repetition, is like the drip, drip, of a tiny stream of water. M. Maeterlinck is difficult to quote, but here, in English, is a passage from Act I. of *La Princesse Maleine*, which will indicate something of this Biblically monotonous style:

> *J cannot see you. Come hither, there is more light here, lean back your head a little towards the sky. You too are strange to-night! Jt is as though my eyes were opened to-night! Jt is as though my heart were half opened to-night! But J think you are strangely beautiful! But you are strangely beautiful, Uglyane! Jt seems to me that J have never looked on you till now! But J think you are strangely beautiful! There is something about you. . . . Let us go elsewhither—under the light—come!*

As an experiment in a new kind of drama, these curious plays do not seem to exactly achieve themselves on the stage; it is difficult to imagine how they could ever be made so impressive, when thus externalized, as they are when all is left to the imagination. *L'Intruse*, for instance, which was given at the Haymarket Theatre on January 27, 1892—not quite faithfully given, it is true—seemed, as one saw it then, too faint in outline, with too little carrying power for scenic effect. But M. Maeterlinck is by no means anxious to be considered merely or mainly as a dramatist. A brooding poet, a mystic, a contemplative spectator of the comedy of death— that is how he presents himself to us in his work; and the introduction which he has prefixed to his translation of *L'Ornement des Noces Spirituelles,* of Ruysbroeck l'Admirable, shows how deeply he has studied the mystical writers of all ages, and how much akin to theirs is his own temper. Plato and Plotinus, St. Bernard and Jacob Boehm, Coleridge and Novalis—he knows them all, and it is with a sort of reverence that he sets himself to the task of translating the astonishing Flemish mystic of the thirteenth century, known till now only by the fragments translated into French by Ernest Hello from a sixteenth century Latin version. This translation and this introduction help to explain the real character of M. Maeterlinck's dramatic work—dramatic as to form, by a sort of accident, but essentially mystical.

Partly akin to M. Maeterlinck by race, more completely alien from him in temper than it is possible to express, Joris Karl Huysmans demands a prominent place in any record of the Decadent movement. His work, like that of the Goncourts, is largely determined by the *maladie fin de siècle*— the diseased nerves that, in his case, have given a curious personal quality of pessimism to his outlook on the world, his view of life. Part of his work—*Marthe, Les Sœurs Vatard, En Ménage, À Vau-l'Eau*—is a minute and searching study of the minor discomforts, the commonplace miseries of life, as seen by a peevishly disordered vision, delighting, for its own self-torture, in the insistent contemplation of human stupidity, of the sordid in existence. Yet these books do but lead up to the unique masterpiece, the astonishing caprice of *À Rebours,* in which he has concentrated all that is delicately depraved, all that is beautifully, curiously poisonous, in modern art. *À Rebours* is the history of a typical Decadent— a study, indeed, after a real man,[8] but a study which seizes the type rather than the personality. In the sensations and ideas of Des Esseintes we see the sensations and ideas of the

[8] The character Des Esseintes is based upon the legends surrounding Robert de Montesquiou—dandy, homosexual, poet.

effeminate, over-civilized, deliberately abnormal creature who is the last product of our society: partly the father, partly the offspring, of the perverse art that he adores. Des Esseintes creates for his solace, in the wilderness of a barren and profoundly uncomfortable world, an artificial paradise. His *Thébaïde raffinée* ["refined" *Thébaïde*, Greek epic] is furnished elaborately for candle-light, equipped with the pictures, the books, that satisfy his sense of the exquisitely abnormal. He delights in the Latin of Apuleius and Petronius, in the French of Baudelaire, Goncourt, Verlaine, Mallarmé, Villiers; in the pictures of Gustave Moreau, the French Burne-Jones, of Odilon Redon, the French Blake. He delights in the beauty of strange, unnatural flowers, in the melodic combination of scents, in the imagined harmonies of the sense of taste. And at last, exhausted by these spiritual and sensory debauches in the delights of the artificial, he is left (as we close the book) with a brief, doubtful choice before him—madness or death, or else a return to nature, to the normal life.

Since *À Rebours*, M. Huysmans has written one other remarkable book, *Là-Bas*, a study in the hysteria and mystical corruption of contemporary Black Magic. But it is on that one exceptional achievement, *À Rebours*, that his fame will rest; it is there that he has expressed not merely himself, but an epoch. And he has done so in a style which carries the modern experiments upon language to their furthest development. Formed upon Goncourt and Flaubert, it has sought for novelty, *l'image peinte*, the exactitude of color, the forcible precision of epithet, wherever words, images, or epithets are to be found. Barbaric in its profusion, violent in its emphasis, wearying in its splendor, it is—especially in regard to things seen—extraordinarily expressive, with all the shades of a painter's palette. Elaborately and deliberately perverse, it is in its very perversity that Huysmans' work—so fascinating, so repellent, so instinctively artificial—comes to represent, as the work of no other writer can be said to do, the main tendencies, the chief results, of the Decadent movement in literature.[9]

[9] When Symons reprinted "The Decadent Movement in Literature" in *Dramatis Personae* (1923), he omitted the discussion that follows.

Such, then, is the typical literature of the Decadence—literature which, as we have considered it so far, is entirely French. But those qualities which we find in the work of Goncourt, Verlaine, Huysmans—qualities which have permeated literature much more completely in France than in any other country—are not wanting in the recent literature of other countries. In Holland there is a new school of Sensitivists, as they call themselves, who have done some remarkable work—Couperus, in *Ecstasy,* for example—very much on the lines of the French art of Impressionism. In Italy, Luigi Capuana (in *Giacinta,* for instance) has done some wonderful studies of morbid sensation; Gabriele d'Annunzio, in that marvellous, malarious *Piacere,* has achieved a triumph of exquisite perversity. In Spain, one of the principal novelists, Señora Pardo-Bazan, has formed herself, with some deliberateness, after Goncourt, grafting his method, curiously enough, upon a typically Spanish Catholicism of her own. In Norway, Ibsen has lately developed a personal kind of Impressionism (in *Hedda Gabler*) and of Symbolism (in *The Master-Builder*)—"opening the door," in his own phrase, "to the younger generation." And in England, too, we find the same influences at work. The prose of Mr. Walter Pater, the verse of Mr. W. E. Henley—to take two prominent examples—are attempts to do with the English language something of what Goncourt and Verlaine have done with the French. Mr. Pater's prose is the most beautiful English prose which is now being written; and, unlike the prose of Goncourt, it has done no violence to language, it has sought after no vivid effects, it has found a large part of mastery in reticence, in knowing what to omit. But how far away from the classic ideals of style is this style in which words have their color, their music, their perfume, in which there is "some strangeness in the proportion" of every beauty! The *Studies in the Renaissance* have made of criticism a new art—have raised criticism almost to the act of creation. And *Marius the Epicurean,* in its study of "sensations and ideas" (the conjunction was Goncourt's before it was Mr. Pater's), and the *Imaginary Portraits,* in their evocations of the Middle Ages, the age of Watteau—have they not that morbid subtlety of analysis, that morbid curiosity of

form, that we have found in the works of the French Decadents? A fastidiousness equal to that of Flaubert has limited
Mr. Pater's work to six volumes, but in these six volumes
there is not a page that is not perfectly finished, with a conscious art of perfection. In its minute elaboration it can be
compared only with goldsmith's work—so fine, so delicate is
the handling of so delicate, so precious a material.

Mr. Henley's work in verse has none of the characteristics
of Mr. Pater's work in prose. Verlaine's definition of his own
theory of poetical writing—"sincerity, and the impression of
the moment followed to the letter"—might well be adopted
as a definition of Mr. Henley's theory or practice. In *A Book
of Verses* and *The Song of the Sword* he has brought into the
traditional conventionalities of modern English verse the
note of a new personality, the touch of a new method. The
poetry of Impressionism can go no further, in one direction,
than that series of rhymes and rhythms named *In Hospital*.
The ache and throb of the body in its long nights on a
tumbled bed, and as it lies on the operating-table awaiting
"the thick, sweet mystery of chloroform," are brought home
to us as nothing else that I know in poetry has ever brought
the physical sensations. And for a sharper, closer truth of
rendering, Mr. Henley has resorted (after the manner of
Heine) to a rhymeless form of lyric verse, which in his
hands, certainly, is sensitive and expressive. Whether this
kind of *vers libre* can fully compensate, in what it gains of
freedom and elasticity, for what it loses of compact form and
vocal appeal, is a difficult question. It is one that Mr. Henley's verse is far from solving in the affirmative, for, in his
work, the finest things, to my mind, are rhymed. In the
purely impressionistic way, do not the *London Voluntaries*,
which are rhymed, surpass all the unrhymed vignettes and
nocturnes which attempt the same quality of result? They
flash before us certain aspects of the poetry of London as
only Whistler had ever done, and in another art. Nor is it
only the poetry of cities, as here, nor the poetry of the disagreeable, as in *In Hospital*, that Mr. Henley can evoke; he
can evoke the magic of personal romance. He has written
verse that is exquisitely frivolous, daintily capricious, wayward and fugitive as the winged remembrance of some mo-

mentary delight. And, in certain fragments, he has come nearer than any other English singer to what I have called the achievement of Verlaine and the ideal of the Decadence: to be a disembodied voice, and yet the voice of a human soul.

EMMY

Emmy's exquisite youth and her virginal air,
Eyes and teeth in the flash of a musical smile,
Come to me out of the past, and I see her there
As I saw her once for a while.

Emmy's laughter rings in my ears, as bright,
Fresh and sweet as the voice of a mountain brook,
And still I hear her telling us tales that night,
Out of Boccaccio's book.

There, in the midst of the villainous dancing-hall,
Leaning across the table, over the beer,
While the music maddened the whirling skirts of the ball,
As the midnight hour drew near,

There with the women, haggard, painted and old,
One fresh bud in a garland withered and stale,
She, with her innocent voice and her clear eyes, told
Tale after shameless tale.

And ever the witching smile, to her face beguiled,
Paused and broadened, and broke in a ripple of fun,
And the soul of a child looked out of the eyes of a child,
Or ever the tale was done.

O my child, who wronged you first, and began
First the dance of death that you dance so well?
Soul for soul: and I think the soul of a man
Shall answer for yours in hell.

[1892]

MAQUILLAGE

The charm of rouge on fragile cheeks,
Pearl-powder, and, about the eyes,
The dark and lustrous eastern dyes;
A voice of violets that speaks
Of perfumed hours of day, and doubtful night
Of alcoves curtained close against the light.

Gracile and creamy white and rose,
Complexioned like the flower of dawn,
Her fleeting colours are as those
That, from an April sky withdrawn,
Fade in a fragrant mist of tears away
When weeping noon leads on the altered day.

[1892]

MORBIDEZZA

White girl, your flesh is lilies
Under a frozen moon,
So still is
The rapture of your swoon
Of whiteness, snow or lilies.

Virginal in revealment,
Your bosom's wavering slope,
Concealment,
In fainting heliotrope,
Of whitest white's revealment,

Is like a bed of lilies,
A jealous-guarded row,
Whose will is

Simply chaste dreams: but oh,
The alluring scent of lilies!

[1892]

PROLOGUE: BEFORE THE CURTAIN

We are the puppets of a shadow-play,
We dream the plot is woven of our hearts,
Passionately we play the self-same parts
Our fathers have played passionately yesterday,
And our sons play to-morrow. There's no speech
In all desire, nor any idle word,
Men have not said and women have not heard;
And when we lean and whisper each to each
Until the silence quickens to a kiss,
Even so the actor and the actress played
The lovers yesterday; when the lights fade
Before our feet, and the obscure abyss
Opens, and darkness falls about our eyes,
'Tis only that some momentary rage
Or rapture blinds us to forget the stage,
Like the wise actor, most in this thing wise.
We pass, and have our gesture; love and pain
And hope and apprehension and regret
Weave ordered lines into a pattern set
Not for our pleasure, and for us in vain.
The gesture is eternal; we who pass
Pass on the gesture; we, who pass, pass on
One after one into oblivion,
As shadows dim and vanish from a glass.

[1895]

PROLOGUE: IN THE STALLS

My life is like a music-hall,
Where, in the impotence of rage,
Chained by enchantment to my stall,
I see myself upon the stage
Dance to amuse a music-hall.

'Tis I that smoke this cigarette,
Lounge here, and laugh for vacancy,
And watch the dancers turn; and yet
It is my very self I see
Across the cloudy cigarette.

My very self that turns and trips,
Painted, pathetically gay,
An empty song upon the lips
In make-believe of holiday:
I, I, this thing that turns and trips!

The light flares in the music-hall,
The light, the sound, that weary us;
Hour follows hour, I count them all,
Lagging, and loud, and riotous:
My life is like a music-hall.

[1895]

TO A DANCER

Intoxicatingly
Her eyes across the footlights gleam,
(The wine of love, the wine of dream)
Her eyes, that gleam for me!

The eyes of all that see
Draw to her glances, stealing fire

From her desire that leaps to my desire;
Her eyes that gleam for me!

Subtly, deliciously,
A quickening fire within me, beat
The rhythms of her poising feet;
Her feet that poise to me!

Her body's melody,
In silent waves of wandering sound,
Thrills to the sense of all around,
Yet thrills alone for me!

And O, intoxicatingly,
When, at the magic moment's close,
She dies into the rapture of repose,
Her eyes that gleam for me!

[1895]

LA MÉLINITE:[1]
MOULIN-ROUGE

Olivier Metra's Waltz of Roses
Sheds in a rhythmic shower
The very petals of the flower;
And all is roses,
The rouge of petals in a shower.

---

[1] Symons first saw La Mélinite in May, 1892, in Le Jardin de Paris. She was, he wrote, "young and girlish, the more provocative because she played as a prude, with an assumed modesty, *décolletée* nearly to the waist, in the oriental fashion. She had long black curls around her face; and had about her a depraved virginity. And she caused in me, even then, a curious sense of depravity that perhaps comes into the verses I wrote on her. There, certainly, on the night of May 22nd, danced in her feverish, her perverse, her enigmatical beauty, La Mélinite, to her own image in the mirror."

Down the long hall the dance returning
Rounds the full circle, rounds
The perfect rose of lights and sounds,
The rose returning
Into the circle of its rounds.

Alone, apart, one dancer watches
Her mirrored, morbid grace;
Before the mirror, face to face,
Alone she watches
Her morbid, vague, ambiguous grace.

Before the mirror's dance of shadows
She dances in a dream,
And she and they together seem
A dance of shadows,
Alike the shadows of a dream.

The orange-rosy lamps are trembling
Between the robes that turn;
In ruddy flowers of flame that burn
The lights are trembling:
The shadows and the dancers turn.

And, enigmatically smiling,
In the mysterious night,
She dances for her own delight,
A shadow smiling
Back to a shadow in the night.

[1895]

JAVANESE DANCERS

Twitched strings, the clang of metal, beaten drums,
Dull, shrill, continuous, disquieting;
And now the stealthy dancer comes
Undulantly with cat-like steps that cling;

Smiling between her painted lids a smile,
Motionless, unintelligible, she twines
Her fingers into mazy lines,
The scarves across her fingers twine the while.

One, two, three, four glide forth, and, to and fro,
Delicately and imperceptibly,
Now swaying gently in a row,
Now interthreading slow and rhythmically,

Still, with fixed eyes, monotonously still,
Mysteriously, with smiles inanimate,
With lingering feet that undulate,
With sinuous fingers, spectral hands that thrill

In measure while the gnats of music whirr,
The little amber-coloured dancers move,
Like painted idols seen to stir
By the idolaters in a magic grove.

[1894]

BY THE POOL AT THE THIRD
ROSSES[1]

I heard the sighing of the reeds
In the grey pool in the green land,
The sea-wind in the long reeds sighing
Between the green hill and the sand.

I heard the sighing of the reeds
Day after day, night after night;
I heard the whirring wild ducks flying,
I saw the sea-gulls' wheeling flight.

[1896]

[1] Near Sligo, where Yeats had taken him on a visit to Ireland.

HALLUCINATION : I

One petal of a blood-red tulip pressed
Between the pages of a Baudelaire :
No more, and I was suddenly aware
Of the white fragrant apple of a breast
On which my lips were pastured; and I knew
That dreaming I remembered an old dream.
Sweeter than any fruit that fruit did seem,
Which, as my hungry teeth devoured it, grew
Ever again, and tantalised my taste.
So, vainly hungering, I seemed to see
Eve and the serpent and the apple-tree,
And Adam in the garden, and God laying waste
Innocent Eden, because man's desire,
Godlike before, now for a woman's sake
Descended through the woman to the snake.
Then as my mouth grew parched, stung as with fire
By that white fragrant apple, once so fair,
That seemed to shrink and spire into a flame,
I cried, and wakened, crying on your name :
One blood-red petal stained the Baudelaire.

[1895]

VIOLET

I. PRELUDE

This was a sweet white wildwood violet
I found among the painted slips that grow
Where, under hot-house glass, the flowers forget
How the sun shines, and how the cool winds blow.

The violet took the orchid's colouring,
Tricked out its dainty fairness like the rest;

Yet still its breath was as the breath of Spring,
And the wood's heart was wild within its breast.

The orchid mostly is the flower I love,
And violets, the mere violets of the wood,
For all their sweetness, have not power to move
The curiosity that rules my blood.

Yet here, in this spice-laden atmosphere,
Where only nature is a thing unreal,
I found in just a violet, planted here,
The artificial flower of my ideal.

[1895]

FROM STÉPHANE MALLARMÉ

I. HÉRODIADE

Hérodiade.
To mine own self I am a wilderness.
You know it, amethyst gardens numberless
Enfolded in the flaming, subtle deep,
Strange gold, that through the red earth's heavy sleep
Has cherished ancient brightness like a dream,
Stones whence mine eyes, pure jewels, have their gleam
Of icy and melodious radiance, you,
Metals, which into my young tresses drew
A fatal splendour and their manifold grace!
Thou, woman, born into these evil days
Disastrous to the cavern sibylline,
Who speakest, prophesying not of one divine,
But of a mortal, if from that close sheath,
My robes, rustle the wild enchanted breath
In the white quiver of my nakedness,
If the warm air of summer, O prophetess,
(And woman's body obeys that ancient claim)

Behold me in my shivering starry shame,
I die!
The horror of my virginity
Delights me, and I would envelop me
In the terror of my tresses, that, by night,
Inviolate reptile, I might feel the white
And glimmering radiance of thy frozen fire,
Thou that art chaste and diest of desire,
White night of ice and of the cruel snow!
Eternal sister, my lone sister, lo
My dreams uplifted before thee! now, apart,
So rare a crystal is my dreaming heart,
I live in a monotonous land alone,
And all about me lives but in mine own
Image, the idolatrous mirror of my pride,
Mirroring this Hérodiade diamond-eyed.
I am indeed alone, O charm and curse!

Nurse.
O lady, would you die then?

Hérodiade.
No, poor nurse;
Be calm, and leave me; prithee, pardon me,
But, ere thou go, close-to the casement; see
How the seraphical blue in the dim glass smiles,
But I abhor the blue of the sky!
Yet miles
On miles of rocking waves! Know'st not a land
Where, in the pestilent sky, men see the hand
Of Venus, and her shadow in dark leaves?
Thither I go.
Light thou the wax that grieves
In the swift flame, and sheds an alien tear
Over the vain gold; wilt not say in mere
Childishness?

Nurse.
Now?

Hérodiade.
Farewell. You lie, O flower
Of these chill lips!
I wait the unknown hour,
Or, deaf to your crying and that hour supreme,
Utter the lamentation of the dream
Of childhood seeing fall apart in sighs
The icy chaplet of its reveries.

[1896]

PREFACE TO THE SECOND
EDITION OF "SILHOUETTES":

BEING A WORD ON BEHALF
OF PATCHOULI

The Prefaces to the second editions of *Silhouettes* (1896)
and of *London Nights* (1897) represent Symons' attempt—
in the face of hostile criticism—to justify artifice in literature, and, more broadly, to extend the range of acceptable
subject matter. As attempts to divorce moral judgment from
choice of subject matter—a major preoccupation of the Aesthetes as well as the realistic novelists—the Prefaces are Symons' clearest and most forthright statements of his position
in the Nineties.

An ingenious reviewer once described some verses of mine as
"unwholesome," because, he said, they had "a faint smell of
Patchouli about them." I am a little sorry he chose Patchouli,
for that is not a particularly favourite scent with me. If he
had only chosen Peau d'Espagne, which has a subtle meaning, or Lily of the Valley, with which I have associations! But
Patchouli will serve. Let me ask, then, in republishing, with

additions, a collection of little pieces, many of which have been objected to, at one time or another, as being somewhat deliberately frivolous, why art should not, if it please, concern itself with the artificially charming, which, I suppose, is what my critic means by Patchouli? All art, surely, is a form of artifice, and thus, to the truly devout mind, condemned already, if not as actively noxious, at all events as needless. That is a point of view which I quite understand, and its conclusion I hold to be absolutely logical. I have the utmost respect for the people who refuse to read a novel, to go to the theatre, or to learn dancing. That is to have convictions and to live up to them. I understand also the point of view from which a work of art is tolerated in so far as it is actually militant on behalf of a religious or moral idea. But what I fail to understand are those delicate, invisible degrees by which a distinction is drawn between this form of art and that; the hesitations, and compromises, and timorous advances, and shocked retreats, of the Puritan conscience once emancipated and yet afraid of liberty. However you may try to convince yourself to the contrary, a work of art can be judged only from two standpoints: the standpoint from which its art is measured entirely by its morality, and the standpoint from which its morality is measured entirely by its art.

Here, for once, in connection with these "Silhouettes," I have not, if my recollection serves me, been accused of actual immorality. I am but a fair way along the "primrose path," not yet within singeing distance of the "everlasting bonfire." In other words, I have not yet written "London Nights," which, it appears (I can scarcely realise it, in my innocent abstraction in æsthetical matters), has no very salutary reputation among the blameless moralists of the press. I need not, therefore, on this occasion, concern myself with more than the curious fallacy by which there is supposed to be something inherently wrong in artistic work which deals frankly and lightly with the very real charm of the lighter emotions and the more fleeting sensations.

I do not wish to assert that the kind of verse which happened to reflect certain moods of mine at a certain period of my life is the best kind of verse in itself, or is likely to seem to me, in other years, when other moods may have made me their own, the best kind of verse for my own expression of myself. Nor do I affect to doubt that the creation of the supreme emotion is a higher form of art than the reflection of the most exquisite sensation, the evocation of the most magical impression. I claim only an equal liberty for the rendering of every mood of that variable and inexplicable and contradictory creature which we call ourselves, of every aspect under which we are gifted or condemned to apprehend the beauty and strangeness and curiosity of the visible world.

Patchouli! Well, why not Patchouli? Is there any "reason in nature" why we should write exclusively about the natural blush, if the delicately acquired blush of rouge has any attraction for us? Both exist; both, I think, are charming in their way; and the latter, as a subject, has, at all events, more novelty. If you prefer your "new-mown hay" in the hayfield, and I, it may be, in a scent-bottle, why may not my individual caprice be allowed to find expression as well as yours? Probably I enjoy the hayfield as much as you do; but I enjoy quite other scents and sensations as well, and I take the former for granted, and write my poem, for a change, about the latter. There is no necessary difference in artistic value between a good poem about a flower in the hedge and a good poem about the scent in a sachet. I am always charmed to read beautiful poems about nature in the country. Only, personally, I prefer town to country; and in the town we have to find for ourselves, as best we may, the *décor* which is the town equivalent of the great natural *décor* of fields and hills. Here it is that artificiality comes in; and if any one sees no beauty in the effects of artificial light, in all the variable, most human, and yet most factitious town landscape, I can only pity him, and go on my own way.

That is, if he will let me. But he tells me that one thing is right and the other is wrong; that one is good art and the other is bad; and I listen in amazement, sometimes not without impatience, wondering why an estimable personal prejudice should be thus exalted into a dogma, and uttered in the name of art. For in art there can be no prejudices, only results. If we are to save people's souls by the writing of verses, well and good. But if not, there is no choice but to admit absolute freedom of choice. And if Patchouli pleases one, why not Patchouli?

[LONDON, *February* 1896]

PREFACE TO THE SECOND EDITION OF "LONDON NIGHTS"
[1897]

The publication of this book was received by the English press with a singular unanimity of abuse.[1] In some cases the abuse was ignoble; for the most part, it was no more than unintelligent. Scarcely any critic did himself the credit of considering with any care the intention or the execution of what offended him by its substance or its subject. I had expected opposition, I was prepared for a reasonable amount of prejudice; but I must confess to some surprise at the nature of the opposition, the extent of the prejudice, which it was my fortune to encounter. Happening to be in France at the time, I reflected, with scarcely the natural satisfaction of the Englishman, that such a reception of a work of art would have been possible in no country but England.

And now, in bringing out a new edition of these poems, which I have neither taken from nor added to, and in which I have found it needful to make but little revision, it is with no hope of persuading any one not already aware of what I have to say that I make this statement on behalf of general principles and my own application of them, but rather on Blake's theory, that you should tell the truth, not to convince those who do not believe, but to confirm those who do.

I have been attacked, then, on the ground of morality, and

---

[1] *The National Observer*, citing the "dreary indecencies" of *London Nights*, commented: "We have no intention of wasting many words over a most disagreeable volume. It is given to a majority of mankind at one time or another to have some such experiences as Mr. Symons describes, but for the most part, thank heaven! they do not gloat over them and roll them on the tongue . . ."

by people who, in condemning my book, not because it is bad art, but because they think it bad morality, forget that they are confusing moral and artistic judgments, and limiting art without aiding morality. I contend on behalf of the liberty of art, and I deny that morals have any right of jurisdiction over it. Art may be served by morality; it can never be its servant. For the principles of art are eternal, while the principles of morality fluctuate with the spiritual ebb and flow of the ages. Show me any commandment of the traditional code of morals which you are at present obeying, and I will show you its opposite among the commandments of some other code of morals which your forefathers once obeyed; or, if you prefer, some righteous instance of its breaking, which you will commend in spite of yourself. Is it for such a shifting guide that I am to forsake the sure and constant leading of art, which tells me that whatever I find in humanity (passion, desire, the spirit or the senses, the hell or heaven of man's heart) is part of the eternal substance which nature weaves in the rough for art to combine cunningly into beautiful patterns? The whole visible world itself, we are told, is but a symbol, made visible in order that we may apprehend ourselves, and not be blown hither and thither like a flame in the night. How laughable is it, then, that we should busy ourselves, with such serious faces, in the commending or condemning, the permission or the exemption, of this accident or that, this or the other passing caprice of our wisdom or our folly, as a due or improper subject for the "moment's monument" of a poem! It is as if you were to say to me, here on these weedy rocks of Rosses Point, where the grey sea passes me continually, flinging a little foam at my feet, that I may write of one rather than another of these waves, which are not more infinite than the moods of men.

The moods of men! There I find my subject, there the region over which art rules; and whatever has once been a mood of mine, though it has been no more than a ripple on the sea, and had no longer than that ripple's duration, I claim the right to render, if I can, in verse; and I claim, from my critics and my readers, the primary understanding, that a mood is after all but a mood, a ripple on the sea, and perhaps with no longer than that ripple's duration. I do not profess that any poem in this book is the record of actual fact; I declare that every poem is the sincere attempt to render a particular mood which has once been mine, and to render it as if, for the moment, there were no other mood for me in the world. I have rendered, well or ill, many moods, and without disguise or preference. If it be objected to me that some of them were moods I had better never have felt, I am ready to answer, Possibly; but I must add, What of that? They have existed; and whatever has existed has achieved the right of artistic existence.

[ROSSES POINT, SLIGO, *September 2, 1896*]

Oscar Wilde

[1854 – 1900]

THE DECAY OF LYING:

AN OBSERVATION

First published in January, 1889, "The Decay of Lying" was intended, Wilde wrote to a friend, "to bewilder the masses by its fantastic form; *au fond,* it is of course serious." To another friend, he wrote that the essay was "only for artistic temperaments."

The dialogue form—no more "fantastic" than Plato's use of it—draws on ideas from Gautier, Baudelaire, and Whistler, who was annoyed at Wilde's borrowings and parody, in the fog passage, of his own famous description in "The Ten O'Clock" lecture four years before, where Whistler speaks of the "evening mist [that] clothes the riverside with poetry, as with a veil, and the poor buildings lose themselves in the dim sky, and the tall chimneys become campanili, and the warehouses are palaces in the night . . ." The speakers in the dialogue are given the names of Wilde's two children.

A Dialogue

PERSONS: *Cyril and Vivian.*

SCENE: *the library of a country house in Nottinghamshire.*

CYRIL (*coming in through the open window from the terrace*): My dear Vivian, don't coop yourself up all day in the library. It is a perfectly lovely afternoon. The air is exquisite. There is a mist upon the woods, like the purple bloom upon a plum. Let us go and lie on the grass and smoke cigarettes and enjoy Nature.

VIVIAN: Enjoy Nature! I am glad to say that I have entirely lost that faculty. People tell us that Art makes us love Nature more than we loved her before; that it reveals her secrets to us; and that after a careful study of Corot [1796–1875: French landscape painter] and Constable [1776–1837: English landscape painter] we see things in her that had escaped our observation. My own experience is that the more we study Art, the less we care for Nature. What Art really reveals to us is Nature's lack of design, her curious crudities, her extraordinary monotony, her absolutely unfinished condition. Nature has good intentions, of course, but, as Aristotle once said, she cannot carry them out. When I look at a landscape I cannot help seeing all its defects. It is fortunate for us, however, that Nature is so imperfect, as otherwise we should have no art at all. Art is our spirited protest, our gallant attempt to teach Nature her proper place. As for the infinite variety of Nature, that is a pure myth. It is not to be found in Nature herself. It resides in the imagination, or fancy, or cultivated blindness of the man who looks at her.

CYRIL: Well, you need not look at the landscape. You can lie on the grass and smoke and talk.

VIVIAN: But Nature is so uncomfortable. Grass is hard and lumpy and damp, and full of dreadful black insects. Why, even Morris's poorest workman[1] could make you a more comfortable seat than the whole of Nature can. Nature pales before the furniture of "the street which from Oxford has borrowed its name," as the poet you love so much once vilely phrased it. I don't complain. If Nature had been comfortable, mankind would never have invented architecture, and I prefer houses to the open air. In a house we all feel of

[1] William Morris (1834–96), English poet, designer, painter, a Pre-Raphaelite who, in 1861, founded Morris and Co., which attempted, under the inspiration of medieval decorative art, to revive public interest in stained glass, fine tapestries, and well-designed furniture.

the proper proportions. Everything is subordinated to us, fashioned for our use and our pleasure. Egotism itself, which is so necessary to a proper sense of human dignity, is entirely the result of indoor life. Out of doors one becomes abstract and impersonal. One's individuality absolutely leaves one. And then Nature is so indifferent, so unappreciative. Whenever I am walking in the park here, I always feel that I am no more to her than the cattle that browse on the slope, or the burdock that blooms in the ditch. Nothing is more evident than that Nature hates Mind. Thinking is the most unhealthy thing in the world, and people die of it just as they die of any other disease. Fortunately, in England at any rate, thought is not catching. Our splendid physique as a people is entirely due to our national stupidity. I only hope we shall be able to keep this great historic bulwark of our happiness for many years to come; but I am afraid that we are beginning to be over-educated; at least everybody who is incapable of learning has taken to teaching—that is really what our enthusiasm for education has come to. In the meantime, you had better go back to your wearisome uncomfortable Nature, and leave me to correct my proofs.

CYRIL: Writing an article! That is not very consistent after what you have just said.

VIVIAN: Who wants to be consistent? The dullard and the doctrinaire, the tedious people who carry out their principles to the bitter end of action, to the *reductio ad absurdum* of practice. Not I. Like Emerson, I write over the door of my library the word "Whim." Besides, my article is really a most salutary and valuable warning. If it is attended to, there may be a new Renaissance of Art.

CYRIL: What is the subject?

VIVIAN: I intend to call it "The Decay of Lying: A Protest."

CYRIL: Lying! I should have thought that our politicians kept up that habit.

VIVIAN: I assure you that they do not. They never rise beyond the level of misrepresentation, and actually condescend to prove, to discuss, to argue. How different from the temper of the true liar, with his frank, fearless statements, his superb irresponsibility, his healthy, natural disdain of proof of any kind! After all, what is a fine lie? Simply that which is its own evidence. If a man is sufficiently unimaginative to produce evidence in support of a lie, he might just as well speak the truth at once. No, the politicians won't do. Something may, perhaps, be urged on behalf of the Bar. The mantle of the Sophist[2] has fallen on its members. Their feigned ardours and unreal rhetoric are delightful. They can make the worse appear the better cause, as though they were fresh from Leontine schools [after Leontius, 6th cent., the first scholastic to apply Aristotle to theology], and have been known to wrest from reluctant juries triumphant verdicts of acquittal for their clients, even when those clients, as often happens, were clearly and unmistakably innocent. But they are briefed by the prosaic, and are not ashamed to appeal to precedent. In spite of their endeavours, the truth will out. Newspapers, even, have degenerated. They may now be absolutely relied upon. One feels it as one wades through their columns. It is always the unreadable that occurs. I am afraid that there is not much to be said in favour of either the lawyer or the journalist. Besides, what I am pleading for is Lying in art. Shall I read you what I have written? It might do you a great deal of good.

CYRIL: Certainly, if you give me a cigarette. Thanks. By the way, what magazine do you intend it for?

VIVIAN: For the *Retrospective Review*. I think I told you that the elect had revived it.

CYRIL: Whom do you mean by "the elect"?

VIVIAN: Oh, The Tired Hedonists, of course. It is a club to which I belong. We are supposed to wear faded roses in our buttonholes when we meet, and to have a sort of cult for Domitian.[3] I am afraid you are not eligible. You are too fond of simple pleasures.

[2] Originally, in ancient Greece, one who taught the sons of the wealthy. Once a respected title, later it acquired pejorative connotations when such sophists as Thrasymachus and Hippias ceased to concern themselves with truth but with teaching skills useful to a political career.

[3] Roman emperor (81–96 A.D.) who devoted his life to pursuit of pleasure and literature until he came to the throne, then instituted rigorous moral reforms.

CYRIL: I should be black-balled on the ground of animal spirits, I suppose?

VIVIAN: Probably. Besides, you are a little too old. We don't admit anybody who is of the usual age.

CYRIL: Well, I should fancy you are all a good deal bored with each other.

VIVIAN: We are. That is one of the objects of the club. Now, if you promise not to interrupt too often, I will read you my article.

CYRIL: You will find me all attention.

VIVIAN (*reading in a very clear voice*): "THE DECAY OF LYING: A PROTEST.—One of the chief causes that can be assigned for the curiously commonplace character of most of the literature of our age is undoubtedly the decay of Lying as an art, a science, and a social pleasure. The ancient historians gave us delightful fiction in the form of fact; the modern novelist presents us with dull facts under the guise of fiction. The Blue-Book[4] is rapidly becoming his ideal both for method and manner. He has his tedious *document humain*, his miserable little *coin de la création* ["corner of the universe"], into which he peers with his microscope. He is to be found at the Librairie Nationale, or at the British Museum, shamelessly reading up his subject. He has not even the courage of other people's ideas, but insists on going directly to life for everything, and ultimately, between encyclopædias and personal experience, he comes to the ground, having drawn his types from the family circle or from the weekly washerwoman, and having acquired an amount of useful information from which never, even in his most meditative moments, can he thoroughly free himself.

"The loss that results to literature in general from this false ideal of our time can hardly be overestimated. People have a careless way of talking about a "born liar," just as they talk about a born poet. But in both cases they are wrong. Lying and poetry are arts—arts, as Plato saw, not unconnected with each other—and they require the most careful study, the most disinterested devotion. Indeed, they have their technique, just as the more material arts of paint-

[4] Any catalog of classified facts. Wilde is here ridiculing the realists and naturalists.

ing and sculpture have their subtle secrets of form and colour, their craft-mysteries, their deliberate artistic methods. As one knows the poet by his fine music, so one can recognise the liar by his rich rhythmic utterance, and in neither case will the casual inspiration of the moment suffice. Here, as elsewhere, practice must precede perfection. But in modern days while the fashion of writing poetry has become far too common, and should, if possible, be discouraged, the fashion of lying has almost fallen into disrepute. Many a young man starts in life with a natural gift for exaggeration which, if nurtured in congenial and sympathetic surroundings, or by the imitation of the best models, might grow into something really great and wonderful. But, as a rule, he comes to nothing. He either falls into careless habits of accuracy—"

CYRIL: My dear fellow!

VIVIAN: Please don't interrupt in the middle of a sentence. "He either falls into careless habits of accuracy, or takes to frequenting the society of the aged and the well-informed. Both things are equally fatal to his imagination, as indeed they would be fatal to the imagination of anybody, and in a short time he develops a morbid and unhealthy faculty of truth-telling, begins to verify all statements made in his presence, has no hesitation in contradicting people who are much younger than himself, and often ends by writing novels which are so life-like that no one can possibly believe in their probability. This is no isolated instance that we are giving. It is simply one example out of many; and if something cannot be done to check, or at least to modify, our monstrous worship of facts, Art will become sterile and beauty will pass away from the land.

"Even Mr. Robert Louis Stevenson, that delightful master of delicate and fanciful prose, is tainted with this modern vice, for we know positively no other name for it. There is such a thing as robbing a story of its reality by trying to make it too true, and *The Black Arrow* is so inartistic as not to contain a single anachronism to boast of, while the transformation of Dr. Jekyll reads dangerously like an experiment out of the *Lancet* [a medical journal]. As for Mr. Rider Haggard, who really has, or had once, the makings of a perfectly magnificent liar, he is now so afraid of being suspected of genius that when he does tell us anything marvellous, he feels bound to invent a personal reminiscence, and to put it into a footnote as a kind of cowardly corroboration. Nor are our other novelists much better. Mr. Henry James writes fiction as if it were a painful duty, and wastes upon mean motives and imperceptible 'points of view' his neat literary style, his felicitous phrases, his swift and caustic satire. Mr. Hall Caine, it is true, aims at the grandiose, but then he writes at the top of his voice. He is so loud that one cannot hear what he says. Mr. James Payn is an adept in the art of concealing what is not worth finding. He hunts down the obvious with the enthusiasm of a short-sighted detective. As one turns over the pages, the suspense of the author becomes almost unbearable. The horses of Mr. William Black's phaeton do not soar towards the sun. They merely frighten the sky at evening into violent chromo-lithographic effects. On seeing them approach, the peasants take refuge in dialect. Mrs. Oliphant prattles pleasantly about curates, lawn-tennis parties, domesticity, and other wearisome things. Mr. Marion Crawford has immolated himself upon the altar of local colour. He is like the lady in the French comedy who keeps talking about *le beau ciel d'Italie* ["the beautiful Italian sky"]. Besides, he has fallen into the bad habit of uttering moral platitudes. He is always telling us that to be good is to be good, and that to be bad is to be wicked. At times he is almost edifying. *Robert Elsmere*[5] is of course a masterpiece —a masterpiece of the *genre ennuyeux* ["boring type"], the one form of literature that the English people seem thoroughly to enjoy. A thoughtful young friend of ours once told us that it reminded him of the sort of conversation that goes on at a meat tea in the house of a serious Nonconformist family, and we can quite believe it. Indeed, it is only in England that such a book could be produced. England is the home of lost ideas. As for that great and daily increasing school of novelists for whom the sun always rises in the East-

---

[5] A best-selling novel (3 vols., 1888) by Mrs. Humphry Ward, who later was one of those responsible for Beardsley's dismissal from *The Yellow Book*. She was one of John Lane's most valued authors.

End, the only thing that can be said about them is that they find life crude, and leave it raw.

"In France, though nothing so deliberately tedious as *Robert Elsmere* had been produced, things are not much better. M. Guy de Maupassant, with his keen mordant irony and his hard vivid style, strips life of the few poor rags that still cover her, and shows us foul sore and festering wound. He writes lurid little tragedies in which everybody is ridiculous; bitter comedies at which one cannot laugh for very tears. M. Zola, true to the lofty principle that he lays down in one of his pronunciamientos on literature, *L'homme de génie n'a jamais d'esprit* ["The man of genius never has any wit"], is determined to show that, if he has not got genius, he can at least be dull. And how well he succeeds! He is not without power. Indeed at times, as in *Germinal,* there is something almost epic in his work. But his work is entirely wrong from beginning to end, and wrong not on the ground of morals, but on the ground of art. From any ethical standpoint it is just what it should be. The author is perfectly truthful, and describes things exactly as they happen. What more can any moralist desire? We have no sympathy at all with the moral indignation of our time against M. Zola. It is simply the indignation of Tartuffe [the religious hypocrite in Molière's play, 1664] on being exposed. But from the standpoint of art, what can be said in favour of the author of *L'Assommoir, Nana* and *Pot-Bouille*? Nothing. Mr. Ruskin once described the characters in George Eliot's novels as being like the sweepings of a Pentonville omnibus, but M. Zola's characters are much worse. They have their dreary vices, and their drearier virtues. The record of their lives is absolutely without interest. Who cares what happens to them? In literature we require distinction, charm, beauty and imaginative power. We don't want to be harrowed and disgusted with an account of the doings of the lower orders. M. Daudet is better. He has wit, a light touch and an amusing style. But he has lately committed literary suicide. Nobody can possibly care for Delobelle with his *Il faut lutter pour l'art* ["It is necessary to struggle for art"], or for Valmajour with his eternal refrain about the nightingale, or for the poet in *Jack* with his *mots cruels* ["cruel words"], now that we have learned from *Vingt Ans de ma Vie Littéraire* [*Twenty Years of my Literary Life*] that these characters were taken directly from life. To us they seem to have suddenly lost all their vitality, all the few qualities they ever possessed. The only real people are the people who never existed, and if a novelist is base enough to go to life for his personages he should at least pretend that they are creations, and not boast of them as copies. The justification of a character in a novel is not that other persons are what they are, but that the author is what he is. Otherwise the novel is not a work of art. As for M. Paul Bourget, the master of the *roman psychologique* ["psychological novel"], he commits the error of imagining that the men and women of modern life are capable of being infinitely analysed for an innumerable series of chapters. In point of fact what is interesting about people in good society—and M. Bourget rarely moves out of the Faubourg St. Germain, except to come to London—is the mask that each one of them wears, not the reality that lies behind the mask. It is a humiliating confession, but we are all of us made out of the same stuff. In Falstaff there is something of Hamlet, in Hamlet there is not a little of Falstaff. The fat knight has his moods of melancholy, and the young prince his moments of coarse humour. Where we differ from each other is purely in accidentals: in dress, manner, tone of voice, religious opinions, personal appearance, tricks of habit and the like. The more one analyses people, the more all reasons for analysis disappear. Sooner or later one comes to that dreadful universal thing called human nature. Indeed, as any one who has ever worked among the poor knows only too well, the brotherhood of man is no mere poet's dream, it is a most depressing and humiliating reality; and if a writer insists upon analysing the upper classes, he might just as well write of match-girls and costermongers at once." However, my dear Cyril, I will not detain you any further just here. I quite admit that modern novels have many good points. All I insist on is that, as a class, they are quite unreadable.

CYRIL: This is certainly a very grave qualification, but I must say that I think you are rather unfair in some of your strictures. I like *The Deemster*, and *The Daughter of Heth*, and *Le Disciple*, and *Mr. Isaacs* [popular works of the time], and as for *Robert Elsmere*, I am quite devoted to it. Not that I can look upon it as a serious work. As a statement of the problems that confront the earnest Christian it is ridiculous and antiquated. It is simply Arnold's *Literature and Dogma* with the literature left out. It is as much behind the age as Paley's *Evidences*, or Colenso's method of Biblical exegesis. Nor could anything be less impressive than the unfortunate hero gravely heralding a dawn that rose long ago, and so completely missing its true significance that he proposes to carry on the business of the old firm under the new name. On the other hand, it contains several clever caricatures, and a heap of delightful quotations, and Green's philosophy very pleasantly sugars the somewhat bitter pill of the author's fiction. I also cannot help expressing my surprise that you have said nothing about the two novelists whom you are always reading, Balzac and George Meredith. Surely they are realists, both of them?

VIVIAN: Ah! Meredith! Who can define him? His style is chaos illumined by flashes of lightning. As a writer he has mastered everything except language: as a novelist he can do everything, except tell a story: as an artist he is everything except articulate. Somebody in Shakespeare—Touchstone [the fool in *As You Like It*], I think—talks about a man who is always breaking his shins over his own wit, and it seems to me that this might serve as the basis for a criticism of Meredith's method. But whatever he is, he is not a realist. Or rather I would say that he is a child of realism who is not on speaking terms with his father. By deliberate choice he has made himself a romanticist. He has refused to bow the knee to Baal, and after all, even if the man's fine spirit did not revolt against the noisy assertions of realism, his style would be quite sufficient of itself to keep life at a respectful distance. By its means he has planted round his garden a hedge full of thorns, and red with wonderful roses. As for Balzac, he was a most remarkable combination of the artistic temperament, with the scientific spirit. The latter he bequeathed to his disciples. The former was entirely his own. The difference between such a book as M. Zola's *L'Assommoir* and Balzac's *Illusions Perdues* [*Lost Illusions*] is the difference between unimaginative realism and imaginative reality. "All Balzac's characters," said Baudelaire, "are gifted with the same ardour of life that animated himself. All his fictions are as deeply coloured as dreams. Each mind is a weapon loaded to the muzzle with will. The very scullions have genius." A steady course of Balzac reduces our living friends to shadows, and our acquaintances to the shadows of shades. His characters have a kind of fervent fiery-coloured existence. They dominate us, and defy scepticism. One of the greatest tragedies of my life is the death of Lucien de Rubempré [character in Balzac's *Illusions Perdues*]. It is a grief from which I have never been able to completely rid myself. It haunts me in my moments of pleasure. I remember it when I laugh. But Balzac is no more a realist than Holbein [1465–1524, German painter] was. He created life, he did not copy it. I admit, however, that he set far too high a value on modernity of form, and that, consequently, there is no book of his that, as an artistic masterpiece, can rank with *Salammbo* [by Flaubert, 1863] or [*Henry*] *Esmond* [by Thackeray, 1852], or *The Cloister and the Hearth* [by Reade, 1861], or the *Vicomte de Bragelonne* [by Dumas père, 1848–50].

CYRIL: Do you object to modernity of form, then?

VIVIAN: Yes. It is a huge price to pay for a very poor result. Pure modernity of form is always somewhat vulgarising. It cannot help being so. The public imagine that, because they are interested in their immediate surroundings, Art should be interested in them also, and should take them as her subject-matter. But the mere fact that they are interested in these things makes them unsuitable subjects for Art. The only beautiful things, as somebody once said, are the things that do not concern us. As long as a thing is useful or necessary to us, or affects us in any way, either for pain or for pleasure, or appeals strongly to our sympathies, or is a vital part of the environment in which we live, it is outside the proper sphere of art. To art's subject-matter we should be more or less indifferent. We should, at any rate have no preferences, no prejudices, no partisan feeling of any kind. It is exactly because Hecuba is nothing to us that her sorrows are such an admirable motive for a tragedy.[6] I do not know anything in the whole history of literature sadder than the artistic career of Charles Reade. He wrote one beautiful book, *The Cloister and the Hearth,* a book as much above *Romola* as *Romola* is above *Daniel Deronda* [both novels by George Eliot], and wasted the rest of his life in a foolish attempt to be modern, to draw public attention to the state of our convict prisons, and the management of our private lunatic asylums. Charles Dickens was depressing enough in all conscience when he tried to arouse our sympathy for the victims of the poor-law administration; but Charles Reade, an artist, a scholar, a man with a true sense of beauty, raging and roaring over the abuses of contemporary life like a common pamphleteer or a sensational journalist, is really a sight for the angels to weep over. Believe me, my dear Cyril, modernity of form and modernity of subject-matter are entirely and absolutely wrong. We have mistaken the common livery of the age for the vesture of the Muses, and spend our days in the sordid streets and hideous suburbs of our vile cities when we should be out on the hillside with Apollo. Certainly we are a degraded race, and have sold our birthright for a mess of facts.

CYRIL: There is something in what you say, and there is no doubt that whatever amusement we may find in reading a purely model novel, we have rarely any artistic pleasure in re-reading it. And this is perhaps the best rough test of what is literature and what is not. If one cannot enjoy reading a book over and over again, there is no use reading it at all. But what do you say about the return to Life and Nature? This is the panacea that is always being recommended to us.

VIVIAN: I will read you what I say on that subject. The passage comes later on in the article, but I may as well give it to you now :—

"The popular cry of our time is 'Let us return to Life and Nature; they will recreate Art for us, and send the red blood coursing through her veins; they will shoe her feet with swiftness and make her hand strong.' But, alas! we are mis-

[6] An allusion to Hamlet's lines concerning the player's speech on Hecuba's death: "What's Hecuba to him or he to Hecuba/That he should weep for her?"

taken in our amiable and well-meaning efforts. Nature is always behind the age. And as for Life, she is the solvent that breaks up Art, the enemy that lays waste her house."

CYRIL: What do you mean by saying that Nature is always behind the age?

VIVIAN: Well, perhaps that is rather cryptic. What I mean is this. If we take Nature to mean natural simple instinct as opposed to self-conscious culture, the work produced under this influence is always old-fashioned, antiquated, and out of date. One touch of Nature may make the whole world kin, but two touches of Nature will destroy any work of Art. If, on the other hand, we regard Nature as the collection of phenomena external to man, people only discover in her what they bring to her. She has no suggestions of her own. Wordsworth went to the lakes, but he was never a lake poet. He found in stones the sermons he had already hidden there. He went moralising about the district, but his good work was produced when he returned, not to Nature but to poetry. Poetry gave him "Laodamia," and the fine sonnets, and the great Ode such as it is. Nature gave him "Martha Ray" and "Peter Bell," and the address to Mr. Wilkinson's spade.

CYRIL: I think that view might be questioned. I am rather inclined to believe in "the impulse from a vernal wood," though of course the artistic value of such an impulse depends entirely on the kind of temperament that receives it, so that the return to Nature would come to mean simply the advance to a great personality. You would agree with that, I fancy. However, proceed with your article.

VIVIAN (*reading*): "Art begins with abstract decoration, with purely imaginative and pleasurable work dealing with what is unreal and non-existent. This is the first stage. Then Life becomes fascinated with this new wonder, and asks to be admitted into the charmed circle. Art takes life as part of her rough material, recreates it, and refashions it in fresh forms, is absolutely indifferent to fact, invents, imagines, dreams, and keeps between herself and reality the impenetrable barrier of beautiful style, of decorative or ideal treatment. The third stage is when Life gets the upper hand, and drives Art out into the wilderness. This is the true decadence, and it is from this that we are now suffering.

"Take the case of the English drama. At first in the hands of the monks Dramatic Art was abstract, decorative and mythological. Then she enlisted Life in her service, and using some of life's external forms, she created an entirely new race of beings, whose sorrows were more terrible than any sorrow man has ever felt, whose joys were keener than lovers' joys, who had the rage of the Titans and the calm of the gods, who had monstrous and marvellous sins, monstrous and marvellous virtues. To them she gave a language different from that of actual use, a language full of resonant music and sweet rhythm, made stately by solemn cadence, or made delicate by fanciful rhyme, jewelled with wonderful words, and enriched with lofty diction. She clothed her children in strange raiment and gave them masks, and at her bidding the antique world rose from its marble tomb. A new Cæsar stalked through the streets of risen Rome, and with purple sail and flute-led oars another Cleopatra passed up the river to Antioch. Old myth and legend and dream took shape and substance. History was entirely re-written, and there was hardly one of the dramatists who did not recognize that the object of Art is not simple truth but complex beauty. In this they were perfectly right. Art itself is really a form of exaggeration; and selection, which is the very spirit of art, is nothing more than an intensified mode of over-emphasis.

"But Life soon shattered the perfection of the form. Even in Shakespeare we can see the beginning of the end. It shows itself by the gradual breaking up of the blank-verse in the later plays, by the predominance given to prose, and by the over-importance assigned to characterisation. The passages in Shakespeare—and there are many—where the language is uncouth, vulgar, exaggerated, fantastic, obscene even, are entirely due to Life calling for an echo of her own voice and rejecting the intervention of beautiful style through which alone should life be suffered to find expression. Shakespeare is not by any means a flawless artist. He is too fond of going directly to life, and borrowing life's natural utterance. He forgets that when Art surrenders her imaginative medium she surrenders everything. Goethe says, somewhere:—

'In der Beschränkung zeigt sich erst der Meister'

"It is in working within limits that the master reveals himself," and the limitation, the very condition of any art is style. However, we need not linger any longer over Shakespeare's realism. *The Tempest* is the most perfect of palinodes. All that we desired to point out was that the magnificent work of the Elizabethan and Jacobean artists contained within itself the seeds of its own dissolution, and that, if it drew some of its strength from using life as rough material, it drew all its weakness from using life as an artistic method. As the inevitable result of this substitution of an imitative for a creative medium, this surrender of an imaginative form, we have the modern English melodrama. The characters in these plays talk on the stage exactly as they would talk off it; they have neither aspirations nor aspirates; they are taken directly from life and reproduce its vulgarity down to the smallest detail; they present the gait, manner, costume and accent of real people; they would pass unnoticed in a third-class railway carriage. And yet how wearisome the plays are! They do not succeed in producing even that impression of reality at which they aim, and which is their only reason for existing. As a method, realism is a complete failure.

"What is true about the drama and the novel is no less true about those arts that we call the decorative arts. The whole history of these arts in Europe is the record of the struggle between Orientalism, with its frank rejection of imitation, its love of artistic convention, its dislike to the actual representation of any object in Nature, and our own imitative spirit. Wherever the former has been paramount, as in Byzantium, Sicily and Spain, by actual contact or in the rest of Europe by the influence of the Crusades, we have had beautiful and imaginative work in which the visible things of life are transmuted into artistic conventions, and the things that Life has not are invented and fashioned for her delight. But wherever we have returned to Life and Nature, our work has always become vulgar, common and uninteresting. Modern tapestry, with its aerial effects, its elaborate perspective, its broad expanses of waste sky, its faithful and laborious realism, has no beauty whatsoever. The pictorial glass of Germany is absolutely detestable. We are beginning to weave possible carpets in England, but only because we have returned to the method and spirit of the East. Our rugs and carpets of twenty years ago, with their solemn depressing truths, their inane worship of Nature, their sordid reproductions of visible objects, have become, even to the Philistine, a source of laughter. A cultured Mahommedan once remarked to us, 'You Christians are so occupied in misinterpreting the fourth commandment ["Remember the Sabbath day."] that you have never thought of making an artistic application of the second ["Thou shall not make unto thee a graven image."].' He was perfectly right, and the whole truth of the matter is this: The proper school to learn art in is not Life but Art."

And now let me read you a passage which seems to me to settle the question very completely.

"It was not always thus. We need not say anything about the poets, for they, with the unfortunate exception of Mr. Wordsworth, have been really faithful to their high mission, and are universally recognised as being absolutely unreliable. But in the works of Herodotus, who, in spite of the shallow and ungenerous attempts of modern sciolists to verify his history, may justly be called the 'Father of Lies'; in the published speeches of Cicero and the biographies of Suetonius; in Tacitus at his best; in Pliny's *Natural History*; in Hanno's *Periplus*; in all the early chronicles; in the Lives of the Saints; in Froissart and Sir Thomas Malory; in the travels of Marco Polo; in Olaus Magnus and Aldrovandus, and Conrad Lycosthenes, with his magnificent *Prodigiorum et Ostentorum Chronicon*; in the autobiography of Benvenuto Cellini; in the memoirs of Casanova; in Defoe's *History of the Plague*; in Boswell's *Life of Johnson*; in Napoleon's despatches, and in the works of our own Carlyle, whose *French Revolution* is one of the most fascinating historical novels ever written, facts are either kept in their proper subordinate position, or else entirely excluded on the general ground of dullness. Now everything is changed. Facts are not merely finding a footing-place in history, but they are usurping the domain of Fancy, and have invaded the kingdom of Romance. Their chilling touch is over everything. They are vulgarising mankind. The crude commercialism of America, its materialising spirit, its indifference to the poetical side of things, and its lack of imagination and of high unattainable ideals, are entirely due to that country having adopted for its national hero a man who, according to his own confession, was incapable of telling a lie, and it is not too much to say that the story of George Washington and the cherry-tree has done more harm, and in a shorter space of time, than any other moral tale in the whole of literature."

CYRIL: My dear boy!

VIVIAN: I assure you it is the case, and the amusing part of the whole thing is that the story of the cherry-tree is an absolute myth. However, you must not think that I am too despondent about the artistic future either of America or of our own country. Listen to this:—

"That some change will take place before this century has drawn to its close we have no doubt whatsoever. Bored by the tedious and improving conversation of those who have neither the wit to exaggerate nor the genius to romance, tired of the intelligent person whose reminiscences are always based upon memory, whose statements are invariably limited by probability, and who is at any time liable to be corroborated by the merest Philistine who happens to be present, Society sooner or later must return to its lost leader, the cultured and fascinating liar. Who he was who first, without ever having gone out to the rude chase, told the wandering cavemen at sunset how he had dragged the Megatherium from the purple darkness of its jasper cave, or slain the Mammoth in single combat and brought back its gilded tusks, we cannot tell, and not one of our modern anthropologists, for all their much-boasted science, has had the ordinary courage to tell us. Whatever was his name or race, he certainly was the true founder of social intercourse. For the aim of the liar is simply to charm, to delight, to give pleasure. He is the very basis of civilised society, and without him a dinner-party, even at the mansions of the great, is as dull as a lecture at the Royal Society, or a debate at the Incorporated Authors, or one of Mr. [Sir Francis Crowley] Burnand's farcical comedies.

"Nor will he be welcomed by society alone. Art, breaking from the prison-house of realism, will run to greet him, and will kiss his false, beautiful lips, knowing that he alone is in possession of the great secret of all her manifestations, the secret that Truth is entirely and absolutely a matter of style; while Life—poor, probable, uninteresting human life—tired of repeating herself for the benefit of Mr. Herbert Spencer [1820–1903, English philosopher of evolution], scientific historians, and the compilers of statistics in general, will follow meekly after him, and try to reproduce, in her own simple and untutored way, some of the marvels of which he talks.

"No doubt there will always be critics who, like a certain writer in the *Saturday Review*, will gravely censure the teller of fairy tales for his defective knowledge of natural history, who will measure imaginative work by their own lack of any imaginative faculty, and will hold up their ink-stained hands in horror if some honest gentleman, who has never been farther than the yew-trees of his own garden, pens a fascinating book of travels like Sir John Mandeville, or, like great Raleigh, writes a whole history of the world, without knowing anything whatsoever about the past. To excuse themselves they will try and shelter under the shield of him who made Prospero the magician, and gave him Caliban and Ariel [characters in Shakespeare's *Tempest*] as his servants, who heard the Tritons blowing their horns round the coral reefs of the Enchanted Isle, and the fairies singing to each other in a wood near Athens, who led the phantom kings in dim procession across the misty Scottish heath, and hid Hecate in a cave with the weird sisters. They will call upon Shakespeare—they always do—and will quote that hackneyed passage forgetting that this unfortunate aphorism about Art holding the mirror up to Nature, is deliberately said by Hamlet in order to convince the bystanders of his absolute insanity in all art-matters."

CYRIL: Ahem! Another cigarette, please.

VIVIAN: My dear fellow, whatever you may say, it is merely a dramatic utterance, and no more represents Shakespeare's real views upon art than the speeches of Iago represent his real views upon morals. But let me get to the end of the passage:—

"Art finds her own perfection within, and not outside of, herself. She is not to be judged by any external standard of resemblance. She is a veil, rather than a mirror. She has

flowers that no forests know of, birds that no woodland possesses. She makes and unmakes many worlds, and can draw
the moon from heaven with a scarlet thread. Hers are the
'forms more real than living man,' and hers the great archetypes of which things that have existence are but unfinished
copies. Nature has, in her eyes, no laws, no uniformity. She
can work miracles at her will, and when she calls monsters
from the deep they come. She can bid the almond-tree blossom in winter, and send the snow upon the ripe cornfield. At
her word the frost lays its silver finger on the burning mouth
of June, and the winged lions creep out from the hollows of
the Lydian hills. The dryads peer from the thicket as she
passes by, and the brown fauns smile strangely at her when
she comes near them. She has hawk-faced gods that worship
her, and the centaurs gallop at her side."

CYRIL: I like that. I can see it. Is that the end?

VIVIAN: No. There is one more passage, but it is purely
practical. It simply suggests some methods by which we
could revive this lost art of Lying.

CYRIL: Well, before you read it to me, I should like to ask
you a question. What do you mean by saying that life,
"poor, probable, uninteresting human life," will try to reproduce the marvels of art? I can quite understand your objection to art being treated as a mirror. You think it would
reduce genius to the position of a cracked looking-glass. But
you don't mean to say that you seriously believe that Life
imitates Art, that Life in fact is the mirror, and Art the reality?

VIVIAN: Certainly I do. Paradox though it may seem—and
paradoxes are always dangerous things—it is none the less
true that Life imitates art far more than Art imitates life. We
have all seen in our own day in England how a certain curious and fascinating type of beauty, invented and emphasised
by two imaginative painters, has so influenced Life that
whenever one goes to a private view, or to an artistic salon
one sees, here the mystic eyes of Rossetti's dream, the long
ivory throat, the strange square-cut jaw, the loosened shadowy hair that he so ardently loved, there the sweet maiden-
hood of "The Golden Stair," the blossom-like mouth and
weary loveliness of the "Laus Amoris," the passion-pale face

of Andromeda, the thin hands and lithe beauty of the Vivian in "Merlin's Dream." And it has always been so. A great artist invents a type, and Life tries to copy it, to reproduce it in a popular form, like an enterprising publisher. Neither Holbein nor Vandyck [1599–1641, Flemish painter] found in England what they have given us. They brought their types with them, and Life with her keen imitative faculty set herself to supply the master with models. The Greeks, with their quick artistic instinct, understood this, and set in the bride's chamber the statue of Hermes or of Apollo, that she might bear children as lovely as the works of art that she looked at in her rapture or her pain. They knew that Life gains from art not merely spirituality, depth of thought and feeling, soul-turmoil or soul-peace, but that she can form herself on the very lines and colours of art, and can reproduce the dignity of Pheidias as well as the grace of Praxiteles [both famous ancient Greek sculptors]. Hence came their objection to realism. They disliked it on purely social grounds. They felt that it inevitably makes people ugly, and they were perfectly right. We try to improve the conditions of the race by means of good air, free sunlight, wholesome water, and hideous bare buildings for the better housing of the lower orders. But these things merely produce health, they do not produce beauty. For this, Art is required, and the true disciples of the great artist are not his studio-imitators, but those who become like his works of art, be they plastic as in Greek days, or pictorial as in modern times; in a world, Life is Art's best, Art's only pupil.

As it is with the visible arts, so it is with literature. The most obvious and the vulgarest form in which this is shown is in the case of the silly boys who, after reading the adventures of Jack Sheppard [7] or Dick Turpin, [8] pillage the stalls of unfortunate apple-women, break into sweet-shops at night, and alarm old gentlemen who are returning home from the city by leaping out on them in suburban lanes, with black masks and unloaded revolvers. This interesting phenomenon,

[7] Hero of William Ainsworth's novel (1839) who is adept at housebreaking and jailbreaking.

[8] Hero of Ainsworth's romance *Rookwood* (1834) based on the life of Richard Turpin (1706–39), English horse-thief.

which always occurs after the appearance of a new edition of either of the books I have alluded to, is usually attributed to the influence of literature on the imagination. But this is a mistake. The imagination is essentially creative, and always seeks for a new form. The boy-burglar is simply the inevitable result of life's imitative instinct. He is Fact, occupied as Fact usually is, with trying to reproduce Fiction, and what we see in him is repeated on an extended scale throughout the whole of life. Schopenhauer has analysed the pessimism that characterises modern thought, but Hamlet invented it. The world has become sad because a puppet was once melancholy. The Nihilist, that strange martyr who has no faith, who goes to the stake without enthusiasm, and dies for what he does not believe in, is a purely literary product. He was invented by Tourguenieff, and completed by Dostoevski. Robespierre came out of the pages of Rousseau as surely as the People's Palace rose out of the *débris* of a novel. Literature always anticipates life. It does not copy it, but moulds it to its purpose. The nineteenth century, as we know it, is largely an invention of Balzac. Our Luciens de Rubempré, our Rastignacs, and De Marsays made their first appearance on the stage of the *Comédie Humaine* [a series of novels by Balzac]. We are merely carrying out, with footnotes and unnecessary additions, the whim or fancy or creative vision of a great novelist. I once asked a lady, who knew Thackeray intimately, whether he had had any model for Becky Sharp. She told me that Becky was an invention, but that the idea of the character had been partly suggested by a governess who lived in the neighbourhood of Kensington Square, and was the companion of a very selfish and rich old woman. I inquired what became of the governess, and she replied that, oddly enough, some years after the appearance of *Vanity Fair*, she ran away with the nephew of the lady with whom she was living, and for a short time made a great splash in society, quite in Mrs. Rawdon Crawley's [Becky Sharp's] style, and entirely by Mrs. Rawdon Crawley's methods. Ultimately she came to grief, disappeared to the Continent, and used to be occasionally seen at Monte Carlo and other gambling places. The noble gentleman from whom the same great sentimentalist drew Colonel Newcome died, a few months after *The Newcomes* had reached a fourth edition, with the word "Adsum" on his lips. Shortly after Mr. Stevenson published his curious psychological story of transformation, a friend of mine, called Mr. Hyde, was in the north of London, and being anxious to get to a railway station, took what he thought would be a short cut, lost his way, and found himself in a network of mean, evil-looking streets. Feeling rather nervous he began to walk extremely fast, when suddenly out of an archway ran a child right between his legs. It fell on the pavement, he tripped over it, and trampled upon it. Being, of course, very much frightened and a little hurt, it began to scream, and in a few seconds the whole street was full of rough people who came pouring out of the houses like ants. They surrounded him, and asked him his name. He was just about to give it when he suddenly remembered the opening incident in Mr. Stevenson's story. He was so filled with horror at having realised in his own person that terrible and well-written scene, and at having done accidentally, though in fact, what the Mr. Hyde of fiction had done with deliberate intent, that he ran away as hard as he could go. He was, however, very closely followed, and finally he took refuge in a surgery, the door of which happened to be open, where he explained to a young assistant, who happened to be there, exactly what had occurred. The humanitarian crowd were induced to go away on his giving them a small sum of money, and as soon as the coast was clear he left. As he passed out, the name on the brass door-plate of the surgery caught his eye. It was "Jekyll." At least it should have been . . .

However, I do not wish to dwell any further upon individual instances. Personal experience is a most vicious and limited circle. All that I desire to point out is the general principle that Life imitates Art far more than Art imitates Life, and I feel sure that if you think seriously about it you will find that it is true. Life holds the mirror up to Art, and either reproduces some strange type imagined by painter or sculptor, or realises in fact what has been dreamed in fiction. Scientifically speaking, the basis of life—the energy of life, as Aristotle would call it—is simply the desire for expression, and Art is always presenting various forms through which the expression can be attained. Life seizes on them and uses them, even if they be to her own hurt. Young men have committed suicide because Rolla [in Sheridan's play *Pizarro*, 1799] did so, have died by their own hand because by his own hand Werther [hero of Goethe's *Sorrows of Young Werther*, 1774] died. Think of what we owe to the imitation of Christ, of what we owe to the imitation of Cæsar.

CYRIL: The theory is certainly a very curious one, but to make it complete you must show that Nature, no less than Life, is an imitation of Art. Are you prepared to prove that?

VIVIAN: My dear fellow, I am prepared to prove anything.

CYRIL: Nature follows the landscape painter, then, and takes her effects from him?

VIVIAN: Certainly. Where, if not from the Impressionists, do we get those wonderful brown fogs that come creeping down our streets, blurring the gas-lamps and changing the houses into monstrous shadows? To whom, if nòt to them and their master, do we owe the lovely silver mists that brood over our river, and turn to faint forms of fading grace, curved bridge and swaying barge? The extraordinary change that has taken place in the climate of London during the last ten years is entirely due to a particular school of Art. You smile. Consider the matter from a scientific or a metaphysical point of view, and you will find that I am right. For what is Nature? Nature is no great mother who has borne us. She is our creation. It is in our brain that she quickens to life. Things are because we see them, and what we see, and how we see it, depends on the Arts that have influenced us. To look at a thing is very different from seeing a thing. One does not see anything until one sees its beauty. Then, and then only, does it come into existence. At present, people see fogs, not because there are fogs, but because poets and painters have taught them the mysterious loveliness of such effects. There may have been fogs for centuries in London. I dare say there were. But no one saw them, and so we do not know anything about them. They did not exist till Art had invented them. Now, it must be admitted, fogs are carried to excess. They have become the mere mannerism of a clique, and the exaggerated realism of their method gives dull people bronchitis. Where the cultured catch an effect, the uncultured catch cold. And so, let us be humane, and invite Art to turn her wonderful eyes elsewhere. She has done so already, indeed. That white quivering sunlight that one sees now in France, with its strange blotches of mauve, and its restless violet shadows, is her latest fancy, and, on the whole, Nature reproduces it quite admirably. Where she used to give us Corots and Daubignys, she gives us now exquisite Monets and entrancing Pissaros [late 19th cent. French impressionists]. Indeed there are moments, rare, it is true, but still to be observed from time to time, when Nature becomes absolutely modern. Of course she is not always to be relied upon. The fact is that she is in this unfortunate position. Art creates an incomparable and unique effect, and, having done so, passes on to other things. Nature, upon the other hand, forgetting that imitation can be made the sincerest form of insult, keeps on repeating this effect until we all become absolutely wearied of it. Nobody of any real culture, for instance, ever talks nowadays about the beauty of a sunset. Sunsets are quite old-fashioned. They belong to the time when Turner [1775–1851, English landscape painter] was the last note in art. To admire them is a distinct sign of provincialism of temperament. Upon the other hand they go on. Yesterday evening Mrs. Arundel insisted on my going to the window and looking at the glorious sky, as she called it. Of course I had to look at it. She is one of those absurdly pretty Philistines to whom one can deny nothing. And what was it? It was simply a very second-rate Turner, a Turner of a bad period, with all the painter's worst faults exaggerated and over-emphasised. Of course I am quite ready to admit that Life very often commits the same error. She produces her false Renés[9] and her sham Vautrins,[10] just as Nature gives us, on one day a doubtful Cuyp [family of Dutch painters, 17th cent.], and on another a more than questionable Rousseau. Still, Nature irritates one more when she does things of that kind. It seems so stupid, so obvious, so unnecessary. A false Vautrin might be delightful. A doubtful Cuyp

[9] René, the central character in Chateaubriand's *Attila* (1801), joins a tribe of Natchez Indians.

[10] The sinister intriguer in Balzac's *Père Goriot* (1835) who is exposed as a criminal.

is unbearable. However, I don't want to be too hard on Nature. I wish the Channel, especially at Hastings, did not look quite so often like a Henry Moore, grey pearl with yellow lights, but then, when Art is more varied, Nature will, no doubt, be more varied also. That she imitates Art, I don't think even her worst enemy would deny now. It is the one thing that keeps her in touch with civilised man. But have I proved my theory to your satisfaction?

CYRIL: You have proved it to my dissatisfaction, which is better. But even admitting this strange imitative instinct in Life and Nature, surely you would acknowledge that Art expresses the temper of its age, the spirit of its time, the moral and social conditions that surround it, and under whose influence it is produced.

VIVIAN: Certainly not! Art never expresses anything but itself.[11] This is the principle of my new æsthetics; and it is this, more than that vital connection between form and substance, on which Mr. Pater dwells,[12] that makes basic the type of all the arts. Of course, nations and individuals, with that healthy natural vanity which is the secret of existence, are always under the impression that it is of them that the Muses are talking, always trying to find in the calm dignity of imaginative art some mirror of their own turbid passions, always forgetting that the singer of life is not Apollo but Marsyas.[13] Remote from reality and with her eyes turned away from the shadows of the cave, Art reveals her own perfection, and the wondering crowd that watches the opening of the marvellous many-petalled rose fancies that it is its own history that is being told to it, its own spirit that is finding expression in a new form. But it is not so. The highest

[11] A paraphrase of Gautier's doctrine of *l'art pour l'art* in the preface to *Mademoiselle de Maupin* (1835).

[12] An allusion to Pater's famous statement "All art constantly aspires towards the condition of music" in his essay on the school of Giorgione in *The Renaissance*.

[13] Having found a flute abandoned and cursed by Athena, Marsyas acquired such skill that he challenged Apollo to a contest. As punishment for his rashness, the Muses—or perhaps the Nysaeans, who decided in Apollo's favor—flayed him alive. Marsyas' statue, erected in several Roman cities, symbolized liberty.

art rejects the burden of the human spirit, and gains more from a new medium or a fresh material than she does from any enthusiasm for art, or from any lofty passion, or from any great awakening of the human consciousness. She develops purely on her own lines. She is not symbolic of any age. It is the ages that are her symbols.

Even those who hold that Art is representative of time and place and people cannot help admitting that the more imitative an art is the less it represents to us the spirit of its age. The evil faces of the Roman emperors look out at us from the foul porphyry and spotted jasper in which the realistic artists of the day delighted to work and we fancy that in those cruel lips and heavy sensual jaws we can find the secret of the ruin of the Empire. But it was not so. The vices of Tiberius [Roman emperor, 42 B.C.–37 A.D.] could not destroy that supreme civilisation any more than the virtues of the Antonines [illustrious family in ancient Rome] could save it. It fell for other, for less interesting reasons. The sibyls and prophets of the Sistine [Chapel] may indeed serve to interpret for some that new birth of the emancipated spirit that we call the Renaissance; but what do the drunken boors and bawling peasants of Dutch art tell us about the great soul of Holland? The more abstract, the more ideal an art is, the more it reveals to us the temper of its age. If we wish to understand a nation by means of its art, let us look at its architecture or its music . . .

CYRIL: But in order to avoid making any error I want you to tell me briefly the doctrines of the new æsthetics.

VIVIAN: Briefly, then, they are these. Art never expresses anything but itself. It has an independent life, just as Thought has, and develops purely on its own lines. It is not necessarily realistic in an age of realism, nor spiritual in an age of faith. So far from being the creation of its time, it is usually in direct opposition to it, and the only history that it preserves for us is the history of its own progress. Sometimes it returns upon its footsteps, and revives some antique form, as happened in the archaistic movement of late Greek Art, and in the pre-Raphaelite movement of our own day. At other times it entirely anticipates its age, and produces in one century work that it takes another century to understand, to appreciate, and to enjoy. In no case does it reproduce its age. To pass from the art of a time to the time itself is the great mistake that all historians commit.

The second doctrine is this. All bad art comes from returning to Life and Nature, and elevating them into ideals. Life and Nature may sometimes be used as part of Art's rough material, but before they are of any real service to Art they must be translated into artistic conventions. The moment Art surrenders its imaginative medium it surrenders everything. As a method Realism is a complete failure, and the two things that every artist should avoid are modernity of form and modernity of subject-matter. To us, who live in the nineteenth century, any century is a suitable subject for art except our own. The only beautiful things are the things that do not concern us. It is, to have the pleasure of quoting myself, exactly because Hecuba is nothing to us that her sorrows are so suitable a motive for a tragedy. Besides, it is only the modern that ever becomes old-fashioned. M. Zola sits down to give us a picture of the Second Empire [in France, 1852–70]. Who cares for the Second Empire now? It is out of date. Life goes faster than Realism, but Romanticism is always in front of Life.

The third doctrine is that Life imitates Art far more than Art imitates Life. This results not merely from Life's imitative instinct, but from the fact that the self-conscious aim of Life is to find expression, and that Art offers it certain beautiful forms through which it may realise that energy. It is a theory that has never been put forward before, but it is extremely fruitful, and throws an entirely new light upon the history of Art.

It follows, as a corollary from this, that external Nature also imitates Art. The only effects that she can show us are effects that we have already seen through poetry, or in paintings. This is the secret of Nature's charm, as well as the explanation of Nature's weakness.

The final revelation is that Lying, the telling of beautiful untrue things, is the proper aim of Art. But of this I think I have spoken at sufficient length. And now let us go out on the terrace, where "droops the milk-white peacock like a ghost," while the evening star "washes the dusk with silver."

At twilight nature becomes a wonderfully suggestive effect, and is not without loveliness, though perhaps its chief use is to illustrate quotations from the poets. Come! We have talked long enough.

SALOMÉ

Inspired by Huysmans' description in *À Rebours* (see Appendix) Wilde wrote *Salomé* in French in 1891, then sent it to the poet Pierre Louÿs for corrections. Rehearsals for the London production, with Sarah Bernhardt in the leading role, were halted, however, when the Lord Chamberlain, in June, 1892, banned the play because it contained Biblical characters. Wilde immediately announced his departure for France, where, he contended, a work of art could be produced. To this, the poet William Watson wrote "Lines to our New Censor":

> *And wilt thou, Oscar, from us flee,*
> *And must we, henceforth, wholly sever?*
> *Shall thy laborious* jeux-d'esprit
> *Sadden our lives no more for ever?*

Replied Wilde: "There is not enough fire in William Watson's poetry to boil a tea-kettle."

The French version of *Salomé* was published simultaneously in Paris and in London, where it was advertised as "the play the Lord Chamberlain refused to license." Annoyed, Wilde wrote to his publisher John Lane: "Please do not do this again. The interest and value of *Salomé* is not that it was suppressed by a foolish official, but that it was written by an artist."

The English version—by Lord Alfred Douglas, after Wilde rejected Beardsley's—was published by the Bodley Head in February, 1894, with Beardsley's illustrations, most of which—grotesque and satirical—are irrelevant to to the play.

A TRAGEDY IN ONE ACT

The Persons of the Play

HEROD ANTIPAS, Tetrarch of Judæa
JOKANAAN, the Prophet
THE YOUNG SYRIAN, Captain of the Guard
TIGELLINUS, a Young Roman
A CAPPADOCIAN
A NUBIAN
FIRST SOLDIER
SECOND SOLDIER
THE PAGE OF HERODIAS
JEWS, NAZARENES, ETC.
A SLAVE
NAAMAN, the Executioner
HERODIAS, Wife of the Tetrarch
SALOMÉ, Daughter of Herodias
THE SLAVES OF SALOMÉ

Scene. A great terrace in the Palace of HEROD, set above the banqueting-hall. Some soldiers are leaning over the balcony. To the right there is a gigantic staircase, to the left, at the back, an old cistern surrounded by a wall of green bronze. The moon is shining very brightly.

THE YOUNG SYRIAN: How beautiful is the Princess Salomé tonight!

THE PAGE OF HERODIAS: Look at the moon. How strange the moon seems! She is like a woman rising from a tomb. She is like a dead woman. One might fancy she was looking for dead things.

THE YOUNG SYRIAN: She has a strange look. She is like a little princess who wears a yellow veil, and whose feet are of silver. She is like a princess who has little white doves for feet. One might fancy she was dancing.

THE PAGE OF HERODIAS: She is like a woman who is dead. She moves very slowly.

(*Noise in the banqueting-hall.*)

THE WOMAN IN THE MOON
Wilde, with his green carnation, is caricatured in the moon

FIRST SOLDIER: What an uproar! Who are those wild beasts howling?

SECOND SOLDIER: The Jews. They are always like that. They are disputing about their religion.

FIRST SOLDIER: Why do they dispute about their religion?

SECOND SOLDIER: I cannot tell. They are always doing it. The Pharisees, for instance, say that there are angels, and the Sadducees declare that angels do not exist.

FIRST SOLDIER: I think it is ridiculous to dispute about such things.

THE YOUNG SYRIAN: How beautiful is the Princess Salomé tonight!

THE PAGE OF HERODIAS: You are always looking at her. You look at her too much. It is dangerous to look at people in such fashion. Something terrible may happen.

THE YOUNG SYRIAN: She is very beautiful tonight.

FIRST SOLDIER: The Tetrarch has a sombre aspect.

SECOND SOLDIER: Yes; he has a sombre aspect.

FIRST SOLDIER: He is looking at something.

SECOND SOLDIER: He is looking at someone.

FIRST SOLDIER: At whom is he looking?

SECOND SOLDIER: I cannot tell.

THE YOUNG SYRIAN: How pale the Princess is! Never have I seen her so pale. She is like the shadow of a white rose in a mirror of silver.

THE PAGE OF HERODIAS: You must not look at her. You look too much at her.

FIRST SOLDIER: Herodias has filled the cup of the Tetrarch.

THE CAPPADOCIAN: Is that the Queen Herodias, she who wears a black mitre sewed with pearls, and whose hair is powdered with blue dust?

FIRST SOLDIER: Yes; that is Herodias, the Tetrarch's wife.

SECOND SOLDIER: The Tetrarch is very fond of wine. He has wine of three sorts. One which is brought from the Island of Samothrace, and is purple like the cloak of Cæsar.

THE CAPPADOCIAN: I have never seen Cæsar.

SECOND SOLDIER: Another that comes from a town called Cyprus, and is as yellow as gold.

THE CAPPADOCIAN: I love gold.

SECOND SOLDIER: And the third is a wine of Sicily. That wine is as red as blood.

THE NUBIAN: The gods of my country are very fond. Twice in the year we sacrifice to them young men and maidens; fifty young men and a hundred maidens. But I am afraid that we never give them quite enough, for they are very harsh to us.

THE CAPPADOCIAN: In my country there are no gods left. The Romans have driven them out. There are some who say that they have hidden themselves in the mountains, but I do not believe it. Three nights I have been on the mountains seeking them everywhere. I did not find them. And at last I called them by their names, and they did not come. I think they are dead.

FIRST SOLDIER: The Jews worship a God that one cannot see.

THE CAPPADOCIAN: I cannot understand that.

FIRST SOLDIER: In fact, they only believe in things that one cannot see.

THE CAPPADOCIAN: That seems to me altogether ridiculous.

THE VOICE OF JOKANAAN: After me shall come another mightier than I. I am not worthy so much as to unloose the latchet of his shoes. When he cometh, the solitary places shall be glad. They shall blossom like the rose. The eyes of the blind shall see the day, and the ears of the deaf shall be opened. The suckling child shall put his hand upon the dragon's lair, he shall lead the lions by their manes.

SECOND SOLDIER: Make him be silent. He is always saying ridiculous things.

FIRST SOLDIER: No, no. He is a holy man. He is very gentle, too. Every day, when I give him to eat he thanks me.

THE CAPPADOCIAN: Who is he?

FIRST SOLDIER: A prophet.

THE CAPPADOCIAN: What is his name?

FIRST SOLDIER: Jokanaan.

THE CAPPADOCIAN: Whence comes he?

FIRST SOLDIER: From the desert where he fed on locusts and wild honey. He was clothed in camel's hair, and round his loins he had a leathern belt. He was very terrible to look upon. A great multitude used to follow him. He even had disciples.

THE CAPPADOCIAN: What is he talking of?

FIRST SOLDIER: We can never tell. Sometimes he says things that affright one, but it is impossible to understand what he says.

THE CAPPADOCIAN: May one see him?

FIRST SOLDIER: No. The Tetrarch has forbidden it.

THE YOUNG SYRIAN: The Princess has hidden her face behind her fan! Her little white hands are fluttering like doves that fly to their dovecots. They are like white butterflies. They are just like white butterflies.

THE PAGE OF HERODIAS: What is that to you? Why do you look at her? You must not look at her. . . . Something terrible may happen.

THE CAPPADOCIAN (*Pointing to the cistern*): What a strange prison!

SECOND SOLDIER: It is an old cistern.

THE CAPPADOCIAN: An old cistern! That must be a poisonous place in which to dwell!

SECOND SOLDIER: Oh no! For instance, the Tetrarch's brother, his elder brother, the first husband of Herodias the Queen, was imprisoned there for twelve years. It did not kill him. At the end of the twelve years he had to be strangled.

THE CAPPADOCIAN: Strangled? Who dared to do that?

SECOND SOLDIER (*Pointing to the Executioner, a huge Negro*): That man yonder, Naaman.

THE CAPPADOCIAN: He was not afraid?

SECOND SOLDIER: Oh no! The Tetrarch sent him the ring.

THE CAPPADOCIAN: What ring?

THE SECOND SOLDIER: The death-ring. So he was not afraid.

THE CAPPADOCIAN: Yet it is a terrible thing to strangle a king.

FIRST SOLDIER: Why? Kings have but one neck, like other folk.

THE CAPPADOCIAN: I think it terrible.

THE YOUNG SYRIAN: The Princess is getting up! She is leaving the table! She looks very troubled. Ah, she is coming this way. Yes, she is coming towards us. How pale she is! Never have I seen her so pale.

THE PAGE OF HERODIAS: I pray you not to look at her.

THE YOUNG SYRIAN: She is like a dove that has strayed. . . . She is like a narcissus trembling in the wind. . . . She is like a silver flower.

(*Enter* SALOMÉ.)

SALOMÉ: I will not stay. I cannot stay. Why does the Tetrarch look at me all the while with his mole's eyes under his shaking eyelids? It is strange that the husband of my mother looks at me like that. I know not what it means. Of a truth I know it too well.

THE YOUNG SYRIAN: You have left the feast, Princess?

SALOMÉ: How sweet is the air here! I can breathe here! Within there are Jews from Jerusalem who are tearing each other in pieces over their foolish ceremonies, and barbarians who drink and drink, and spill their wine on the pavement, and Greeks from Smyrna with painted eyes and painted cheeks, and frizzed hair curled in columns, and Egyptians silent and subtle, with long nails of jade and russet cloaks, and Romans brutal and coarse, with their uncouth jargon. Ah! how I loathe the Romans! They are rough and common, and they give themselves the airs of noble lords.

THE YOUNG SYRIAN: Will you be seated, Princess?

THE PAGE OF HERODIAS: Why do you speak to her? Oh! something terrible will happen. Why do you look at her?

SALOMÉ: How good to see the moon! She is like a little piece of money, a little silver flower. She is cold and chaste. I am sure she is a virgin. Yes, she is a virgin. She has never defiled herself. She has never abandoned herself to men, like the other goddesses.

THE VOICE OF JOKANAAN: Behold! the Lord hath come. The son of man is at hand. The centaurs have hidden themselves in the rivers, and the nymphs have left the rivers, and are lying beneath the leaves of the forest.

SALOMÉ: Who was that who cried out?

SECOND SOLDIER: The prophet, Princess.

SALOMÉ: Ah, the prophet! He of whom the Tetrarch is afraid?

THE PEACOCK SKIRT
A superb example of Art Nouveau

SECOND SOLDIER: We know nothing of that, Princess. It was the prophet Jokanaan who cried out.

THE YOUNG SYRIAN: Is it your pleasure that I bid them bring your litter, Princess? The night is fair in the garden.

SALOMÉ: He says terrible things about my mother, does he not?

SECOND SOLDIER: We never understand what he says, Princess.

SALOMÉ: Yes; he says terrible things about her.

(*Enter a slave.*)

THE SLAVE: Princess, the Tetrarch prays you to return to the feast.

THE YOUNG SYRIAN: Pardon me, Princess, but if you return not some misfortune may happen.

SALOMÉ: Is he an old man, this prophet?

THE YOUNG SYRIAN: Princess, it were better to return. Suffer me to lead you in.

SALOMÉ: This prophet . . . is he an old man?

FIRST SOLDIER: No, Princess, he is quite young.

SECOND SOLDIER: One cannot be sure. There are those who say he is Elias.

SALOMÉ: Who is Elias?

SECOND SOLDIER: A prophet of this country in bygone days, Princess.

THE SLAVE: What answer may I give the Tetrarch from the Princess?

THE VOICE OF JOKANAAN: Rejoice not, O land of Palestine, because the rod of him who smote thee is broken. For from the seed of the serpent shall come a basilisk, and that which is born of it shall devour the birds.

SALOMÉ: What a strange voice! I would speak with him.

FIRST SOLDIER: I fear it may not be, Princess. The Tetrarch does not suffer anyone to speak with him. He has even forbidden the high priest to speak with him.

SALOMÉ: I desire to speak with him.

FIRST SOLDIER: It is impossible, Princess.

SALOMÉ: I will speak with him.

THE YOUNG SYRIAN: Would it not be better to return to the banquet?

SALOMÉ: Bring forth this prophet. (*Exit the slave.*)

FIRST SOLDIER: We dare not, Princess.

SALOMÉ (*Approaching the cistern and looking down into it*): How black it is, down there! It must be terrible to be in so black a hole! It is like a tomb. . . . (*To the soldiers.*) Did you not hear me? Bring out the prophet. I would look on him.

SECOND SOLDIER: Princess, I beg you do not require this of us.

SALOMÉ: You are making me wait upon your pleasure.

FIRST SOLDIER: Princess, our lives belong to you, but we cannot do what you have asked of us. And indeed, it is not of us that you should ask this thing.

SALOMÉ (*Looking at the young Syrian*): Ah!

THE PAGE OF HERODIAS: Oh! what is going to happen? I am sure that something terrible will happen.

SALOMÉ (*Going up to the young Syrian*): Thou wilt do this thing for me, wilt thou not, Narraboth? Thou wilt do this thing for me. I have ever been kind towards thee. Thou wilt do it for me. I would but look at him, this strange prophet. Men have talked so much of him. Often I have heard the Tetrarch talk of him. I think he is afraid of him, the Tetrarch. Art thou, even thou, also afraid of him, Narraboth?

THE YOUNG SYRIAN: I fear him not, Princess; there is no man I fear. But the Tetrarch has formally forbidden that any man should raise the cover of this well.

SALOMÉ: Thou wilt do this thing for me, Narraboth, and tomorrow when I pass in my litter beneath the gate-way of the idol-sellers I will let fall for thee a little flower, a little green flower.[1]

THE YOUNG SYRIAN: Princess, I cannot, I cannot.

SALOMÉ (*Smiling*): Thou wilt do this thing for me, Narraboth. Thou knowest that thou wilt do this thing for me. And on the morrow when I shall pass in my litter by the bridge of the idol-buyers, I will look at thee through the muslin veils, I will look at thee, Narraboth, it may be I will

[1] Wilde habitually wore a green carnation as his symbol of the superiority of artifice over nature. Beardsley's illustrations use the flower to mock Wilde, and Robert Hichens' satire of Wilde bears the title *The Green Carnation*. (See Appendix)

THE BLACK CAPE

The illustration, irrelevant to the play, is an exquisite satire of contemporary fashion

smile at thee. Look at me, Narraboth, look at me. Ah! thou knowest that thou wilt do what I ask of thee. Thou knowest it. . . . I know that thou wilt do this thing.

THE YOUNG SYRIAN (*Signing to the third soldier*) : Let the prophet come forth. . . . The Princess Salomé desires to see him.

SALOMÉ : Ah!

THE PAGE OF HERODIAS : Oh! How strange the moon looks. Like the hand of a dead woman who is seeking to cover herself with a shroud.

THE YOUNG SYRIAN : She has a strange aspect! She is like a little princess, whose eyes are eyes of amber. Through the clouds of muslin she is smiling like a little princess.

(*The prophet comes out of the cistern.* SALOMÉ *looks at him and steps slowly back.*)

JOKANAAN : Where is he whose cup of abominations is now full? Where is he, who in a robe of silver shall one day die in the face of all the people? Bid him come forth, that he may hear the voice of him who hath cried in the waste places and in the houses of kings.

SALOMÉ : Of whom is he speaking?

THE YOUNG SYRIAN : No one can tell, Princess.

JOKANAAN : Where is she who saw the images of men painted on the walls, even the images of the Chaldeans painted with colours, and gave herself up unto the lust of her eyes, and sent ambassadors into the land of Chaldæa?

SALOMÉ : It is of my mother that he is speaking.

THE YOUNG SYRIAN : Oh, no, Princess.

SALOMÉ : Yes; it is of my mother that he is speaking.

JOKANAAN : Where is she who gave herself unto the Captains of Assyria, who have baldricks on their loins, and crowns of many colours on their heads? Where is she who hath given herself to the young men of the Egyptians, who are clothed in fine linen and hyacinth, whose shields are of gold, whose helmets are of silver, whose bodies are mighty? Go, bid her rise up from the bed of her abominations, from the bed of her incestuousness, that she may hear the words of him who prepareth the way of the Lord, that she may repent her of her iniquities. Though she will not repent, but will stick fast in her abominations; go, bid her come, for the fan of the Lord is in His hand.

SALOMÉ: Ah, but he is terrible, he is terrible!

THE YOUNG SYRIAN: Do not stay here, Princess, I beseech you.

SALOMÉ: It is his eyes above all that are terrible. They are like black holes burned by torches in a tapestry of Tyre. They are like the black caverns of Egypt in which the dragons make their lairs. They are like black lakes troubled by fantastic moons. . . . Do you think he will speak again?

THE YOUNG SYRIAN: Do not stay here, Princess. I pray you do not stay here.

SALOMÉ: How wasted he is! He is like a thin ivory statue. He is like an image of silver. I am sure he is chaste as the moon is. He is like a moonbeam, like a shaft of silver. I would look closer at him. I must look at him closer.

THE YOUNG SYRIAN: Princess! Princess!

JOKANAAN: Who is this woman who is looking at me? I will not have her look at me. Wherefore doth she look at me with her golden eyes, under her gilded eyelids. I know not who she is. I do not desire to know who she is. Bid her begone. It is not to her that I would speak.

SALOMÉ: I am Salomé, daughter of Herodias, Princess of Judæa.

JOKANAAN: Back! daughter of Babylon! Come not near the chosen of the Lord. Thy mother hath filled the earth with the wine of her iniquities, and the cry of her sinning hath come up even to the ears of God.

SALOMÉ: Speak again, Jokanaan. Thy voice is as music to mine ear.

THE YOUNG SYRIAN: Princess! Princess! Princess!

SALOMÉ: Speak again! Speak again, Jokanaan, and tell me what I must do.

JOKANAAN: Daughter of Sodom, come not near me! But cover thy face with a veil, and scatter ashes upon thine head, and get thee to the desert and seek out the Son of Man.

SALOMÉ: Who is he, the Son of Man? Is he as beautiful as thou art, Jokanaan?

JOKANAAN: Get thee behind me! I hear in the palace the beating of the wings of the angel of death.

JOHN AND SALOMÉ
Suppressed in the first edition, it appeared in later printings

THE YOUNG SYRIAN: Princess, I beseech thee to go within.

JOKANAAN: Angel of the Lord God, what dost thou here with thy sword? Whom seekest thou in this palace? The day of him who shall die in a robe of silver has not yet come.

SALOMÉ: Jokanaan!

JOKANAAN: Who speaketh?

SALOMÉ: I am amorous of thy body, Jokanaan! Thy body is white like the lilies of a field that the mower hath never mowed. Thy body is white like the snows that lie on the mountains of Judæa, and come down into the valleys. The roses in the garden of the Queen of Arabia are not so white as thy body. Neither the roses of the garden of the Queen of Arabia, the garden of spices of the Queen of Arabia, nor the feet of the dawn when they light on the leaves, nor the breast of the moon when she lies on the breast of the sea. . . . There is nothing in the world so white as thy body. Suffer me to touch thy body.

JOKANAAN: Back! daughter of Babylon! By woman came evil into the world. Speak not to me. I will not listen to thee. I listen but to the voice of the Lord God.

SALOMÉ: Thy body is hideous. It is like the body of a leper. It is like a plastered wall where vipers have crawled; like a plastered wall where the scorpions have made their nest. It is like a whitened sepulchre full of loathsome things. It is horrible, thy body is horrible. It is thy hair that I am enamoured of, Jokanaan. Thy hair is like clusters of grapes, like the clusters of black grapes that hang from the vine-trees of Edom in the land of the Edomites. Thy hair is like the cedars of Lebanon, like the great cedars of Lebanon that give their shade to the lions and to the robbers who would hide them by day. The long black nights, when the moon hides her face, when the stars are afraid, are not so black as thy hair. The silence that dwells in the forest is not so black. There is nothing in the world that is so black as thy hair. . . . Suffer me to touch thy hair.

JOKANAAN: Back, daughter of Sodom! Touch me not. Profane not the temple of the Lord God.

SALOMÉ: Thy hair is horrible. It is covered with mire and dust. It is like a knot of serpents coiled round thy neck. I love not thy hair. . . . It is thy mouth that I desire,

Jokanaan. Thy mouth is like a band of scarlet on a tower of ivory. It is like a pomegranate cut in twain with a knife of ivory. The pomegranate flowers that blossom in the gardens of Tyre, and are redder than roses, are not so red. The red blasts of trumpets that herald the approach of kings, and make afraid the enemy, are not so red. Thy mouth is redder than the feet of the doves who inhabit the temples and are fed by the priests. It is redder than the feet of him who cometh from a forest where he hath slain a lion, and seen gilded tigers. Thy mouth is like a branch of coral that fishers have found in the twilight of the sea, the coral that they keep for the kings! . . . It is like the vermilion that the Moabites find in the mines of Moab, the vermilion that the kings take from them. It is like the bow of the King of the Persians, that is painted with vermilion, and is tipped with coral. There is nothing in the world so red as thy mouth. . . . Suffer me to kiss thy mouth.

JOKANAAN: Never! daughter of Babylon! Daughter of Sodom! Never.

SALOMÉ: I will kiss thy mouth, Jokanaan. I will kiss thy mouth.

THE YOUNG SYRIAN: Princess, Princess, thou who art like a garden of myrrh, thou who art the dove of all doves, look not at this man, look not at him! Do not speak such words to him. I cannot endure it. . . . Princess, do not speak these things.

SALOMÉ: I will kiss thy mouth, Jokanaan.

THE YOUNG SYRIAN: Ah! (*He kills himself and falls between* SALOMÉ *and* JOKANAAN.)

THE PAGE OF HERODIAS: The young Syrian has slain himself! The young captain has slain himself! He has slain himself who was my friend! I gave him a little box of perfumes and ear-rings wrought in silver, and now he has killed himself! Ah, did he not say that some misfortune would happen? I too said it, and it has come to pass. Well I knew that the moon was seeking a dead thing, but I knew not that it was he whom she sought. Ah! why did I not hide him from the moon? If I had hidden him in a cavern she would not have seen him.

FIRST SOLDIER: Princess, the young captain has just slain himself.

SALOMÉ: Suffer me to kiss thy mouth, Jokanaan.

JOKANAAN: Art thou not afraid, daughter of Herodias? Did I not tell thee that I had heard in the palace the beatings of the wings of the angel of death, and hath he not come, the angel of death?

SALOMÉ: Suffer me to kiss thy mouth.

JOKANAAN: Daughter of adultery, there is but one who can save thee, it is He of whom I speak. Go seek Him. He is in a boat on the sea of Galilee, and He talketh with His disciples. Kneel down on the shore of the sea, and call unto Him by His name. When He cometh to thee (and to all who call on Him He cometh), bow thyself at His feet and ask of Him the remissions of thy sins.

SALOMÉ: Suffer me to kiss thy mouth.

JOKANAAN: Cursed be thou! daughter of an incestuous mother, be thou accursed!

SALOMÉ: I will kiss thy mouth, Jokanaan.

JOKANAAN: I will not look at thee, thou art accursed, Salomé, thou art accursed. (*He goes down into the cistern.*)

SALOMÉ: I will kiss thy mouth, Jokanaan; I will kiss thy mouth.

FIRST SOLDIER: We must bear away the body to another place. The Tetrarch does not care to see dead bodies, save the bodies of those whom he himself has slain.

THE PAGE OF HERODIAS: He was my brother, and nearer to me than a brother. I gave him a little box full of perfumes, and a ring of agate that he wore always on his hand. In the evening we were wont to walk by the river, and among the almond trees, and he used to tell me of the things of his country. He spake ever very low. The sound of his voice was like the sound of the flute, of one who playeth upon the flute. Also he had much joy to gaze at himself in the river. I used to reproach him for that.

SECOND SOLDIER: You are right; we must hide the body. The Tetrarch must not see it.

FIRST SOLDIER: The Tetrarch will not come to this place. He never comes on the terrace. He is too much afraid of the prophet.

ENTER HERODIAS

 This is Beardsley's original drawing. In the published version, Lane insisted that the right-hand figure be decorously draped. Compromising, Beardsley added a fig leaf. The figure in the lower right is, of course, another caricature of Wilde

(*Enter* HEROD, HERODIAS, *and all the Court.*)

HEROD: Where is Salomé? Where is the Princess? Why did she not return to the banquet as I commanded her? Ah! there she is!

HERODIAS: You must not look at her! You are always looking at her!

HEROD: The moon has a strange look tonight. Has she not a strange look? She is like a mad woman who is seeking everywhere for lovers. She is naked too. She is quite naked. The clouds are seeking to clothe her nakedness, but she will not let them. She shows herself naked in the sky. She reels through the clouds like a drunken woman. . . . I am sure she is looking for lovers. Does she not reel like a drunken woman? She is like a mad woman, is she not?

HERODIAS: No; the moon is like the moon, that is all. Let us go within. . . . We have nothing to do here.

HEROD: I will stay here! Manasseh, lay carpets there. Light torches, bring forth the ivory table, and the tables of jasper. The air here is sweet. I will drink more wine with my guests. We must show all honours to the ambassadors of Cæsar.

HERODIAS: It is not because of them that you remain.

HEROD: Yes; the air is very sweet. Come, Herodias, our guests await us. Ah! I have slipped! I have slipped in blood! It is an ill omen. Wherefore is there blood here? . . . and this body, what does this body here? Think you I am like the King of Egypt, who gives no feast to his guests but that he shows them a corpse? Whose is it? I will not look on it.

FIRST SOLDIER: It is our captain, sire. He is the young Syrian whom you made captain of the guard but three days gone.

HEROD: I issued no order that he should be slain.

SECOND SOLDIER: He slew himself, sire.

HEROD: For what reason? I had made him captain of my guard.

SECOND SOLDIER: We do not know, sire. But with his own hand he slew himself.

HEROD: That seems strange to me. I had thought it was but the Roman philosophers who slew themselves. Is it not true, Tigellinus, that the philosophers at Rome slay themselves?

TIGELLINUS: There be some who slay themselves, sire. They are the Stoics. The Stoics are people of no cultivation. They are ridiculous people. I myself regard them as being perfectly ridiculous.

HEROD: I also. It is ridiculous to kill oneself.

TIGELLINUS: Everybody at Rome laughs at them. The Emperor has written a satire against them. It is recited everywhere.

HEROD: Ah! he has written a satire against them? Cæsar is wonderful. He can do everything. . . . It is strange that the young Syrian has slain himself. I am sorry he has slain himself. I am very sorry; for he was fair to look upon. He was even very fair. He had very languorous eyes. I remember that I saw that he looked languorously at Salomé. Truly, I thought he looked too much at her.

HERODIAS: There are others who look too much at her.

HEROD: His father was a king. I drove him from his kingdom. And of his mother, who was a queen, you made a slave —Herodias. So he was here as my guest, as it were, and for that reason I made him my captain. I am sorry he is dead. Ho! why have you left the body here? I will not look at it—away with it! (*They take away the body.*) It is cold here. There is a wind blowing. Is there not a wind blowing?

HERODIAS: No; there is no wind.

HEROD: I tell you there is a wind that blows. . . . And I hear in the air something that is like the beating of wings, like the beating of vast wings. Do you not hear it?

HERODIAS: I hear nothing.

HEROD: I hear it no longer. But I heard it. It was the blowing of the wind. It has passed away. But no, I hear it again. Do you not hear it? It is just like the beating of wings.

HERODIAS: I tell you there is nothing. You are ill. Let us go within.

HEROD: I am not ill. It is your daughter who is sick to death. Never have I seen her so pale.

HERODIAS: I have told you not to look at her.

HEROD: Pour me forth wine. (*Wine is brought.*) Salomé, come drink a little wine with me. I have here a wine that is exquisite. Cæsar himself sent it me. Dip into it thy little red lips, that I may drain the cup.

SALOMÉ: I am not thirsty, Tetrarch.

HEROD: You hear how she answers me, this daughter of yours?

HERODIAS: She does right. Why are you always gazing at her?

HEROD: Bring me ripe fruits. (*Fruits are brought*.) Salomé, come and eat fruits with me. I love to see in a fruit the mark of thy little teeth. Bite but a little of this fruit that I may eat what is left.

SALOMÉ: I am not hungry, Tetrarch.

HEROD (*To* HERODIAS): You see how you have brought up this daughter of yours.

HERODIAS: My daughter and I come of a royal race. As for thee, thy father was a camel driver! He was a thief and a robber to boot!

HEROD: Thou liest!

HERODIAS: Thou knowest well that it is true.

HEROD: Salomé, come and sit next to me. I will give thee the throne of thy mother.

SALOMÉ: I am not tired, Tetrarch.

HERODIAS: You see in what regard she holds you.

HEROD: Bring me—what is it that I desire? I forget. Ah! ah! I remember.

THE VOICE OF JOKANAAN: Behold the time is come! That which I foretold has come to pass. The day that I spoke of is at hand.

HERODIAS: Bid him be silent. I will not listen to his voice. This man is for ever hurling insults against me.

HEROD: He has said nothing against you. Besides, he is a very great prophet.

HERODIAS: I do not believe in prophets. Can a man tell what will come to pass? No man knows it. Also he is for ever insulting me. But I think you are afraid of him. . . . I know well that you are afraid of him.

HEROD: I am not afraid of him. I am afraid of no man.

HERODIAS: I tell you, you are afraid of him. If you are not afraid of him why do you not deliver him to the Jews who for these six months past have been clamouring for him?

A JEW: Truly, my lord, it were better to deliver him into our hands.

HEROD: Enough on this subject. I have already given you my answer. I will not deliver him into your hands. He is a holy man. He is a man who has seen God.

A JEW: That cannot be. There is no man who hath seen God since the prophet Elias. He is the last man who saw God face to face. In these days God doth not show Himself. God hideth Himself. Therefore great evils have come upon the land.

ANOTHER JEW: Verily, no man knoweth if Elias the prophet did indeed see God. Peradventure it was but the shadow of God that he saw.

A THIRD JEW: God is at no time hidden. He showeth Himself at all times and in all places. God is in what is evil even as He is in what is good.

A FOURTH JEW: Thou shouldst not say that. It is a very dangerous doctrine. It is a doctrine that cometh from Alexandria, where men teach the philosophy of the Greeks. And the Greeks are Gentiles: They are not even circumcised.

A FIFTH JEW: No one can tell how God worketh. His ways are very dark. It may be that the things which we call evil are good, and that the things which we call good are evil. There is no knowledge of anything. We can but bow our heads to His will, for God is very strong. He breaketh in pieces the strong together with the weak, for He regardeth not any man.

FIRST JEW: Thou speaketh truly. Verily God is terrible; He breaketh in pieces the strong and the weak as a man breaks corn in a mortar. But as for man, he hath never seen God. No man hath seen God since the prophet Elias.

HERODIAS: Make them be silent. They weary me.

HEROD: But I have heard it said that Jokanaan is in very truth your prophet Elias.

THE JEW: That cannot be. It is more than three hundred years since the days of the prophet Elias.

HEROD: There be some who say that this man is Elias the prophet.

A NAZARENE: I am sure that he is Elias the prophet.

THE JEW: Nay, but he is not Elias the prophet.

THE VOICE OF JOKANAAN: Behold the day is at hand, the day of the Lord, and I hear upon the mountains the feet of Him who shall be the Saviour of the world.

HEROD: What does that mean? The Saviour of the world?

TIGELLINUS: It is a title that Cæsar adopts.

HEROD: But Cæsar is not coming into Judæa. Only yesterday I received letters from Rome. They contained nothing concerning this matter. And you, Tigellinus, who were at Rome during the winter, you heard nothing concerning this matter, did you?

TIGELLINUS: Sire, I heard nothing concerning the matter. I was explaining the title. It is one of Cæsar's titles.

HEROD: But Cæsar cannot come. He is too gouty. They say that his feet are like the feet of an elephant. Also there are reasons of State. He who leaves Rome loses Rome. He will not come. Howbeit, Cæsar is lord, he will come if such be his pleasure. Nevertheless, I think he will not come.

FIRST NAZARENE: It was not concerning Cæsar that the prophet spake these words, sire.

HEROD: How?—it was not concerning Cæsar?

FIRST NAZARENE: No, my lord.

HEROD: —Concerning whom then did he speak?

FIRST NAZARENE: Concerning Messias who has come.

A JEW: Messias hath not come.

FIRST NAZARENE: He hath come, and everywhere He worketh miracles.

HERODIAS: Ho! ho! miracles! I do not believe in miracles. I have seen too many. (*To the Page.*) My fan.

FIRST NAZARENE: This Man worketh true miracles. Thus, at a marriage which took place in a little town of Galilee, a town of some importance, He changed water into wine. Certain persons who were present related it to me. Also He healed two lepers that were seated before the Gate of Capernaum simply by touching them.

SECOND NAZARENE: Nay, it was blind men that He healed at Capernaum.

FIRST NAZARENE: Nay; they were lepers. But He hath healed blind people also, and He was seen on a mountain talking with angels.

A SADDUCEE: Angels do not exist.

A PHARISEE: Angels exist, but I do not believe that this Man has talked with them.

FIRST NAZARENE: He was seen by a great multitude of people talking with angels.

HERODIAS: How these men weary me! They are ridiculous! (*To the Page.*) Well! my fan! (*The Page gives her the fan.*) You have a dreamer's look; you must not dream. It is only sick people who dream. (*She strikes the Page with her fan.*)

SECOND NAZARENE: There is also the miracle of the daughter of Jairus.

FIRST NAZARENE: Yea, that is sure. No man can gainsay it.

HERODIAS: These men are mad. They have looked too long on the moon. Command them to be silent.

HEROD: What is this miracle of the daughter of Jairus?

FIRST NAZARENE: The daughter of Jairus was dead. This Man raised her from the dead.

HEROD: How! He raises people from the dead?

FIRST NAZARENE: Yea, sire, He raiseth the dead.

HEROD: I do not wish Him to do that. I forbid Him to do that. I suffer no man to raise the dead. This Man must be found and told that I forbid Him to raise the dead. Where is this Man at present?

SECOND NAZARENE: He is in every place, my lord, but it is hard to find Him.

FIRST NAZARENE: It is said that He is now in Samaria.

A JEW: It is easy to see that this is not Messias, if He is in Samaria. It is not to the Samaritans that Messias shall come. The Samaritans are accursed. They bring no offerings to the Temple.

SECOND NAZARENE: He left Samaria a few days since. I think that at the present moment He is in the neighbourhood of Jerusalem.

FIRST NAZARENE: No; He is not there. I have just come from Jerusalem. For two months they have had no tidings of Him.

HEROD: No matter! But let them find Him, and tell Him, thus saith Herod the King, "I will not suffer Thee to raise the dead!" To change water into wine, to heal the lepers and the blind. . . . He may do these things if He will. I say nothing against these things. In truth I hold it a kindly deed to heal a leper. But no man shall raise the dead. It would be terrible if the dead came back.

THE VOICE OF JOKANAAN: Ah! the wanton one! The harlot! Ah! the daughter of Babylon with her golden eyes and her gilded eyelids! Thus saith the Lord God, Let there come up against her a multitude of men. Let the people take stones and stone her. . . .

HERODIAS: Command him to be silent.

THE VOICE OF JOKANAAN: Let the captains of the hosts pierce her with their swords, let them crush her beneath their shields.

HERODIAS: Nay, but it is infamous.

THE VOICE OF JOKANAAN: It is thus that I will wipe out all wickedness from the earth, and that all women shall learn not to imitate her abominations.

HERODIAS: You hear what he says against me? You suffer him to revile her who is your wife?

HEROD: He did not speak your name.

HERODIAS: What does that matter? You know well that it is I whom he seeks to revile. And I am your wife, am I not?

HEROD: Of a truth, dear and noble Herodias, you are my wife, and before that you were the wife of my brother.

HERODIAS: It was thou didst snatch me from his arms.

HEROD: Of a truth I was stronger than he was. . . . But let us not talk of that matter. I do not desire to talk of it. It is the cause of the terrible words that the prophet has spoken. Peradventure on account of it a misfortune will come. Let us not speak of this matter. Noble Herodias, we are not mindful of our guests. Fill thou my cup, my well-beloved. Ho! fill with wine the great goblets of silver, and the great goblets of glass. I will drink to Cæsar. There are Romans here, we must drink to Cæsar.

ALL: Cæsar! Cæsar!

HEROD: Do you not see your daughter, how pale she is?

HERODIAS: What is that to you if she be pale or not?

HEROD: Never have I seen her so pale.

HERODIAS: You must not look at her.

THE VOICE OF JOKANAAN: In that day the sun shall become black like sackcloth of hair, and the moon shall become like blood, and the stars of the heaven shall fall upon the earth like unripe figs that fall from the fig tree, and the kings of the earth shall be afraid.

HERODIAS: Ah! Ah! I should like to see that day of which he speaks, when the moon shall become like blood, and when the stars shall fall upon the earth like unripe figs. This prophet talks like a drunken man . . . but I cannot suffer the sound of his voice. I hate his voice. Command him to be silent.

HEROD: I will not. I cannot understand what it is that he saith, but it may be an omen.

HERODIAS: I do not believe in omens. He speaks like a drunken man.

HEROD: It may be he is drunk with the wine of God.

HERODIAS: What wine is that, the wine of God? From what vineyards is it gathered? In what winepress may one find it?

HEROD (*From this point he looks all the while at* SALOMÉ): Tigellinus, when you were at Rome of late, did the Emperor speak with you on the subject of . . . ?

TIGELLINUS: On what subject, my Lord?

HEROD: On what subject? Ah! I asked you a question, did I not? I have forgotten what I would have asked you.

HERODIAS: You are looking again at my daughter. You must not look at her. I have already said so.

HEROD: You say nothing else.

HERODIAS: I say it again.

HEROD: And that restoration of the Temple about which they have talked so much, will anything be done? They say the veil of the Sanctuary has disappeared, do they not?

HERODIAS: It was thyself didst steal it. Thou speakest at random and without wit. I will not stay here. Let us go within.

HEROD: Dance for me, Salomé.

HERODIAS: I will not have her dance.

SALOMÉ: I have no desire to dance, Tetrarch.

HEROD: Salomé, daughter of Herodias, dance for me.

HERODIAS: Peace! let her alone.

THE EYES OF HÉROD
Again, Wilde is caricatured

HEROD: I command thee to dance, Salomé.

SALOMÉ: I will not dance, Tetrarch.

HERODIAS (*Laughing*): You see how she obeys you.

HEROD: What is it to me whether she dance or not? It is naught to me. Tonight I am happy, I am exceeding happy. Never have I been so happy.

FIRST SOLDIER: The Tetrarch has a sombre look. Has he not a sombre look?

SECOND SOLDIER: Yes, he has a sombre look.

HEROD: Wherefore should I not be happy? Cæsar, who is lord of the world, Cæsar, who is lord of all things, loves me well. He has just sent me most precious gifts. Also he has promised me to summon to Rome the King of Cappadocia, who is my enemy. It may be that at Rome he will crucify him, for he is able to do all things that he has a mind to. Verily, Cæsar is lord. Therefore I do well to be happy. There is nothing in the world that can mar my happiness.

THE VOICE OF JOKANAAN: He shall be seated on this throne. He shall be clothed in scarlet and purple. In his hand he shall bear a golden cup full of his blasphemies. And the angel of the Lord shall smite him. He shall be eaten of worms.

HERODIAS: You hear what he says about you. He says that you will be eaten of worms.

HEROD: It is not of me that he speaks. He speaks never against me. It is of the King of Cappadocia that he speaks; the King of Cappadocia who is mine enemy. It is he who shall be eaten of worms. It is not I. Never has he spoken word against me, this prophet, save that I sinned in taking to wife the wife of my brother. It may be he is right. For, of a truth, you are sterile.

HERODIAS: I am sterile, I? You say that, you that are ever looking at my daughter, you that would have her dance for your pleasure? You speak as a fool. I have borne a child. You have gotten no child, no, not on one of your slaves. It is you who are sterile, not I.

HEROD: Peace, woman! I say that you are sterile. You have borne me no child, and the prophet says that our marriage is not a true marriage. He says that it is a marriage of incest, a marriage that will bring evils. . . . I fear he is

THE TOILETTE OF SALOMÉ. I.

*This did not appear in the first edition. The second version
(see the illustration following) was deemed less offensive*

right; I am sure that he is right. I would be happy at this. Of a truth, I am happy. There is nothing I lack.

HERODIAS: I am glad you are of so fair a humour tonight. It is not your custom. But it is late. Let us go within. Do not forget that we hunt at sunrise. All honours must be shown to Cæsar's ambassadors, must they not?

SECOND SOLDIER: The Tetrarch has a sombre look.

FIRST SOLDIER: Yes, he has a sombre look.

HEROD: Salomé, Salomé, dance for me. I pray thee dance for me. I am sad tonight. Yes; I am passing sad tonight. When I came hither I slipped in blood, which is an evil omen; also I heard in the air a beating of wings, a beating of giant wings. I cannot tell what they mean. . . . I am sad tonight. Therefore dance for me. Dance for me, Salomé, I beseech thee. If thou dancest for me thou mayest ask of me what thou wilt, and I will give it thee, even unto the half of my kingdom.

SALOMÉ (Rising) : Will you indeed give me whatsoever I shall ask of thee, Tetrarch?

HERODIAS: Do not dance, my daughter.

HEROD: Whatsoever thou shalt ask of me, even unto the half of my kingdom.

SALOMÉ: You swear it, Tetrarch?

HEROD: I swear it, Salomé.

HERODIAS: Do not dance, my daughter.

SALOMÉ: By what will you swear this thing, Tetrarch?

HEROD: By my life, by my crown, by my gods. Whatsoever thou shalt desire I will give it thee, even to the half of my kingdom, if thou wilt but dance for me. O Salomé, Salomé, dance for me!

SALOMÉ: You have sworn an oath, Tetrarch.

HEROD: I have sworn an oath.

HERODIAS: My daughter, do not dance.

HEROD: Even to the half of my kingdom. Thou wilt be passing fair as a queen, Salomé, if it please thee to ask for the half of my kingdom. Will she not be fair as a queen? Ah! it is cold here! There is an icy wind, and I hear . . . wherefore do I hear in the air this beating of wings? Ah! one might fancy a huge black bird that hovers over the terrace. Why can I not see it, this bird? The beat of its wings is terrible.

THE TOILETTE OF SALOMÉ. II.

Beardsley's choice of books in his drawings is frequently revealing. Here there are books by Zola and the Marquis de
Sade

The breath of the wind of its wings is terrible. It is a chill wind. Nay, but it is not cold, it is hot. I am choking. Pour water on my hands. Give me snow to eat. Loosen my mantle. Quick! quick! loosen my mantle. Nay, but leave it. It is my garland that hurts me, my garland of roses. The flowers are like fire. They have burned my forehead. (*He tears the wreath from his head and throws it on the table.*) Ah! I can breathe now. How red those petals are! They are like stains of blood on the cloth. That does not matter. It is not wise to find symbols in everything that one sees. It makes life too full of terrors. It were better to say that stains of blood are as lovely as rose petals. It were better far to say that. . . . But we will not speak of this. Now I am happy. I am passing happy. Have I not the right to be happy? Your daughter is going to dance for me. Wilt thou not dance for me, Salomé? Thou hast promised to dance for me.

HERODIAS: I will not have her dance.

SALOMÉ: I will dance for you, Tetrarch.

HEROD: You hear what your daughter says. She is going to dance for me. Thou doest well to dance for me, Salomé. And when thou hast danced for me, forget not to ask of me whatsoever thou hast a mind to ask. Whatsoever thou shalt desire I will give it thee, even to the half of my kingdom. I have sworn it, have I not?

SALOMÉ: Thou hast sworn it, Tetrarch.

HEROD: And I have never broken my word. I am not of those who break their oaths. I know not how to lie. I am the slave of my word, and my word is the word of a king. The King of Cappadocia had ever a lying tongue, but he is no true king. He is a coward. Also he owes me money that he will not repay. He has even insulted my ambassadors. He has spoken words that were wounding. But Cæsar will crucify him when he comes to Rome. I know that Cæsar will crucify him. And if he crucify him not, yet will he die, being eaten of worms. The prophet has prophesied it. Well! wherefore dost thou tarry, Salomé?

SALOMÉ: I am waiting until my slaves bring perfumes to me and the seven veils, and take from off my feet my sandals. (*Slaves bring perfumes and the seven veils, and take off the sandals of* SALOMÉ.)

HEROD: Ah, thou art to dance with naked feet. 'Tis well! 'Tis well. Thy little feet will be like white doves. They will be like little white flowers that dance upon the trees. . . . No, no, she is going to dance on blood. There is blood spilt on the ground. She must not dance on blood. It were an evil omen.

HERODIAS: What is it to thee if she dance on blood? Thou hast waded deep enough in it. . . .

HEROD: What is it to me? Ah! look at the moon! She has become red. She has become red as blood. Ah! the prophet prophesied truly. He prophesied that the moon would become as blood. Did he not prophesy it? All of ye heard him prophesying it. And now the moon has become as blood. Do ye not see it?

HERODIAS: Oh, yes, I see it well, and the stars are falling like unripe figs, are they not? and the sun is becoming black like sackcloth of hair, and the kings of the earth are afraid. That at least one can see. The prophet is justified of his words in that at least, for truly the kings of the earth are afraid. . . . Let us go within. You are sick. They will say at Rome that you are mad. Let us go within, I tell you.

THE VOICE OF JOKANAAN: Who is this who cometh from Edom, who is this who cometh from Bozra, whose raiment is dyed with purple, who shineth in the beauty of his garments, who walketh mighty in his greatness? Wherefore is thy raiment stained with scarlet?

HERODIAS: Let us go within. The voice of that man maddens me. I will not have my daughter dance while he is continually crying out. I will not have her dance while you look at her in this fashion. In a word, I will not have her dance.

HEROD: Do not rise, my wife, my queen, it will avail thee nothing. I will not go within till she hath danced. Dance, Salomé, dance for me.

HERODIAS: Do not dance, my daughter.

SALOMÉ: I am ready, Tetrarch.

(SALOMÉ *dances the dance of the seven veils.*)

HEROD: Ah! wonderful! wonderful! You see that she has danced for me, your daughter. Come near, Salomé, come near, that I may give thee thy fee. Ah! I pay a royal price to

THE STOMACH DANCE

those who dance for my pleasure. I will pay thee royally. I will give thee whatsoever thy soul desireth. What wouldst thou have? Speak.

SALOMÉ (*Kneeling*) : I would that they presently bring me in a silver charger. . . .

HEROD (*Laughing*) : In a silver charger? Surely yes, in a silver charger. She is charming, is she not? What is it thou wouldst have in a silver charger, O sweet and fair Salomé, thou art fairer than all the daughters of Judæa? What wouldst thou have them bring thee in a silver charger? Tell me. Whatsoever it may be, thou shalt receive it. My treasures belong to thee. What is it that thou wouldst have, Salomé?

SALOMÉ (*Rising*) : The head of Jokanaan.

HERODIAS : Ah! that is well said, my daughter.

HEROD : No, no!

HERODIAS : That is well said, my daughter.

HEROD : No, no, Salomé. It is not that thou desirest. Do not listen to thy mother's voice. She is ever giving thee evil counsel. Do not heed her.

SALOMÉ : It is not my mother's voice that I heed. It is for mine own pleasure that I ask the head of Jokanaan in a silver charger. You have sworn an oath, Herod. Forget not that you have sworn an oath.

HEROD : I know it. I have sworn an oath by my gods. I know it well. But I pray thee, Salomé, ask of me something else. Ask of me the half of my kingdom, and I will give it thee. But ask not of me what thy lips have asked.

SALOMÉ : I ask of you the head of Jokanaan.

HEROD : No, no, I will not give it thee.

SALOMÉ : You have sworn an oath, Herod.

HERODIAS : Yes, you have sworn an oath. Everybody heard you. You swore it before everybody.

HEROD : Peace, woman! It is not to you I speak.

HERODIAS : My daughter has done well to ask the head of Jokanaan. He has covered me with insults. He has said unspeakable things against me. One can see that she loves her mother well. Do not yield, my daughter. He has sworn an oath, he has sworn an oath.

HEROD : Peace! Speak not to me! . . . Salomé, I pray

thee be not stubborn. I have ever been kind toward thee. I have ever loved thee. . . . It may be that I have loved thee too much. Therefore ask not this thing of me. This is a terrible thing, an awful thing to ask of me. Surely, I think thou art jesting. The head of a man that is cut from his body is ill to look upon, is it not? It is not meet that the eyes of a virgin should look upon such a thing. What pleasure couldst thou have in it? There is no pleasure that thou couldst have in it. No, no, it is not that thou desirest. Hearken to me. I have an emerald, a great emerald, thou canst see that which passeth afar off. Cæsar himself carries such an emerald when he goes to the circus. But my emerald is the larger. I know well that it is the larger. It is the largest emerald in the whole world. Thou wilt take that, wilt thou not? Ask it of me and I will give it thee.

SALOMÉ: I demand the head of Jokanaan.

HEROD: Thou art not listening. Thou art not listening. Suffer me to speak, Salomé.

SALOMÉ: The head of Jokanaan.

HEROD: No, no, thou wouldst not have that. Thou sayest that but to trouble me, because I have looked at thee and ceased not this night. It is true, I have looked at thee and ceased not this night. Thy beauty has troubled me. Thy beauty has grievously troubled me, and I have looked at thee over-much. Nay, but I will look at thee no more. One should not look at anything. Neither at things, nor at people should one look. Only in mirrors is it well to look, for mirrors do but show us masks. Oh! oh! bring wine! I thirst. . . . Salomé, Salomé, let us be as friends. Bethink thee. . . . Ah! what would I say? What was't? Ah! I remember it! . . . Salomé—nay but come nearer to me; I fear thou wilt not hear my words—Salomé, thou knowest my white peacocks, my beautiful white peacocks, that walk in the garden between the myrtles and the tall cypress trees. Their beaks are gilded with gold and the grains that they eat are smeared with gold, and their feet are stained with purple. When they cry out the rain comes, and the moon shows herself in the heavens when they spread their tails. Two by two they walk between the cypress trees and the black myrtles, and each has a slave to tend it. Sometimes they fly across the trees, and anon they crouch in the grass, and round the pools of the water. There are not in all the world birds so wonderful. I know that Cæsar himself has no birds so fair as my birds. I will give thee fifty of my peacocks. They will follow thee whithersoever thou goest, and in the midst of them thou wilt be like unto the moon in the midst of a great white cloud. . . . I will give them to thee all. I have but a hundred, and in the whole world there is no king who has peacocks like unto my peacocks. But I will give them all to thee. Only thou must loose me from my oath, and must not ask of me that which thy lips have asked of me. (*He empties the cup of wine.*)

SALOMÉ: Give me the head of Jokanaan.

HERODIAS: Well said, my daughter! As for you, you are ridiculous with your peacocks.

HEROD: Ah! thou art not listening to me. Be calm. As for me, am I not calm? I am altogether calm. Listen. I have jewels hidden in this place—jewels that thy mother even has never seen; jewels that are marvellous to look at. I have a collar of pearls, set in four rows. They are like unto moons chained with rays of silver. They are even as half a hundred moons caught in a golden net. On the ivory breast of a queen they have rested. Thou shalt be as fair as a queen when thou wearest them. I have amethysts of two kinds, one that is black like wine, and one that is red like wine that one has coloured with water. I have topazes, yellow as are the eyes of tigers, and topazes that are pink as the eyes of a wood pigeon, and green topazes that are as the eyes of cats. I have opals that burn always, with a flame that is cold as ice, opals that make sad men's minds, and are afraid of the shadows. I have onyxes like the eyeballs of a dead woman. I have moonstones that change when the moon changes, and are wan when they see the sun. I have sapphires big like eggs, and as blue as blue flowers. The sea wanders within them and the moon comes never to trouble the blue of their waves. I have chrysolites and beryls and chrysoprases and rubies. I have sardonyx and hyacinth stones, and stones of chalcedony, and I will give them all unto thee, all, and other things will I add to them. The King of the Indies has but even now sent me four fans fashioned from the feathers of parrots, and the King of Numidia a garment of ostrich feathers. I have a crys-

A PLATONIC LAMENT

Again, an irrelevant illustration. Another caricature of Wilde may be seen in the sky

tal, into which it is not lawful for a woman to look, nor may young men behold it until they have been beaten with rods. In a coffer of nacre I have three wondrous turquoises. He who wears them on his forehead can imagine things which are not, and he who carries them in his hand can turn the fruitful woman into a woman that is barren. These are great treasures above all price. But this is not all. In an ebony coffer I have two cups, amber, that are like apples of pure gold. If an enemy pour poison into these cups they become like apples of silver. In a coffer incrusted with amber I have sandals incrusted with glass. I have mantles that have been brought from the land of the Seres, and bracelets decked about with carbuncles and with jade that come from the city of Euphrates. . . . What desirest thou more than this, Salomé! Tell me the thing that thou desirest, and I will give it thee. All that thou askest I will give thee, save one thing only. I will give thee all that is mine, save only the head of one man. I will give thee the mantle of the high priest. I will give thee the veil of the Sanctuary.

THE JEWS: Oh! oh!

SALOMÉ: Give me the head of Jokanaan.

HEROD (*Sinking back in his seat*): Let her be given what she asks! Of a truth she is her mother's child! (*The first Soldier approaches.* HERODIAS *draws from the hand of the Tetrarch the ring of death, and gives it to the Soldier, who straightway bears it to the Executioner. The Executioner looks scared.*) Who has taken my ring? There was a ring on my right hand. Who has drunk my wine? There was wine in my cup. It was full of wine. Someone has drunk it! Oh! surely some evil will befall someone. (*The Executioner goes down into the cistern.*) Ah! Wherefore did I give my oath? Hereafter let no king swear an oath. If he keep it not, it is terrible, and if he keep it, it is terrible also.

HERODIAS: My daughter has done well.

HEROD: I am sure that some misfortune will happen.

SALOMÉ (*She leans over the cistern and listens*): There is no sound. I hear nothing. Why does he not cry out, this man? Ah! if any man sought to kill me, I would cry out, I would struggle, I would not suffer. . . . Strike, strike, Naaman, strike, I tell you. . . . No, I hear nothing. There is a

THE DANCER'S REWARD

silence, a terrible silence. Ah! something has fallen upon the ground. I heard something fall. He is afraid, this slave. He is a coward, this slave! Let soldiers be sent. (*She sees the Page of* HERODIAS *and addresses him.*) Come thither, thou wert the friend of him who is dead, wert thou not? Well, I tell thee, there are not dead men enough. Go to the soldiers and bid them go down and bring me the thing I ask, the thing the Tetrarch has promised me, the thing that is mine. (*The Page recoils. She turns to the soldiers.*) Hither, ye soldiers. Get ye down into this cistern and bring me the head of this man. Tetrarch, Tetrarch, command your soldiers that they bring me the head of Jokanaan.

(*A huge black arm, the arm of the Executioner, comes forth from the cistern, bearing on a silver shield the head of* JOKANAAN. SALOMÉ *seizes it.* HEROD *hides his face with his cloak.* HERODIAS *smiles and fans herself. The Nazarenes fall on their knees and begin to pray.*)

Ah! thou wouldst not suffer me to kiss thy mouth, Jokanaan. Well, I will kiss it now. I will bite it with my teeth as one bites a ripe fruit. Yes, I will kiss thy mouth, Jokanaan. I said it; did I not say it? I said it. Ah! I will kiss it now. . . . But, wherefore dost thou not look at me, Jokanaan? Thine eyes that were so terrible, so full of rage and scorn, are shut now. Wherefore are they shut? Open thine eyes! Lift up thine eyelids, Jokanaan! Wherefore dost thou not look at me? Art thou afraid of me, Jokanaan, that thou wilt not look at me? . . . And thy tongue, that was like a red snake darting poison, it moves no more, it speaks no words, Jokanaan, that scarlet viper that spat its venom upon me. It is strange, is it not? How is it that the red viper stirs no longer? . . . Thou wouldst have none of me, Jokanaan. Thou rejectedst me. Thou didst speak evil words against me. Thou didst bear thyself toward me as to a harlot, as to a woman that is a wanton, to me, Salomé, daughter of Herodias, Princess of Judæa! Well, I still live, but thou art dead, and thy head belongs to me. I can do with it what I will. I can throw it to the dogs and to the birds of the air. That which the dogs leave, the birds of the air shall devour. . . . Ah, Jokanaan, thou wert the man that I loved alone among men. All other men were hateful to me. But thou wert beautiful! Thy body

THE CLIMAX
A different version, which appeared in The Studio. No. 1, *of April, 1893, was probably the drawing which resulted in the commission to illustrate Salomé*

was a column of ivory set upon feet of silver. It was a garden full of doves and lilies of silver. It was a tower of silver decked with shields of ivory. There was nothing in the world so white as thy body. There was nothing in the world so black as thy hair. In the whole world there was nothing so red as thy mouth. Thy voice was a censer that scattered strange perfumes, and when I looked on thee I heard a strange music. Ah! wherefore didst thou not look at me, Jokanaan? With the cloak of thine hands and with the cloak of thy blasphemies thou didst hide thy face. Thou didst put upon thine eyes the covering of him who would see his God. Well, thou hast seen thy God, Jokanaan, but me, me, thou didst never see. If thou hadst seen me thou hadst loved me. I saw thee, and I loved thee. Oh, how I loved thee! I love thee yet, Jokanaan, I love only thee. . . . I am athirst for thy beauty; I am hungry for thy body; and neither wine nor apples can appease my desire. What shall I do now, Jokanaan? Neither the floods nor the great waters can quench my passion. I was a princess, and thou didst scorn me. I was a virgin, and thou didst take my virginity from me. I was chaste, and thou didst fill my veins with fire. . . . Ah! ah! wherefore didst thou not look at me? If thou hadst looked at me thou hadst loved me. Well I know that thou wouldst have loved me, and the mystery of love is greater than the mystery of death.

HEROD: She is monstrous, thy daughter, I tell thee she is monstrous. In truth, what she has done is a great crime. I am sure that it is. A crime against some unknown God.

HERODIAS: I am well pleased with my daughter. She has done well. And I would stay here now.

HEROD (*Rising*): Ah! There speaks my brother's wife! Come! I will not stay in this place. Come, I tell thee. Surely some terrible thing will befall. Manasseh, Issadar, Zias, put out the torches. I will not look at things, I will not suffer things to look at me. Put out the torches! Hide the moon! Hide the stars! Let us hide ourselves in our palace, Herodias. I begin to be afraid.

(*The slaves put out the torches. The stars disappear. A great cloud crosses the moon and conceals it completely. The* stage becomes quite dark. The Tetrarch begins to climb the staircase.)

THE VOICE OF SALOMÉ : Ah! I have kissed thy mouth, Jokanaan, I have kissed thy mouth. There was a bitter taste on my lips. Was it the taste of blood? . . . Nay; but perchance it was the taste of love. . . . They say that love hath a bitter taste. . . . But what matter? what matter? I have kissed thy mouth.

HEROD (*Turning round and seeing* SALOMÉ) : Kill that woman!

(*The soldiers rush forward and crush beneath their shields* SALOMÉ, *daughter of* HERODIAS, *Princess of Judæa.*)

CURTAIN

TAILPIECE
  An enormous powderpuff and box as Salomé's final resting place is Beardsley's final satiric thrust

PHRASES AND PHILOSOPHIES FOR THE USE OF THE YOUNG[1]

The first duty in life is to be as artificial as possible. What the second duty is no one has as yet discovered.

Wickedness is a myth invented by good people to account for the curious attractiveness of others.

If the poor only had profiles there would be no difficulty in solving the problem of poverty.

Those who see any difference between soul and body have neither.

A really well-made buttonhole is the only link between Art and Nature.

Religions die when they are proved to be true. Science is the record of dead religions.

The well-bred contradict other people. The wise contradict themselves.

Nothing that actually occurs is of the smallest importance.

Dullness is the coming of age of seriousness.

In all unimportant matters, style, not sincerity, is the essential. In all important matters, style, not sincerity, is the essential.

If one tells the truth, one is sure, sooner or later, to be found out.

Pleasure is the only thing one should live for. Nothing ages like happiness.

It is only by not paying one's bills that one can hope to live in the memory of the commercial classes.

[1] These epigrams appeared at the beginning of *The Chameleon*. (See note 3 of the Introduction.)

No crime is vulgar, but all vulgarity is crime. Vulgarity is the conduct of others.

Only the shallow know themselves.

Time is waste of money.

One should always be a little improbable.

There is a fatality about all good resolutions. They are invariably made too soon.

The only way to atone for being occasionally a little over-dressed is by being always absolutely over-educated.

To be premature is to be perfect.

Any preoccupation with ideas of what is right or wrong in conduct shows an arrested intellectual development.

Ambition is the last refuge of the failure.

A truth ceases to be true when more than one person believes in it.

In examinations the foolish ask questions that the wise cannot answer.

Greek dress was in its essence inartistic. Nothing should reveal the body but the body.

One should either be a work of art, or wear a work of art.

It is only the superficial qualities that last. Man's deeper nature is soon found out.

Industry is the root of all ugliness.

The ages live in history through their anachronisms.

It is only the gods who taste of death. Apollo has passed

away, but Hyacinth,[2] whom men say he slew, lives on.
Nero and Narcissus are always with us.

The old believe everything: the middle-aged suspect everything: the young know everything.

The condition of perfection is idleness: the aim of perfection
is youth.

Only the great masters of style ever succeed in being obscure.

There is something tragic about the enormous number of
young men there are in England at the present moment
who start life with perfect profiles, and end by adopting
some useful profession.

To love oneself is the beginning of a life-long romance.

SYMPHONY IN YELLOW

An omnibus across the bridge
    Crawls like a yellow butterfly,
    And, here and there, a passer-by
Shows like a little restless midge.

Big barges full of yellow hay
    Are moored against the shadowy wharf,
    And, like a yellow silken scarf,
The thick fog hangs along the quay.

The yellow leaves begin to fade
    And flutter from the Temple elms,
    And at my feet the pale green Thames
Lies like a rod of rippled jade.

[2] See Olive Custance's "Hyacinthus" and Lord Alfred Douglas' "Rejected."

THE HARLOT'S HOUSE

We caught the tread of dancing feet,
We loitered down the moonlit street,
And stopped beneath the Harlot's House.
Inside, above the din and fray,
We heard the loud musicians play
The *Treues Liebes Herz* of Strauss.

Like strange mechanical grotesques,
Making fantastic arabesques,
The shadows raced across the blind.
We watched the ghostly dancers spin,
To sound of horn and violin,
Like black leaves wheeling in the wind.

Like wire-pulled Automatons,
Slim silhouetted skeletons
Went sidling through the slow quadrille,
Then took each other by the hand,
And danced a stately saraband;
Their laughter echoed thin and shrill.

Sometimes a clock-work puppet pressed
A phantom lover to her breast,
Sometimes they seemed to try and sing.
Sometimes a horrible Marionette
Came out and smoked its cigarette
Upon the steps like a live thing.

Then turning to my love I said,
"The dead are dancing with the dead,
The dust is whirling with the dust."
But she, she heard the violin,
And left my side and entered in:
Love passed into the House of Lust.

Then suddenly the tune went false,
   The dancers wearied of the waltz,
The shadows ceased to wheel and whirl,
   And down the long and silent street,
   The dawn with silver-sandalled feet,
Crept like a frightened girl.

IMPRESSION DU MATIN

The Thames nocturne of blue and gold
   Changed to a Harmony in gray:
   A bare with ochre-colored hay
Dropt from the wharf: and chill and cold

The yellow fog came creeping down
   The bridges, till the houses' walls
   Seemed changed to shadows, and St. Paul's
Loomed like a bubble o'er the town.

Then suddenly arose the clang
   Of waking life; the streets were stirred
   With country wagons: and a bird
Flew to the glistening roofs and sang.

But one pale woman all alone,
   The daylight kissing her wan hair,
   Loitered beneath the gas lamps' flare,
With lips of flame and heart of stone.

HÉLAS!

To drift with every passion till my soul
Is a stringed lute on which all winds can play,
Is it for this that I have given away

Mine ancient wisdom, and austere control?—
Methinks my life is a twice-written scroll
Scrawled over on some boyish holiday
With idle songs for pipe and virelay
Which do but mar the secret of the whole.
Surely there was a time I might have trod
The sunlit heights, and from life's dissonance
Struck one clear chord to reach the ears of God;
Is that time dead? lo! with a little rod
I did but touch the honey of romance—[1]
And must I lose a soul's inheritance?

[1] An allusion to Jonathan's reply to Saul in the First Book of Samuel (14:43): "I did but taste a little honey with the end of the rod that was in mine hand, and lo! I must die." Wilde's poem—with its phallic suggestion and alteration of the Biblical passage—denies moral consequences. Pater uses the entire Biblical passage in his essay on Winckelmann in *The Renaissance*, perhaps the "source" of Wilde's poem.

Theodore Wratislaw

[1 8 7 1 – 1 9 3 3]

From CAPRICES [1893]

Highly derivative, Wratislaw's verse embodies such characteristic themes of the Decadents as artifice, perversity, satiety, and the beauty of evil, while displaying such wares as
exotic perfumes (opoponax and frangipani), music halls,
fetid hothouses, and tainted orchids. Reviewing *Caprices*, the
New York *Critic* (June, 1894) identified Wratislaw as a
Symbolist, a term used with little differentiation from "Decadent" in the late nineteenth century:

> *The aim of every writer in this school is to say as much
> about nothing as will delude one into thinking it is some-
> thing. Most of Mr. Wratislaw's Caprices are evidently the
> outcome of wine, women, song, and insomnia.*

OPOPONAX

Blonde perfume of the painted girl!
You where the heated dancers whirl
In mazes of the midnight ball
Or in the glittering music-hall,
Uplift your rich and cloying scent
Until the banal blandishment

Of whispers and inviting eyes
Seems tempting even to the wise.
But here your honeyed vapours bring
To me in solitude the ring
Of certain voices and the glance
Of eyelids fluttered in the dance
That once I knew: and bring again
The memories of ancient pain,
Of burning day and rose-red night . . .
Till I forget them in delight
Of your superb luxurious fume
About the scented curtained room.

SATIETY

I weary of the heat of hell,
The perfumed palace of thy love;
I need the cliff, the bubbling well,
The wind-swept grass, the blue above.

I weary of the panting dawn
That finds mine arms encircling thee;
I seek the silent mountain lawn,
The waking murmur of the sea.

I weary of the tangled hair,
The kiss, the passionate clasp, the sigh;
I pass into the keen sweet air,
The vague immensity of sky.

FRANGIPANI

Perfume! That lingerest round the throat,
Between the breasts and in the hair
I kiss, and risest up to float
About the room, a southern note
Of sultry isles and swooning air,

Thou leavest on the languid skin
Outworn with nights of amorous toil,
A spice of health that blossoms in
Hot lands that tropic fragrance win
From marvellous flowers and scented oil.

Thou bring'st from far away to me
The savour of spice and southern palm,
Of naked wild-foot girls that flee
By sunlit fountains and the calm
Low murmur of a burning sea.

PALM SUNDAY

The clouds of incense mounting in the air,
    The heavy fervent smell,
Palm-branches waving by the altar-stair,
    While we redeemed from hell,

We knelt together humbly, she and I,
    Before the red-stained East,
To seek for mercy from our sin, as high
    The purple-vestured priest

Held up the chalice to the face of God,
    And a long silence fell,
Three times and as the wine became God's blood
    Thrice rang the smitten bell.

Then like two slaves regaining liberty,
    When the long mass was done,
With prayer and sadness left behind us, we
    Emerged into the sun.

Forgot what hearts had felt or eyes had seen
    And gave ourselves to mark
Friends' faces as we talked and strolled between
    The toilettes of Hyde Park.

From ORCHIDS [1896]

ORCHIDS

Orange and purple, shot with white and mauve,
Such in a greenhouse wet with tropic heat
One sees these delicate flowers whose parents throve
In some Pacific island's hot retreat.

Their ardent colours that betray the rank
Fierce hotbed of corruption whence they rose
Please eyes that long for stranger sweets than prank
Wild meadow-blooms and what the garden shows.

Exotic flowers! How great is my delight
To watch your petals curiously wrought,
To lie among your splendours day and night
Lost in a subtle dream of subtler thought.

Bathed in your clamorous orchestra of hues,
The palette of your perfumes, let me sleep
While your mesmeric presences diffuse
Weird dreams: and then bizarre sweet rhymes shall creep

Forth from my brain and slowly form and make
Sweet poems as a weaving spider spins,
A shrine of loves that laugh and swoon and ache,
A temple of coloured sorrows and perfumed sins!

WHITE LILIES

Flowers rare and sweet I sent, whose delicate white
Should, grouping at her corsage, interlace
Their purity with her corrupted grace,
With the full throat and mouth of my delight.

Evil design! To see the pale flowers slight
The beauty of the worn and powdered face,

Mingling their costly virtue with the trace
Of ancient loves that live in time's despite.

How soon they died, poor blossoms! at her throat
Ere of the last valse died the last sad note:
No more than love of her meant to endure,

For all the savour of her lips, the spice
Of her frail spirit steeped in cultured vice,
Gracefully bad and delicately impure!

SONNET MACABRE

I love you for the grief that lurks within
Your languid spirit, and because you wear
Corruption with a vague and childish air,
And with your beauty know the depths of sin;

Because shame cuts and holds you like a gin,
And virtue dies in you slain by despair,
Since evil has you tangled in its snare
And triumphs on the soul good cannot win.

I love you since you know remorse and tears,
And in your troubled loveliness appears
The spot of ancient crimes that writhe and hiss:

I love you for your hands that calm and bless,
The perfume of your sad and slow caress,
The avid poison of your subtle kiss.

HOTHOUSE FLOWERS

I hate the flower of wood or common field.
I cannot love the primrose nor regret
The death of any shrinking violet,
Nor even the cultured garden's banal yield.

The silver lips of lilies virginal,
The full deep bosom of the enchanted rose
Please less than flowers glass-hid from frosts and snows
For whom an alien heat makes festival.

I love those flowers reared by man's careful art,
Of heady scents and colours: strong of heart
Or weak that die beneath the touch or knife,

Some rich as sin and some as virtue pale,
And some as subtly infamous and frail
As she whose love still eats my soul and life.

William Butler Yeats

[1865–1939]

THE LAKE ISLE OF INNISFREE[1]

I will arise and go now, and go to Innisfree,
And a small cabin build there, of clay and wattles made;
Nine bean rows will I have there, a hive for the honey bee,
And live alone in the bee-loud glade.

And I shall have some peace there, for peace comes dropping
    slow,
Dropping from the veils of the morning to where the cricket
    sings;
There midnight's all a glimmer, and noon a purple glow,
And evening full of the linnet's wings.

I will arise and go now, for always night and day
I hear lake water lapping with low sounds by the shore;

[1] Of Innisfree, in Lough Gill, Sligo, Yeats wrote in his autobiography:
"My father had read to me some passage out of *Walden*, and I
planned to live some day in a cottage on a little island called Innisfree . . ."

While I stand on the roadway, or on the pavements gray,
I hear it in the deep heart's core.

[1890]

THE WHITE BIRDS

I would that we were, my beloved, white birds on the foam
    of the sea!
We tire of the flame of the meteor, before it can fade and
    flee;
And the flame of the blue star of twilight, hung low on the
    rim of the sky,
Has awaked in our hearts, my beloved, a sadness that may
    not die.

A weariness comes from those dreamers, dew dabbled, the
    lily and rose;
Ah, dream not of them, my beloved, the flame of the meteor
    that goes,
Or the flame of the blue star that lingers hung low in the fall
    of the dew:
For I would we were changed to white birds on the wander-
    ing foam: I and you!

I am haunted by numberless islands, and many a Danaan
    shore,
Where Time would surely forget us, and Sorrow come near
    us no more;
Soon far from the rose and the lily, and fret of the flames
    would we be,
Were we only white birds, my beloved, buoyed out on the
    foam of the sea!

[1892]

ROSA MUNDI[1]

Who dreamed that beauty passes like a dream?
For these red lips with all their mournful pride—
Mournful that no new wonder may betide—
Troy passed away in one high funeral gleam,
And Usna's children died.[2]

We and the labouring world are passing by:
Amid men's souls that day by day give place,
More fleeting than the sea's foam-fickle face,
Under the passing stars, foam of the sky,
Lives on this lonely face.

Bow down, archangels, in your dim abode;
Before ye were, or any hearts to beat,
Weary and kind one stood beside His seat;
He made the worlds to be a grassy road
Before her wandering feet.

[1892]

TO THE ROSE UPON THE ROOD OF TIME

Red Rose, proud Rose, sad Rose of all my days!
Come near me, while I sing the ancient ways:
Cuchulain[1] battling with the bitter tide;
The Druid, gray, wood-nurtured, quiet-eyed,

---

[1] Retitled "The Rose of the World" in *The Countess Kathleen and Various Legends and Lyrics* (1892). The rose, conventional symbol of Love, is also associated with Ireland and mystical beauty—"the Eternal Rose of Beauty and Peace," as Yeats said, "but suffering with man and not as something pursued and seen from afar."
[2] Betrayed and killed by Conchobar, king of Ulster.
[1] Legendary hero of the early Irish epics.

Who cast round Fergus² dreams, and ruin untold;
And thine own sadness, whereof stars, grown old
In dancing silver sandalled on the sea,
Sing in their high and lonely melody.
Come near, that no more blinded by man's fate,
I find under the boughs of love and hate,
In all poor foolish things that live a day,
Eternal beauty wandering on her way.
Come near, come near, come near—Ah, leave me still
A little space for the rose-breath to fill!
Lest I no more hear common things that crave;
The weak worm hiding down in its small cave,
The field mouse running by me in the grass,
And heavy mortal hopes that toil and pass;
But seek alone to hear the strange things said
By God to the bright hearts of those long dead,
And learn to chaunt a tongue men do not know.
Come near; I would, before my time to go,
Sing of old Eire and the ancient ways:
Red Rose, proud Rose, sad Rose of all my days.

[1892]

O'SULLIVAN RUA TO
MARY LAVELL¹

When my arms wrap you round, I press
My heart upon the loveliness
That has long faded in the world;

² Bard of the Fenians, warriors led by Finn, who defended Ireland
against possible invaders.
¹ Appeared in *Wind Among the Reeds* (1899) as "Michael Robartes
Remembers Forgotten Beauty" and in other printings as "He Remembers Forgotten Beauty." O'Sullivan Rua, like Aedh (see "Aedh Wishes
for the Cloths of Heaven") and Michael Robartes, represents, said
Yeats in the notes he added to *Wind Among the Reeds*, a principle of
the mind (or a facet of Yeats himself). Robartes is "the pride of the
imagination brooding upon the greatness of its possessions."

The jewelled crowns that kings have hurled
In shadowy pools, when armies fled;
The love-tales wove with silken thread
By dreaming ladies upon cloth
That has made fat the murderous moth;
The roses that of old time were
Woven by ladies in their hair,
Before they drowned their lovers' eyes
In twilight shaken with low sighs;
The dew-cold lilies ladies bore
Through many a sacred corridor
Where a so sleepy incense rose
That only God's eyes did not close:
For that dim brow and lingering hand
Come from a more dream-heavy land,
A more dream-heavy hour than this;
And, when you sigh from kiss to kiss,
I hear pale Beauty sighing too,
For hours when all must fade like dew
Till there be naught but throne on throne
Of seraphs, brooding, each alone,
A sword upon his iron knees
On her most lonely mysteries.

[1896]

THE SECRET ROSE[1]

Far off, most secret, and inviolate Rose,
Enfold me in my hour of hours; where those
Who sought thee in the Holy Sepulchre,
Or in the wine vat, dwell beyond the stir
And tumult of defeated dreams; and deep
Among pale eyelids, heavy with the sleep
Men have named beauty. Thy great leaves enfold

[1] First appeared under the title "O'Sullivan Rua to the Secret Rose" in *The Savoy*, September, 1896, and later also as "To the Secret Rose."

The ancient beards, the helms of ruby and gold
Of the crowned Magi; and the king whose eyes
Saw the Pierced Hands and Rood of elder rise
In druid vapour and make the torches dim;
Till vain frenzy awoke and he died; and him
Who met Fand walking among flaming dew
By a gray shore where the wind never blew,
And lost the world and Emer[2] for a kiss;
And him who drove the gods out of their liss,
And till a hundred morns had flowered red,
Feasted and wept the barrows of his dead;
And the proud dreaming king who flung the crown
And sorrow away, and calling bard and clown
Dwelt among wine-stained wanderers in deep woods;
And him who sold tillage, and house, and goods,
And sought through lands and islands numberless years,
Until he found with laughter and with tears,
A woman of so shining loveliness,
That men threshed corn at midnight by a tress,
A little stolen tress. I, too, await
The hour of thy great wind of love and hate.
When shall the stars be blown about the sky,
Like the sparks blown out of a smithy, and die?
Surely thine hour has come, thy great wind blows,
Far off, most secret, and inviolate Rose?

[1896]

THE SONG OF WANDERING AENGUS[1]

I went out to the hazel wood,
Because a fire was in my head,

[2] Wife of Cuchulain.
[1] "Angus—god of youth, beauty, and poetry. He reigned in Tir-nam-Oge, the country of the young" [Yeats's note]. The poem's original title was "A Mad Song."

And cut and peeled a hazel wand,
And hooked a berry to a thread;
And when white moths were on the wing,
And moth-like stars were flickering out,
I dropped the berry in a stream
And caught a little silver trout.

When I had laid it on the floor
I went to blow the fire a-flame,
But something rustled on the floor,
And some one called me by my name:

It had become a glimmering girl
With apple blossom in her hair
Who called me by my name and ran
And faded through the brightening air.

Though I am old with wandering
Through hollow lands and hilly lands,
I will find out where she has gone,
And kiss her lips and take her hands;
And walk among long dappled grass,
And pluck till time and times are done,
The silver apples of the moon,
The golden apples of the sun.

[1897]

AEDH² WISHES FOR THE CLOTHS OF HEAVEN

Had I the heavens' embroidered cloths,
Enwrought with golden and silver light,
The blue and the dim and the dark cloths
Of night and light and the half light,

² The Gaelic word for "fire," Aedh is the symbolic representation of the rejected Lover.

I would spread the cloths under your feet:
But I, being poor, have only my dreams;
I have spread my dreams under your feet;
Tread softly because you tread on my dreams.

[1899]

APPENDIX

Walter Pater

[1 8 3 9 – 1 8 9 4]

From STUDIES IN THE HISTORY OF THE RENAISSANCE [1873][1]

PREFACE

Many attempts have been made by writers on art and poetry to define beauty in the abstract, to express it in the most general terms, to find a universal formula for it. The value of such attempts has most often been in the suggestive and penetrating things said by the way. Such discussions help us very little to enjoy what has been well done in art or poetry, to discriminate between what is more and what is less excellent in them, or to use words like beauty, excellence, art, poetry,

[1] Changed to *The Renaissance: Studies in Art and Poetry* in subsequent editions.

with more meaning than they would otherwise have. Beauty, like all other qualities presented to human experience, is relative; and the definition of it becomes unmeaning and useless in proportion to its abstractness. To define beauty, not in the most abstract, but in the most concrete terms possible, to find, not a universal formula for it, but the formula which expresses most adequately this or that special manifestation of it, is the aim of the true student of æsthetics.

"To see the object as in itself it really is," [2] has been justly said to be the aim of all true criticism whatever; and in æsthetic criticism the first step toward seeing one's object as it really is, is to know one's own impression as it really is, to discriminate it, to realize it distinctly. The objects with which æsthetic criticism deals, music, poetry, artistic and accomplished forms of human life, are indeed receptacles of so many powers or forces; they possess, like natural elements, so many virtues or qualities. What is this song or picture, this engaging personality presented in life or in a book, to *me*? What effect does it really produce on me? Does it give me pleasure? And if so, what sort or degree of pleasure? How is my nature modified by its presence, and under its influence? The answers to these questions are the original facts with which the æsthetic critic has to do; and, as in the study of light, of morals, of number, one must realize such primary data for oneself, or not at all. And he who experiences these impressions strongly, and drives directly at the discrimination and analysis of them, need not trouble himself with the abstract question what beauty is in itself, or what its exact relation to truth or experience—metaphysical questions, as unprofitable as metaphysical questions elsewhere. He may pass them all by as being, answerable or not, of no interest to him.

The æsthetic critic, then, regards all the objects with which he has to do, all works of art, and the fairer forms of nature and human life, as powers or forces producing pleasurable sensations, each of a more or less peculiar and unique kind. This influence he feels, and wishes to explain, analyzing it,

---

[2] From the concluding paragraph of Matthew Arnold's second lecture in *On Translating Homer* (1861).

and reducing it to its elements. To him, the picture, the land-scape, the engaging personality in life or in a book, *La Gio-conda*,[3] the hills of Carrara,[4] Pico of Mirandola,[5] are valua-ble for their virtues, as we say in speaking of a herb, a wine, a gem; for the property each has of affecting one with a special, unique impression of pleasure. Our education be-comes complete in proportion as our susceptibility to these impressions increases in depth and variety. And the function of the æsthetic critic is to distinguish, analyze, and separate from its adjuncts, the virtue by which a picture, a landscape, a fair personality in life or in a book, produces this special impression of beauty or pleasure, to indicate what the source of that impression is, and under what conditions it is experi-enced. His end is reached when he has disengaged that vir-tue, and noted it, as a chemist notes some natural element, for himself and others; and the rule for those who would reach this end is stated with great exactness in the words of a recent critic of Sainte-Beuve: *De se borner à connaître de près les belles choses, et à s'en nourrir en exquis amateurs, en humanistes accomplis.*[6]

What is important, then, is not that the critic should pos-sess a correct abstract definition of beauty for the intellect, but a certain kind of temperament, the power of being deeply moved by the presence of beautiful objects. He will remember always that beauty exists in many forms. To him all periods, types, schools of taste, are in themselves equal. In all ages there have been some excellent workmen, and some excellent work done. The question he asks is always: In whom did the stir, the genius, the sentiment of the period find itself? Who was the receptacle of its refinement, its ele-

---

[3] Leonardo da Vinci's famous portrait, better known as the *Mona Lisa*, which hangs in the Louvre in Paris. It was believed that Lady Lisa, third wife of Francisco del Giocondo, of Florence, sat for the portrait.

[4] In northern Italy, where the famous marble is obtained.

[5] Giovanni Pico, Count of Mirandola (1463–94), Italian humanist who is the subject of one of Pater's essays in *The Renaissance*.

[6] "To confine themselves to knowing beautiful objects at first-hand and to nourish themselves on these as refined amateurs and accom-plished humanists."

vation, its taste? "The ages are all equal," says William Blake, "but genius is always above its age."

Often it will require great nicety to disengage this virtue from the commoner elements with which it may be found in combination. Few artists, not Goethe or Byron even, work quite cleanly, casting off all debris, and leaving us only what the heat of their imagination has wholly fused and transformed. Take for instance the writings of Wordsworth. The heat of his genius, entering into the substance of his work, has crystallized a part, but only a part, of it; and in that great mass of verse there is much which might well be forgotten. But scattered up and down it, sometimes fusing and transforming entire compositions, like the stanzas on *Resolution and Independence,* and the ode on the *Recollections of Early Childhood,*[7] sometimes, as if at random, turning a fine crystal here and there, in a matter it does not wholly search through and transform, we trace the action of his unique, incommunicable faculty, that strange, mystical sense of a life in natural things, and of man's life as a part of nature, drawing strength and color and character from local influences, from the hills and streams, and from natural sights and sounds. Well! That is the *virtue,* the active principle in Wordsworth's poetry; and then the function of the critic of Wordsworth is to trace that active principle, to disengage it, to mark the degree in which it penetrates his verse.

The subjects of the following studies are taken from the history of the Renaissance, and touch what I think the chief points in that complex, many-sided movement. I have explained in the first of them what I understand by the word, giving it a much wider scope than was intended by those who originally used it to denote only that revival of classical antiquity in the fifteenth century, which was but one of many results of a general excitement and enlightening of the human mind, and of which the great aim and achievements of what, as Christian art, is often falsely opposed to the Renaissance, were another result. This outbreak of the human spirit may be traced far into the Middle Ages itself, with its qualities already clearly pronounced, the care for physical

[7] The complete title is "Ode: Intimations of Immortality from Recollections of Early Childhood."

beauty, the worship of the body, the breaking down of those limits which the religious system of the Middle Ages imposed on the heart and the imagination. I have taken as an example of this movement, this earlier Renaissance within the Middle Ages itself, and as an expression of its qualities, two little compositions in early French; not because they constitute the best possible expression of them, but because they help the unity of my series, inasmuch as the Renaissance ends also in France, in French poetry, in a phase of which the writings of Joachim du Bellay are in many ways the most perfect illustration; the Renaissance thus putting forth in France an aftermath, a wonderful later growth, the products of which have to the full the subtle and delicate sweetness which belongs to a refined and comely decadence; just as its earliest phases have the freshness which belongs to all periods of growth in art, the charm of *ascesis*,[8] of the austere and serious girding of the loins in youth.

But it is in Italy, in the fifteenth century, that the interest of the Renaissance mainly lies, in that solemn fifteenth century which can hardly be studied too much, not merely for its positive results in the things of the intellect and the imagination, its concrete works of art, its special and prominent personalities, with their profound æsthetic charm, but for its general spirit and character, for the ethical qualities of which it is a consummate type.

The various forms of intellectual activity which together make up the culture of an age, move for the most part from different starting points, and by unconnected roads. As products of the same generation they partake indeed of a common character, and unconsciously illustrate each other; but of the producers themselves, each group is solitary, gaining what advantage or disadvantage there may be in intellectual isolation. Art and poetry, philosophy and the religious life, and that other life of refined pleasure and action in the open places of the world, are each of them confined to its own circle of ideas, and those who prosecute either of them are generally little curious of the thoughts of others. There come, however, from time to time, eras of more favorable

[8] Pater defines this term in his essay "Style" as "self-restraint, a skilful economy of means."

conditions, in which the thoughts of men draw nearer together than is their wont, and the many interests of the intellectual world combine in one complete type of general culture. The fifteenth century in Italy is one of these happier
eras; and what is sometimes said of the Age of Pericles is
true of that of Lorenzo[9]—it is an age productive in personalities, many-sided, centralized, complete. Here, artists and
philosophers and those whom the action of the world has
elevated and made keen do not live in isolation, but breathe
a common air, and catch light and heat from each other's
thoughts. There is a spirit of general elevation and enlighten-
ment in which all alike communicate. It is the unity of this
spirit which gives unity to all the various products of the Renaissance; and it is to this intimate alliance with mind, this
participation in the best thoughts which that age produced,
that the art of Italy in the fifteenth century owes much of its
grave dignity and influence.

I have added an essay on Winckelmann,[10] as not incongruous with the studies which precede it, because Winckelmann,
coming in the eighteenth century, really belongs in spirit to
an earlier age. By his enthusiasm for the things of the intellect and the imagination for their own sake, by his Hellenism, his lifelong struggle to attain to the Greek spirit, he is in
sympathy with the humanists of an earlier century. He is the
last fruit of the Renaissance, and explains in a striking way
its motive and tendencies.

[LA GIOCONDA]

La Gioconda[11] is, in the truest sense, Leonardo's masterpiece, the revealing instance of his mode of thought and
work. In suggestiveness, only the *Melancholia* of Dürer[12] is

[9] Pericles, Athenian statesman of the fifth century B.C.; Lorenzo de'
Medici (1449–92), called "The Magnificent," Florentine prince and
patron of the arts.
[10] Johann Joachim Winckelmann (1717–68), the renowned German
archaeologist and historian of classical art.
[11] See note 3.
[12] Albrecht Dürer (1471–1528), German painter and engraver.

comparable to it; and no crude symbolism disturbs the effect of its subdued and graceful mystery. We all know the face and hands of the figure, set in its marble chair, in that cirque of fantastic rocks, as in some faint light under sea. Perhaps of all ancient pictures time has chilled it least.[13] As often happens with works in which invention seems to reach its limit, there is an element in it given to, not invented by, the master. In that inestimable folio of drawings, once in the possession of Vasari, were certain designs by Verrocchio, faces of such impressive beauty that Leonardo in his boyhood copied them many times. It is hard not to connect with these designs of the elder, by-passed master, as with its germinal principle, the unfathomable smile, always with a touch of something sinister in it, which plays over all Leonardo's work. Besides, the picture is a portrait. From childhood we see this image defining itself on the fabric of his dreams; and but for express historical testimony, we might fancy that this was but his ideal lady, embodied and beheld at last. What was the relationship of a living Florentine to this creature of his thought? By means of what strange affinities had the person and the dream grown up thus apart, and yet so closely together? Present from the first, incorporeal in Leonardo's thought, dimly traced in the designs of Verrocchio, she is found present at last in Il Giocondo's house. That there is much of mere portraiture in the picture is attested by the legend that by artificial means, the presence of mimes and flute players, that subtle expression was protracted on the face. Again, was it in four years, and by renewed labor never really completed, or in four months, and as by stroke of magic, that the image was projected?

The presence that thus rose so strangely beside the waters, is expressive of what in the ways of a thousand years man had come to desire. Hers is the head upon which all "the ends of the world are come," and the eyelids are a little weary. It is a beauty wrought out from within upon the flesh, the deposit, little cell by cell, of strange thoughts and fantastic reveries and exquisite passions. Set it for a moment beside

[13] "Yet for Vasari [1511–74, Italian painter, architect, and art historian] there was some further magic of crimson in the lips and cheeks, lost to us" [Pater's note].

one of those white Greek goddesses or beautiful women of antiquity, and how would they be troubled by this beauty, into which the soul with all its maladies has passed? All the thoughts and experience of the world have etched and molded there, in that which they have of power to refine and make expressive the outward form, the animalism of Greece, the lust of Rome, the reverie of the Middle Ages with its spiritual ambition and imaginative loves, the return of the pagan world, the sins of the Borgias. She is older than the rocks among which she sits; like the vampire, she has been dead many times, and learned the secrets of the grave; and has been a diver in deep seas, and keeps their fallen day about her; and trafficked for strange webs with Eastern merchants; and, as Leda, was the mother of Helen of Troy, and, as Saint Anne, the mother of Mary; and all this has been to her but as the sound of lyres and flutes, and lives only in the delicacy with which it has molded the changing lineaments, and tinged the eyelids and the hands. The fancy of a perpetual life, sweeping together ten thousand experiences, is an old one; and modern thought has conceived the idea of humanity as wrought upon by, and summing up in itself, all modes of thought and life. Certainly Lady Lisa might stand as the embodiment of the old fancy, the symbol of the modern idea.

CONCLUSION

Λέγει που 'Ηράκλειτος ὅτι πάντα χωρεῖ καὶ οὐδὲν μένει [14]

To regard all things and principles of things as inconstant modes or fashions has more and more become the tendency of modern thought. Let us begin with that which is without —our physical life. Fix upon it in one of its more exquisite intervals, the moment, for instance, of delicious recoil from the flood of water in summer heat. What is the whole physical life in that moment but a combination of natural elements to which science gives their names? But these elements,

[14] Pater's translation in his *Plato and Platonism*: "Heraclitus says, 'All things give way; nothing remaineth.'"

phosphorus and lime and delicate fibers, are present not in the human body alone: we detect them in places most remote from it. Our physical life is a perpetual motion of them—the passage of the blood, the wasting and repairing of the lenses of the eye, the modification of the tissues of the brain under every ray of light and sound—processes which science reduces to simpler and more elementary forces. Like the elements of which we are composed, the action of these forces extends beyond us: it rusts iron and ripens corn. Far out on every side of us those elements are broadcast, driven in many currents; and birth and gesture and death and the springing of violets from the grave are but a few out of ten thousand resultant combinations. That clear, perpetual outline of face and limb is but an image of ours, under which we group them—a design in a web, the actual threads of which pass out beyond it. This at least of flamelike our life has, that it is but the concurrence, renewed from moment to moment, of forces parting sooner or later on their ways.

Or if we begin with the inward world of thought and feeling, the whirlpool is still more rapid, the flame more eager and devouring. There it is no longer the gradual darkening of the eye, and fading of color from the wall—the movement of the shoreside, where the water flows down indeed, though in apparent rest—but the race of the midstream, a drift of momentary acts of sight and passion and thought. At first sight experience seems to bury us under a flood of external objects, pressing upon us with a sharp and importunate reality, calling us out of ourselves in a thousand forms of action. But when reflection begins to play upon those objects they are dissipated under its influence; the cohesive force seems suspended like a trick of magic; each object is loosed into a group of impressions—color, odor, texture—in the mind of the observer. And if we continue to dwell in thought on this world, not of objects in the solidity with which language invests them, but of impressions, unstable, flickering, inconsistent, which burn and are extinguished with our consciousness of them, it contracts still further: the whole scope of observation is dwarfed to the narrow chamber of the individual mind. Experience, already reduced to a swarm of impressions, is ringed round for each one of us by that thick wall of personality through which no real voice has ever pierced on its way to us, or from us to that which we can only conjecture to be without. Every one of those impressions is the impression of the individual in his isolation, each mind keeping as a solitary prisoner its own dream of a world. Analysis goes a step farther still, and assures us that those impressions of the individual mind to which, for each one of us, experience dwindles down, are in perpetual flight; that each of them is limited by time, and that as time is infinitely divisible, each of them is infinitely divisible also; all that is actual in it being a single moment, gone while we try to apprehend it, of which it may ever be more truly said that it has ceased to be than that it is. To such a tremulous wisp constantly reforming itself on the stream, to a single sharp impression, with a sense in it, a relic more or less fleeting of such moments gone by, what is real in our life fines itself down. It is with this movement, with the passage and dissolution of impressions, images, sensations, that analysis leaves off—that continual vanishing away, that strange, perpetual weaving and unweaving of ourselves.

Philosophiren, says Novalis, *ist dephlegmatisiren vivificiren.*[15] The service of philosophy, of speculative culture, toward the human spirit, is to rouse, to startle it to a life of constant and eager observation. Every moment some form grows perfect in hand or face; some tone on the hills or the sea is choicer than the rest; some mood of passion or insight or intellectual excitement is irresistibly real and attractive to us,—for that moment only. Not the fruit of experience, but experience itself, is the end. A counted number of pulses only is given to us of a variegated dramatic life. How may we see in them all that is to be seen in them by the finest senses? How shall we pass most swiftly from point to point, and be present always at the focus where the greatest number of vital forces unite in their purest energy?

To burn always with this hard, gemlike flame, to maintain this ecstasy, is success in life. In a sense it might even be said that our failure is to form habits: for, after all, habit is rela-

[15] "To philosophize is to throw off inertia, to come to life." "Novalis" is the pseudonym of the German Romantic poet and philosopher Friedrich von Hardenberg (1772–1801).

tive to a stereotyped world, and meantime it is only the roughness of the eye that makes any two persons, things, situations, seem alike. While all melts under our feet, we may well grasp at any exquisite passion, or any contribution to knowledge that seems by a lifted horizon to set the spirit free for a moment, or any stirring of the senses, strange dyes, strange colors, and curious odors, or work of the artist's hands, or the face of one's friend. Not to discriminate every moment some passionate attitude in those about us, and in the very brilliancy of their gifts some tragic dividing of forces on their ways, is, on this short day of frost and sun, to sleep before evening. With this sense of the splendor of our experience and of its awful brevity, gathering all we are into one desperate effort to see and touch, we shall hardly have time to make theories about the things we see and touch. What we have to do is to be forever curiously testing new opinions and courting new impressions, never acquiescing in a facile orthodoxy of Comte, or of Hegel, or of our own. Philosophical theories or ideas, as points of view, instruments of criticism, may help us to gather up what might otherwise pass unregarded by us. "Philosophy is the microscope of thought." The theory or idea or system which requires of us the sacrifice of any part of this experience, in consideration of some interest into which we cannot enter, or some abstract theory we have not identified with ourselves, or of what is only conventional, has no real claim upon us.

One of the most beautiful passages in the writings of Rousseau is that in the sixth book of the *Confessions,* where he describes the awakening in him of the literary sense. An undefinable taint of death had clung always about him, and now in early manhood he believed himself smitten by mortal disease. He asked himself how he might make as much as possible of the interval that remained; and he was not biased by anything in his previous life when he decided that it must be by intellectual excitement, which he found just then in the clear, fresh writings of Voltaire. Well! we are all *condamnés,* as Victor Hugo says: we are all under sentence of death but with a sort of indefinite reprieve—*les hommes sont tous condamnés à mort avec des sursis indéfinis:* we have an interval, and then our place knows us no more. Some spend this interval in listlessness, some in high passions, the wisest, at least among "the children of this world," [10] in art and song. For our one chance lies in expanding that interval, in getting as many pulsations as possible into the given time. Great passions may give us this quickened sense of life, ecstasy and sorrow of love, the various forms of enthusiastic activity, disinterested or otherwise, which come naturally to many of us. Only be sure it is passion—that it does yield you this fruit of quickened, multiplied consciousness. Of this wisdom, the poetic passion, the desire of beauty, the love of art for art's sake, has most, for art comes to you, proposing frankly to give nothing but the highest quality to your moments as they pass, and simply for those moments' sake.

[10] From Luke XVI:8: ". . . the children of this world are wiser in their generation than the children of light."

Joris-Karl Huysmans

[1 8 4 8 – 1 9 0 7]

From AGAINST THE GRAIN [1884][1]

So, in a spirit of hate and scorn of his unhappy boyhood, he
had suspended from the ceiling of the room we speak of, a
little cage of silver wire in which a cricket was kept prisoner
to chirp as they had been used to do in old days among the
cinders in the great fireplaces at the Château de Lourps.
Whenever he heard this sound, which he had so often listened to on many an evening of constraint and silence in his
mother's chamber, all the miseries of a wretched and neglected childhood would come crowding before the eye of
memory. At such times, roused from his reveries by the
movements of the woman he was fondling mechanically at
the moment and whose words and laughter interrupted his
thoughts of the past and recalled him to reality, there as he
lay in the pink boudoir, a sudden commotion would shake
his soul, a longing for revenge on dreary hours endured in
former times, a mad craving to befoul with base and carnal
acts his recollections of bygone family life, an overmastering
temptation to assuage his lustful propensities on the soft
cushion of a woman's body, to drain the cup of sensuality to
its last and bitterest dregs.

Other times again, when despondency weighed heavy on

[1] For a discussion of Huysmans' *Against the Grain* (translation of *À
Rebours*), see the Introduction and Arthur Symons' "The Decadent
Movement in Literature."

his spirit, when on rainy Autumn days he felt a sick aversion for everything,—for the streets, for his own house, for the dingy mud-coloured sky, for the stony-looking clouds, he would fly to this refuge, set the cricket's cage swinging gently to and fro and watch its movement repeated *ad infinitum* in the surrounding mirrors, till at last his eyes would grow dazed and he seemed to see the cage itself at rest, but all the room tossing and turning, filling the whole apartment with a dizzy whirl of pink walls.

Then, in the days when Des Esseintes still deemed it incumbent on him to play the eccentric, he had also installed strange and elaborate dispositions of furniture and fittings, partitioning off his salon into a series of niches, each differently hung and carpeted, and each harmonizing in a subtle likeness by a more or less vague similarity of tints, gay or sombre, refined or barbaric, with the special character of the Latin and French books he loved. He would then settle himself down to read in whichever of these recesses displayed in its scheme of decoration the closest correspondence with the intimate essence of the particular book his caprice of the moment led him to peruse.

Last fancy of all, he had prepared a lofty hall in which to receive his tradesmen. These would march in, take seats side by side in a row of church stalls; then he would mount an imposing pulpit and preach them a sermon on dandyism, adjuring his bookmakers and tailors to conform with the most scrupulous fidelity to his commandments in the matter of cut and fashion, threatening them with the penalty of pecuniary excommunication if they failed to follow out to the letter the instructions embodied in his monitories and bulls.

He won a great reputation as an eccentric,—a reputation he crowned by adopting a costume of black velvet worn with a gold-fringed waistcoat and sticking by way of cravat a bunch of Parma violets in the opening of a very low-necked shirt. Then he would invite parties of literary friends to dinners that set all the world talking. In one instance in particular, modelling the entertainment on a banquet of the eighteenth century, he had organized a funeral feast in celebration of the most unmentionable of minor personal calamities. The dining-room was hung with black and looked out on a

strangely metamorphosed garden, the walks being strewn
with charcoal, the little basin in the middle of the lawn bor-
dered with a rim of black basalt and filled with ink; and the
ordinary shrubs superseded by cypresses and pines. The dinner itself was served on a black cloth, decorated with baskets
of violets and scabiosæ and illuminated by candelabra in
which tall tapers flared.

While a concealed orchestra played funeral marches, the
guests were waited on by naked negresses wearing shoes and
stockings of cloth of silver besprinkled with tears.

The viands were served on black-bordered plates,—turtle
soup, Russian black bread, ripe olives from Turkey, caviar,
mule steaks, Frankfurt smoked sausages, game dished up in
sauces coloured to resemble liquorice water and boot-black-
ing, truffles in jelly, chocolate-tinted creams, puddings, nectar-
ines, fruit preserves, mulberries and cherries. The wines were
drunk from dark-tinted glasses,—wines of the Limagne and
Rousillon vintages, wines of Tenedos, the Val de Penas and
Oporto. After the coffee and walnuts came other unusual
beverages, kwas, porter and stout.

The invitations, which purported to be for a dinner in
pious memory of the host's (temporarily) lost virility, were
couched in the regulation phraseology of letters summoning
relatives to attend the obsequies of a defunct kinsman.

But these extravagances, that had once been his boast, had
died a natural death; nowadays his only feeling was one of
self-contempt to remember these puerile and out-of-date displays of eccentricity,—the extraordinary clothes he had
donned and the grotesque decorations he had lavished on his
house. His only thought henceforth was to arrange, for his
personal gratification only and no longer in order to startle
other people, a home that should be comfortable, yet at the
same time rich and rare in its appointments, to contrive himself a peaceful and exquisitely organized abode, specially
adapted to meet the exigencies of the solitary life he proposed to lead.

When at length the new house at Fontenay was ready and
fitted up in accordance with his wishes and intentions by the
architect he had engaged; when nothing else was left save to
settle the scheme of furniture and decoration, once again he

passed in review, carefully and methodically, the whole series of available tints.

What he wanted was colours the effect of which was confirmed and strengthened under artificial light; little he cared even if by daylight they should appear insipid or crude, for he lived practically his whole life at night, holding that then a man was more truly at home, more himself and his own master, and that the mind found its only real excitant and effective stimulation in contact with the shades of evening; moreover, he reaped a special and peculiar satisfaction from finding himself in a room brilliantly lighted up, the only place alive and awake among surrounding houses all buried in sleep and darkness,—a sort of enjoyment that is not free from a touch of vanity, a selfish mode of gratification familiar enough to belated workers when, drawing aside the window curtains, they note how all about them the world lies inert, dumb and dead.

To tell the truth, artifice was in Des Esseintes' philosophy the distinctive mark of human genius.

As he used to say, Nature has had her day; she has definitely and finally tired out by the sickening monotony of her landscapes and skyscapes the patience of refined temperaments. When all is said and done, what a narrow, vulgar affair it all is, like a petty shopkeeper selling one article of goods to the exclusion of all others; what a tiresome store of green fields and leafy trees, what a wearisome commonplace collection of mountains and seas!

In fact, not one of her inventions, deemed so subtle and so wonderful, which the ingenuity of mankind cannot create; no Forest of Fontainebleau, no fairest moonlight landscape but can be reproduced by stage scenery illuminated by the electric light; no waterfall but can be imitated by the proper application of hydraulics, till there is no distinguishing the copy from the original; no mountain crag but painted pasteboard can adequately represent; no flower but well chosen silks and dainty shreds of paper can manufacture the like of!

Yes, there is no denying it, she is in her dotage and has long ago exhausted the simple-minded admiration of the true artist; the time is undoubtedly come when her productions must be superseded by art.

Why, to take the one of all her works which is held to be
the most exquisite, the one of all her creations whose beauty
is by general consent deemed the most original and most
perfect,—woman to wit, have not men, by their own unaided
effort, manufactured a living, yet artificial organism that is
every whit her match from the point of view of plastic
beauty? Does there exist in this world of ours a being, conceived in the joys of fornication and brought to birth amid
the pangs of motherhood, the model, the type of which is
more dazzlingly, more superbly beautiful than that of the
two locomotives lately adopted for service on the Northern
Railroad of France?

One, the Crampton, an adorable blonde, shrill-voiced,
slender-waisted, with her glittering corset of polished brass,
her supple, catlike grace, a fair and fascinating blonde, the
perfection of whose charms is almost terrifying when, stiffen-
ing her muscles of steel, pouring the sweat of steam down
her hot flanks, she sets revolving the puissant circle of her
elegant wheels and darts forth a living thing at the head of
the fast express or racing seaside special!

The other, the Engerth, a massively built, dark-browed
brunette, of harsh, hoarse-toned utterance, with thick-set
loins, panoplied in armour-plating of sheet iron, a giantess
with dishevelled mane of black eddying smoke, with her six
pairs of low, coupled wheels, what overwhelming power
when, shaking the very earth, she takes in tow, slowly, deliberately, the ponderous train of goods waggons.

Of a certainty, among women, frail, fair-skinned beauties
or majestic, brown-locked charmers, no such consummate
types of dainty slimness and of terrifying force are to be
found. Without fear of contradiction may we say: man has
done, in his province, as well as the God in whom he believes.

. . . . . .

[SALOMÉ]

Simultaneously with his craving to escape a hateful world of
degrading restrictions and pruderies, the longing never again

to see pictures representing the human form toiling in Paris between four walls or roaming the streets in search of money, had obtained a more and more complete mastery over his mind.

Having once divorced himself from contemporary existence, he was resolved to suffer in his hermit's cell no spectres of old repugnances and bygone dislikes; accordingly he had chosen only to possess pictures of a subtle, exquisite refinement, instinct with dreams of Antiquity, reminiscent it may be of antique corruption, but at any rate remote from our modern times and modern manners.

He had selected for the diversion of his mind and the delight of his eyes works of a suggestive charm, introducing him to an unfamiliar world, revealing to him traces of new possibilities, stirring the nervous system by erudite phantasies, complicated dreams of horror, visions of careless wickedness and cruelty.

Of all others there was one artist who most ravished him with unceasing transports of pleasure,—Gustave Moreau.

He had purchased his two masterpieces, and night after night he would stand dreaming in front of one of these, a picture of Salomé.

The conception of the work was as follows: A throne, like the high altar of a Cathedral, stood beneath an endless vista of vaulted arches springing from thick-set columns resembling the pillars of a Romanesque building, encased in many coloured brickwork, incrusted with mosaics, set with lapis lazuli and sardonyx, in a Palace that recalled a basilica of an architecture at once Saracenic and Byzantine.

In the centre of the tabernacle surmounting the altar, which was approached by steps in the shape of a recessed half circle, the Tetrach Herod was seated, crowned with a tiara, his legs drawn together, with hands on knees.

The face was yellow, like parchment, furrowed with wrinkles, worn with years; his long beard floated like a white cloud over the starry gems that studded the gold-fringed robe that moulded his breast.

Round about his figure, that sat motionless as a statue, fixed in a hieratic pose like some Hindu god, burned cressets from which rose clouds of scented vapour. Through this gleamed, like the phosporic glint of wild beasts' eyes, the flash of the jewels set in the walls of the throne; then the smoke rolled higher, under the arcades of the roof, mingling its misty blue with the gold dust of the great beams of sunlight pouring in from the domes.

Amid the heady odour of the perfumes, in the hot, stifling atmosphere of the great basilica, Salomé, the left arm extended in a gesture of command, the right bent, holding up beside the face a great lotus-blossom, glides slowly forward on the points of her toes, to the accompaniment of a guitar whose strings a woman strikes, sitting crouched on the floor.

Her face wore a thoughtful, solemn, almost reverent expression as she began the wanton dance that was to rouse the dormant passions of the old Herod; her bosoms quiver and touched lightly by her swaying necklets, their rosy points stand pouting; on the moist skin of her body glitter clustered diamonds; from bracelets, belts, rings, dart sparks of fire; over her robe of triumph, bestrewn with pearls, broidered with silver, studded with gold, a corselet of chased goldsmith's work, each mesh of which is a precious stone, seems ablaze with coiling fiery serpents, crawling and creeping over the pink flesh like gleaming insects with dazzling wings of brilliant colours, scarlet with bands of yellow like the dawn, with patterned diapering like the blue of steel, with stripes of peacock green.

With concentrated gaze and the fixed eyes of a sleepwalker, she sees neither the Tetrarch, who sits there quivering, nor her mother, the ruthless Herodias, who watches her, nor the hermaphrodite or eunuch who stands sabre in hand on the lowest step of the throne, a terrible figure, veiled to below the eyes, the sexless dugs of the creature hanging like twin gourds under his tunic barred with orange stripes.

The thought of this Salomé, so full of haunting suggestion to the artist and the poet, had fascinated Des Esseintes for years. How often had he read in the old Bible of Pierre Variquet, translated by the Doctors in Theology of the University of Louvain, the Gospel of St. Matthew where it recounts in brief, naïve phrases the beheading of the Precursor; how often had he dreamed dreams between the simple lines:

"But when Herod's birthday was kept, the daughter of Herodias danced before them, and pleased Herod.

"Whereupon, he promised with an oath to give her whatsoever she would ask.

"And she, being before instructed of her mother, said 'Give me here John Baptist's head in a charger.'

"And the king was sorry: nevertheless, for the oath's sake, and them which sat with him at meat, he commanded it to be given her.

"And he sent, and beheaded John in the prison.

"And his head was brought in a charger, and given to the damsel: and she brought it to her mother."

But neither St. Matthew, nor St. Mark, nor St. Luke, nor any other of the Sacred Writers had enlarged on the maddening charms and the active allurements of the dancer. She had always remained a dim, obliterated figure, lost with her mysterious fascination in the far-off mist of the centuries, not to be realized by exact and pedestrian minds, only appealing to brains shaken and sharpened, made visionary as it were by hysteria; she had always eluded the grasp of fleshy painters, such as Rubens who travestied her as a Flemish butcher's wife; always baffled the comprehension of writers who have never yet succeeded in rendering the delirious frenzy of the wanton, the subtle grandeur of the murderess.

In the work of Gustave Moreau, going for its conception altogether beyond the meagre facts supplied by the New Testament, Des Esseintes saw realized at last the Salomé, weird and superhuman, he had dreamed of. No longer was she merely the dancing-girl who extorts a cry of lust and concupiscence from an old man by the lascivious contortions of her body; who breaks the will, masters the mind of a King by the spectacle of her quivering bosoms, heaving belly and tossing thighs; she was now revealed in a sense as the symbolic incarnation of world-old Vice, the goddess of immortal Hysteria, the Curse of Beauty supreme above all other beauties by the cataleptic spasm that stirs her flesh and steels her muscles,—a monstrous Beast of the Apocalypse, indifferent, irresponsible, insensible, poisoning, like Helen of Troy of the old Classic fables, all who come near her, all who see her, all who touch her.

So understood, she belonged to the ancient Theogonies of the Far East; no longer she drew her origin from Biblical tradition; could not even be likened to the living image of Babylonish Whoredom, or the Scarlet Woman, the Royal Harlot of Revelations, bedecked like her with precious stones and purple, tired and painted like her; for *she* was not driven by a fateful power, by a supreme, irresistible force, into the alluring perversities of debauch.

Moreover, the painter seemed to have wished to mark his deliberate purpose to keep outside centuries of history; to give no definite indication of race or country or period, setting as he does his Salomé in the midst of this strange Palace, with its confused architecture of a grandiose complexity; clothing her in sumptuous, fantastic robes, crowning her with a diadem of no land or time shaped like a Phœnician tower such as Salammbô wears, putting in her hand the sceptre of Isis, the sacred flower of Egypt and of India, the great lotus-blossom.

Des Esseintes strove to fathom the meaning of this emblem. Did it bear the phallic signification the primordial religions of India give it; did it proclaim to the old Tetrarch a sacrifice of a woman's virginity, an exchange of blood, an incestuous embrace asked for and offered on the express condition of a murder? Or was it intended to suggest the allegory of Fertility, the Hindu myth of Life, an existence held betwixt the fingers of woman, snatched away and defiled by the lustful hands of man, who is seized by a sudden madness, bewildered by the cry of the flesh?

Perhaps, too, in arming his enigmatic goddess with the revered lotus-flower, the painter had thought of the dancing harlot of all times, the mortal woman the temple of whose body is defiled,—cause of all the sins and all the crimes; perhaps he had remembered the sepulchral rites of ancient Egypt, the ritual ceremonies of the embalmment, when surgeons and priests stretch the dead woman's body on a slab of jasper, then with curved needles extract her brains through the nostrils, her entrails through an incision opened in the left side; finally, before gilding the nails and teeth, before coating the corpse with bitumen and precious essences, insert into her sexual parts, to purify them, the chaste petals of the divine flower.

Be this as it may, an irresistible fascination breathed from the canvas; but the water-colour entitled "The Apparition" was perhaps even yet more troubling to the senses.

In it, Herod's Palace towered aloft like an Alhambra on light columns iridescent with Moorish chequer-work, joined as with silver mortar, consolidated with cement of gold; arabesques surrounded lozenges of lapis lazuli and wound all along the cupolas, where on marquetries of mother-of-pearl, wandered glittering rainbows, flashes of prismatic colour.

The murder had been done; now the headsman stood there impassive, his hands resting on the pommel of his long sword, stained with blood.

The decapitated head of the Saint had risen up from the charger where it lay on the flags, and the eyes were gazing out from the livid face with its discoloured lips and open mouth; the neck all crimson, dripping tears of gore.

A mosaic encircled the face whence shone an aureola darting gleams of fire under the porticoes, illuminating the ghastly lifting of the head, revealing the glassy eyeballs, that seemed fixed, glued to the figure of the dancing wanton.

With a gesture of horror, Salomé repulses the appalling vision that holds her nailed to the floor, balanced on her toe tips; her eyes are dilated, her hand grips her throat convulsively.

She is almost naked; in the ardour of the dance the veils have unwound themselves, the brocaded draperies of her robes have slipped away; she is clad now only in goldsmith's artistries and translucent gems; a gorget clips her waist like a corselet; and for clasp a superb, a wondrous jewel flashes lightnings in the furrow between her bosoms; lower, on the hips, a girdle swathes her, hiding the upper thighs, against which swings a gigantic pendant, a falling river of carbuncles and emeralds; to complete the picture: where the body shows bare betwixt gorget and girdle, the belly bulges, dimpled by the hollow of the navel that recalls a graven seal of onyx with its milky sheen and tint as of a rosy finger-nail.

Beneath the ardent rays flashing from the Precursor's head, every facet of her jewelled bravery catches fire; the stones burn, outlining the woman's shape in flaming figures; neck, legs, arms, glitter with points of light, now red as burning brands, now violet as jets of gas, now blue as flames of alcohol, now white as moonbeams.

The dreadful head flashes and flames, bleeding always, dripping gouts of dark purple that point the beard and hair. Visible to Salomé, alone, it embraces in the stare of its dead eyes neither Herodias, who sits dreaming of her hate satiated at last, nor the Tetrarch, who, leaning rather forward with hands on knees, still pants, maddened by the sight of the woman's nakedness, reeking with heady fumes, dripping with balms and essences, alluring with scents of incense and myrrh.

Like the old King, Des Esseintes was overwhelmed, overmastered, dizzied before this figure of the dancing-girl, less majestic, less imposing, but more ensnaring to the senses than the Salomé of the oil painting.

In the callous and pitiless statue, in the innocent and deadly idol, the emotion, the terror of the human being had dawned; the great lotus-flower had disappeared, the goddess vanished; an atrocious nightmare now gripped the throat of the mime, intoxicated by the whirl of the dance, of the courtesan, petrified, hypnotized by terror.

In this, she was altogether feminine, obedient to her temperament of a passionate, cruel woman; she was active and alive, more refined and yet more savage, more hateful and yet more exquisite; she was shown awakening more powerfully the sleeping passions of man; bewitching, subjugating more surely his will, with her unholy charm as of a great flower of concupiscence, born of a sacrilegious birth, reared in a hot-house of impiety.

Robert Smythe Hichens

[1864–1950]

From THE GREEN CARNATION
[1894]

While traveling in Egypt, Hichens, a London journalist, met Lord Alfred Douglas, who later introduced him to Wilde. Hichens, who came to know Wilde quite well, wrote that he once saw him in a theatre wearing a green carnation with "five ultra-smart youths, all decorated with similar green carnations," which, Hichens says, was the source of the title of his first novel, published anonymously.

Wilde and Douglas, aware that Hichens was the author, sent him witty telegrams, Douglas advising him, with mock solemnity, to flee from forthcoming vengeance. Because the novel brilliantly captured the cadence and style of Wilde's epigrammatic wit, it was widely believed that Wilde himself was its author. In a letter to the *Pall Mall Gazette* on October 1, 1894, Wilde rejected the suggestion advanced by the journal:

> *I invented that magnificent flower. But with the middle-class and mediocre book that usurps its strangely beautiful name, I have, I need hardly say, nothing whatsoever to do. The flower is a work of art. The book is not.*

Privately, however, Wilde had confessed to his friend, the novelist Ada Leverson: "Hichens I did not think capable of anything so clever."

The Green Carnation is a *roman à clef*—a novel in which actual persons appear with fictitious names—Wilde portrayed as Esmé Amarinthe and Lord Alfred Douglas as Lord Reggie Hastings. Most of the novel takes place in Lady Locke's summer cottage, which is adorned with yew hedges cut into "monstrous shapes." Scrupulously unplotted, the novel consists primarily of random conversations in which Esmé and Lord Reggie expound their "higher philosophy." Satiric paraphrases from Pater and Wilde abound. At one point, for example, Esmé exclaims:

> *Eleven! I had no idea it was so early. I am going to sit up all night with Reggie, saying mad scarlet things, such as Walter Pater loves, and waking the night with silver silences. . . . Let us be brilliant, dear boy, or I feel that I shall weep for sheer wittiness and die, as so many have died, with all my epigrams still in me.*

In 1895, Hichens was revealed as the author when his name appeared on the title page of the fourth impression. In that year, when Wilde was tried and convicted, the publisher halted all sales of the book.

He slipped a green carnation into his evening coat, fixed it in its place with a pin, and looked at himself in the glass, the long glass that stood near the window of his London bedroom. The summer evening was so bright that he could see his double clearly, even though it was just upon seven o'clock. There he stood in his favourite and most characteristic attitude, with his left knee slightly bent, and his arms hanging at his sides, gazing, as a woman gazes at herself before she starts for a party. The low and continuous murmur of Piccadilly, like the murmur of a flowing tide on a smooth beach, stole to his ears monotonously, and inclined him insensibly to a certain thoughtfulness. Floating through the curtained window the soft lemon light sparkled on the silver backs of the brushes that lay on the toilet-table, on the dressing-gown of spun silk that hung from a hook behind the door, on the great mass of Gloire de Dijon roses, that dreamed in an ivory-white bowl set on the writing-table of ruddy-brown wood. It caught the gilt of the boy's fair hair and turned it into brightest gold, until, despite the white weariness of his face, the pale fretfulness of his eyes, he looked like some angel in a church window designed by [Sir Edward] Burne-Jones [1833–98, English Pre-Raphaelite painter], some angel a little blasé from the injudicious conduct of its life. He frankly admired himself as he watched his reflection, occasionally changing his pose, presenting himself to himself, now full face, now three-quarters face, leaning backward or forward, advancing one foot in its silk stocking and shining shoe, assuming a variety of interesting expressions. In his own opinion he was very beautiful, and he thought it right to appreciate his own qualities of mind and of body. He hated those fantastic creatures who are humble even in their self-communings, cowards who dare not acknowledge even to themselves how exquisite, how delicately fashioned they are. Quite frankly he told other people that he was very wonderful, quite frankly he avowed it to himself. There is a nobility in fearless truthfulness, is there not? and about the magic of his personality he could never be induced to tell a lie.

It is so interesting to be wonderful, to be young, with pale gilt hair and blue eyes, and a face in which the shadows of fleeting expressions come and go, and a mouth like the mouth of Narcissus. It is so interesting to oneself. Surely one's beauty, one's attractiveness, should be one's own greatest delight. It is only the stupid, and those who still cling to Exeter Hall as to a Rock of Ages, who are afraid, or ashamed, to love themselves, and to express that love, if need be. Reggie Hastings, at least, was not ashamed. The mantelpiece in his sitting-room bore only photographs of himself, and he explained this fact to inquirers by saying that he worshipped beauty. Reggie was very frank. When he could not be witty, he often told the naked truth; and truth, without any clothes on, frequently passes for epigram. It is daring, and so it seems clever. Reggie was considered very clever by his friends, but more clever by himself. He knew that he was great, and he said so often in Society. And Society smiled and murmured that it was a pose. Everything is a pose nowadays, especially genius.

This evening Reggie stood before the mirror till the Sèvres clock on the chimneypiece gently chimed seven. Then he drew out of their tissue paper a pair of lavender gloves, and pressed the electric bell.

"Call me a hansom, Flynn," he said to his valet.

He threw a long buff-coloured overcoat across his arm, and went slowly downstairs. A cab was at the door, and he entered it and told the man to drive to Belgrave Square. As they turned the corner of Half Moon Street into Piccadilly, he leant forward over the wooden apron and lazily surveyed the crowd. Every second cab he passed contained an immaculate man going out to dinner, sitting bolt upright, with a severe expression of countenance, and surveying the world with steady eyes over an unyielding rampart of starched collar. Reggie exchanged nods with various acquaintances. Presently he passed an elderly gentleman with a red face and small side-whiskers. The elderly gentleman stared him in the face, and sniffed ostentatiously.

"What a pity my poor father is so plain," Reggie said to himself with a quiet smile. Only that morning he had received a long and vehement diatribe from his parent, showering abuse upon him, and exhorting him to lead a more reputable life. He had replied by wire—

"What a funny little man you are.—Reggie."

The funny little man had evidently received his message.

As his cab drew up for a moment at Hyde Park Corner to allow a stream of pedestrians to cross from the Park, he saw several people pointing him out. Two well-dressed women looked at him and laughed, and he heard one murmur his name to the other. He let his blue eyes rest upon them calmly as they peacocked across to St. George's Hospital, still laughing, and evidently discussing him. He did not know them, but he was accustomed to being known. His life had never been a cautious one. He was too modern to be very reticent, and he liked to be wicked in the eye of the crowd. Secret wickedness held little charm for him. He preferred to preface his failings with an overture on the orchestra, to draw up the curtain, and to act his drama of life to a crowded audience of smart people in the stalls. When they hissed him, he only pitied them, and wondered at their ignorance. His social position kept him in Society, however much Society murmured against him; and, far from fearing scandal, he loved it. He chose his friends partly for their charm, and partly for their bad reputations; and the white flower of a blameless life was much too inartistic to have any attraction for him. He believed that Art showed the way to Nature, and worshipped the abnormal with all the passion of his impure and subtle youth.

.   .   .   .   .

[*A dialogue between Lady Locke and Reggie, in whom she takes a great interest. Here, Reggie is speaking.*]

"We none of us live up to our ideals, I suppose. But really I have none. I agree with Esmé that nothing is so limited as to have an ideal."

"And yet you look sometimes as if you might have many," she said, as if half to herself. The curious motherly feeling had come upon her again, a kind of tenderness that often leads to preaching.

Reggie glanced up at her quickly, and with a pleased expression. A veiled tribute to his good looks delighted him, whether it came from man or woman. Only an unveiled one surpassed it in his estimation.

"Ah! but that means nothing," he said. "It is quite a mistake to believe, as many people do, that the mind shows itself in the face. Vice may sometimes write itself in lines and changes of contour, but that is all. Our faces are really masks given to us to conceal our minds with. Of course occasionally the mask slips partly off, generally when we are stupid and emotional. But that is an inartistic accident. Outward revelations of what is going on inside of us take place far more seldom than silly people suppose. No more preposterous theory has ever been put forward than that of the artist revealing himself in his art. The writer, for instance, has at least three minds—his Society mind, his writing mind, and his real mind. They are all quite separate and distinct, or they ought to be. When his writing mind and his real mind get mixed up together, he ceases to be an artist. That is why Swinburne has gone off so much. If you want to write really fine erotic poetry, you must live an absolutely rigid and entirely respectable life. The *Laus Veneris*[1] could only have been produced by a man who had a Nonconformist conscience. I am certain that Mrs. Humphry Ward[2] is the most strictly orthodox Christian whom we have. Otherwise, her books against the accepted Christianity could never have brought her in so many thousands of pounds. I never read her, of course. Life is far too long and lovely for that sort of thing; but a bishop once told me that she was a great artist, and that if she had a sense of gravity, she would rival George Eliot. Dickens had probably no sense of humour. That is why he makes second-rate people die of laughing. Oscar Wilde was utterly mistaken when he wrote *The Picture of Dorian Gray*. After Dorian's act of cruelty, the picture ought to have grown more sweet, more saintly, more angelic in expression."

"I never read that book."

"Then you have gained a great deal. Poor Oscar! He is terribly truthful. He reminds me so much of George Washington."[3]

. . . . .

[1] The famous poem by Swinburne—meaning "Praise of Venus"—which, when it appeared in *Poems and Ballads* (1866), was singled out for attack by hostile critics for its verbal fleshliness.

[2] The popular Victorian novelist, whose *Robert Elsmere* Oscar Wilde ridiculed in "The Decay of Lying." (See note 5 of Wilde's essay in this volume.)

[3] In "The Decay of Lying," Wilde had written: "The crude commercialism of America, its materialising spirit, its indifference to the poetical side of things, and its lack of imagination and of high unattainable ideals, are entirely due to that country having adopted for its national hero a man who, according to his own confession, was incapable of telling a lie, and it is not too much to say that the story of George Washington and the cherry-tree has done more harm, and in a shorter space of time, than any other moral tale in the whole of literature."

She found Lord Reggie alone in the room reading his letters. He was dressed in loose white flannel, and in the buttonhole of his thin jacket a big green carnation was stuck. It looked perfectly fresh.

"How do you manage to keep that flower alive so long?" asked Lady Locke, as they sat down opposite to one another. For there was no formality at this meal, and people began just when they felt inclined.

"I don't understand," Reggie answered, looking at her across his mushrooms.

"Why, you have worn it for two days already."

"This? No. Esmé and I have some sent down every morning from a florist's in Covent Garden."

"Really! Is it worth while?"

"I think that sort of thing is the only sort of thing that is worth while. Most people are utterly wrong, they worship what they call great things. I worship little details. This flower is a detail. I worship it."

"Do you regard it as an emblem, then?"

"No. I hate emblems. The very word makes one think of mourning-rings, and everlasting flowers, and urns, and mementoes of all sorts. Why are people so afraid of forgetting? There is nothing more beautiful than to forget, except, perhaps, to be forgotten. I wear this flower because its colour is exquisite. I have no other reason."

"But its colour is not natural."

"Not yet. Nature has not followed art so far. She always requires time. Esmé invented this flower two months ago. Only a few people wear it, those who are followers of the higher philosophy."

"The higher philosophy! What is that?"

"The philosophy to be afraid of nothing, to dare to live as one wishes to live, not as the middle-classes wish one to live; to have the courage of one's desires, instead of only the cowardice of other people's."

"Mr. Amarinth is the high priest of this philosophy, I suppose?"

"Esmé is the bravest man I know," said Reggie, taking some marmalade. "I think sometimes that he sins even more perfectly than I do. He is so varied. And he escapes those absurd things, consequences. His sin always finds him out. He is never at home to it by any chance. Why do you look at me so strangely?"

"Do I look at you strangely?" she asked, with a sudden curious nervousness. "Perhaps it is because you are so strange, so unlike the men whom I have been accustomed to. Your aims are different from theirs."

"That is impossible, Lady Locke."

"Impossible! Why?"

"Because I have no aims; I have only emotions. If we live for aims we blunt our emotions. If we live for aims, we live for one minute, for one day, for one year, instead of for every minute, every day, every year. The moods of one's life are life's beauties. To yield to all one's moods is to really live."

·　·　·　·　·

[*Esmé has been asked to address a group of choir boys from the local school who have been invited to Lady Locke's cottage.*]

. . . "People teach in order to conceal their ignorance, as people smile in order to conceal their tears, or sin, too often, merely to draw away a curious observation from the amplitude and endurance of their virtue. The beautiful falling generation are learning to do things for their own sake, and not for the sake of Mrs. Grundy,[4] who will soon sit alone in her dowdy disorder, a chaperon bereft of her débutante, the hopeless and frowsy leader of a lost and discredited cause. Yes, wisdom has nearly had its day, and the stars are beginning to twinkle in the violet skies of folly.

"It is not, alas! given to all of us to be properly foolish. The custom of succeeding ages has rendered wisdom a hereditary habit with thousands upon thousands of us, and even the destructive influence of myself, of Lord Reginald"—here

---

[4] In Thomas Morton's play *Speed the Plough* (1798), a character who never appears on stage. Whenever anything occurs or is proposed, the question raised is "What will Mrs. Grundy say?" In the nineteenth century, she personified ultra-respectability, generally with pejorative connotations.

he indicated Reggie, with one plump, white hand—"and of a few, a very few others, among whom I can include Mr. Oscar Wilde, has so far failed to uproot that pestilent plant from its home in the retentive soil of humanity. What was bad enough for our ridiculous fathers is still bad enough for too many of us. We are still content with the old virtues, and still timorous of the new vices. We still fear to clasp the radiant hands of folly, and drown our good impulses in the depths of her enchanted eyes. But many of us are comparatively elderly, and, believe me, the elderly quickly lose the divine power of faculty of disobedience. If it were my first word to you, children, I would say to you—learn to disobey. To know how to be disobedient is to know how to live."

The national schoolmaster at this point planted his feet in the first position with sudden violence, and gave vent to an ahem that was a revelation of keen though inarticulate emotion. Esmé indicated that he had heard the sound by slightly elevating his voice.

"Learn," he said, "to disobey the cold dictates of reason; for reason acts upon life as the breath of frosts acts upon water, and binds the leaping streams of the abnormal in the congealing and icy band of the normal. All that is normal is to be sedulously avoided. That is what the modern pupil will teach in the future his old-fashioned masters. That is what you may, if you will have the courage, impress upon the pastors and masters, who must learn to look to you for guidance."

Extreme disorder of mind was now made manifest in the fantastic postures assumed by the entire staff of teachers, who began to turn their feet in, to construct strange patterns with their fingers, and in all other known ways to express mutely the dire forebodings of those who feel that their empire is passing away from them.

"It has hitherto been the privilege of age to rule the world. In the blessed era of folly that privilege will be transferred to youth. Never forget, therefore, to be young, to be young, and, if possible, consciously foolish."

The expressions of the children at this point indicated intelligent acquiescence, and Esmé's face was irradiated with a tranquil smile.

"It is very difficult to be young, especially up to the age of thirty," he continued, "and very difficult to be properly foolish up to any age at all; but we must not despair. Genius is the art of not taking pains, and genius is more common than is generally supposed. If we do not take proper pains, there is no reason why even the cleverest among us should not in time learn to practise beautifully the beautiful art of folly. It is always well to be personal, and as egoism is scarcely less artistic than its own brother, vanity, I shall make no apology for now alluding, in as marked a manner as possible, to myself. "I"—he spoke here with superb emphasis—"I am absurd. For years I have tried in vain not to hide it. For years I have striven to call public attention to my exquisite gift, to impress its existence upon a heartless world, to lift it up as a darkness that all may see, and for years I have practically failed. I have practically failed, but I am not without hope. I believe that my absurdity is at last beginning to obtain a meed of recognition. I believe that a few fine spirits are beginning to understand that artistic absurdity, the perfection of folly, has a bright and glorious future before it. I am absurd, and have been so for very many years, and in very many ways. I have been an æsthete. I have lain upon hearth-rugs and eaten passion-flowers. I have clothed myself in breeches of white samite, and offered my friends yellow jonquils instead of afternoon tea. But when æstheticism became popular in Bayswater—a part of London built for the delectation of the needy rich—I felt that it was absurd no longer, and I turned to other things. It was then, one golden summer day among the flowering woods of Richmond, that I invented a new art, the art of preposterous conversation. A middle-class country has prevented me from patenting my exquisite invention, which has been closely imitated by dozens of people much older and much stupider than myself; but nobody so far has been able to rival me in my own particular line of business, and my society 'turns' at luncheon parties, dances, and dinners are invariably received with an applause which is almost embarrassing, and which is scarcely necessary to one so admirably conceited as myself."

At this point, Esmé, whose face had been gradually assuming a pained and irritated expression, paused, and looking towards the west, which was barred with green and gold, and flecked with squadrons of rose-coloured cloudlets, exclaimed in a voice expressive of weakness:

"That sky is becoming so terribly imitative that I can hardly go on. Why are modern sunsets so intolerably true to Turner?"

He looked round as if for an answer; but, since nobody had anything to say, he passed one hand over his eyes, as if to shut out some dreadful vision, and continued with rather less vivacity:

"For the true artist is always conceited, just as the true Philistine is always fond of going to the Royal Academy. I have brought the art of preposterous conversation to the pitch of perfection; but I have been greatly handicapped in my efforts by the egregious wisdom of a world that insists upon taking me seriously. There is nothing that should be taken seriously, except, possibly, an income or the music-halls, and I am not an income or a music-hall, although I am intensely and strangely refined. Yet I have been taken seriously throughout my career. My lectures have been gravely discussed. My plays have been solemnly criticized by the amusing failures in literature who love to call themselves 'the gentlemen of the press.' My poems have been boycotted by prurient publishers; and my novel, *The Soul of Bertie Brown*,[5] has ruined the reputation of a magazine that had been successful in shocking the impious for centuries. Bishops have declared that I am a monster, and monsters have declared that I ought to be a bishop. And all this has befallen me because I am an artist in absurdity, a human being who dares to be ridiculous. I practise the exquisite art of folly, an art that will in the future take rank with the arts of painting, of music, of literature. I was born to be absurd. I have lived to be absurd. I shall die to be absurd; for nothing can be more absurd than the death of a man who has lived to sin, instead of having lived to suffer. I married to be absurd; for marriage is one of the most brilliant absurdities ever invented by a prolific imagination. We are all absurd; but we are not all artists, because we are not all self-conscious. The artist

[5] An allusion, obviously, to Wilde's *Picture of Dorian Gray*.

must be self-conscious. If we marry seriously, if we live solemnly, and die with a decent gravity, we are being absurd;
but we do not know it, and therefore our absurdity has no
value. I am an artist, because I am consciously absurd; and I
wish to impress upon you to-day, that if you wish to live
improperly, you must be consciously absurd too. You must
commit follies; but you must not be under the impression
that you are performing sensible acts, otherwise you will
take rank with sensible people, who are invariably and hope-
lessly middle-class."

An interruption occurred here—one of the smallest children who was stationed in the front of the group under the
cedar tree suddenly bursting into a flood of tears, and having
to be led, shrieking, away to a distant corner of the garden.
Esmé followed its convulsed form with his eyes, and then
remarked:

"That child is being absurd; but that child is not an artist,
because it is not conscious of its absurdity. Remember, then,
to be self-conscious, to set aside the normal, to be young,
and to be eternally foolish. Take nothing seriously, except
yourselves, if possible. Do not be deceived into thinking the
mind greater than the face, or the soul grander than the
body. Strike the words virtue and wickedness out of your
dictionaries. There is nothing good and nothing evil. There is
only art. Despise the normal, and flee from everything that is
hallowed by custom, as you would flee from the seven
deadly virtues. Cling to the abnormal. Shrink from the cold
and freezing touch of Nature. One touch of Nature makes
the whole world commonplace. Forget your Catechism, and
remember the words of Flaubert and of Walter Pater, and
remember this, too, that the folly of self-conscious fools is
the only true wisdom! And now sing to us your hymn, sing
to us under the cedar tree self-consciously, and we will listen
self-consciously, even as Ulysses listened to——"

But here a gentle and penetrating "Hush!" broke from the
lips of Mrs. Windsor, and Esmé paused.

"Sing to us," he said, "and we will listen, as the old listen
to the voices of youth, as the nightingale listens to the properly trained vocalist, as Nature listens to Art. Sing to us,
beautiful rose-coloured children, until we forget that you are

singing a hymn, and remember only that you are young, and that some day, in the long-delayed fulness of time, you will be no longer innocent."

He uttered the last words in a tone so soft and so seductive that it was like honey and the honeycomb, and then stood with his eyes fixed dreamily upon the children, who had been getting decidedly red and fidgety, unaccustomed to be directly addressed, and in so fantastic a manner. The relief of the teachers at the cessation of Amarinth's address was tumultuously obvious. They once more turned out their toes. The anguished expression died away from their faces, and they ceased to twist their fingers into curious patterns suggestive of freehand drawings. The national schoolmaster, unlocking his countenance, and delightedly assuming his wonted air of proud authority, stepped forward and called for the Old Hundredth; and in the gentle evening air the well-known tune ascended like incense to the darkening heavens. Shrilly the youthful voices rose and fell, until the amen came as a full stop. Then the little troop was marshalled two and two, made a collective obeisance to Mrs. Windsor and her guests, and wheeled out of the garden into the drive at a quick-step, warbling poignantly, *Onward, Christian Soldiers.* Gradually the sound decreased in volume, decreased in a long diminuendo, and at last faded away into silence.

The Second Coming of Arthur

During the trial of Oscar Wilde in 1895, an ingenious satire of *The Yellow Book*, written by Mostyn Piggott under the pseudonym "Testudo," appeared in the London *World*. Combining Lewis Carroll's jabberwocky with allusions to Aubrey Beardsley ("Aub-Aub Bird"), Max Beerbohm ("Beerbomax"), the Bodley Head (publisher of *The Yellow Book*) located in Vigo Street, the Philistines ("Philerotes"), and the Decadents ("Daycadongs"), the poem, subtitled "A Certain Past Adapted to a Possible Future," is based on the legend that Arthur would return to rescue Britain when in danger. The comic analogy, in which Arthur—representing the forces of respectability—slays the "Yallerbock," suggests the upheaval which resulted in Beardsley's dismissal from *The Yellow Book* (see Introduction) and also the possibility of the journal's eventual death.

'Twas rollog, and the minim potes
    Did mime and mimble in the cafe;
All footly were the Philerotes,
    And Daycadongs outstrafe.

Beware the Yallerbock, my son!
    The aims that rile, the art that racks,
Beware the Aub-Aub Bird, and shun
    The stumious Beerbomax.

He took Excalibur in hand:
  Long time the canxome foe he sought—
So rested he by the Jonbul tree,
  And stood awhile in thought.

Then, as veep Vigo's marge he trod,
  The Yallerbock, with tongue of blue,
Came piffling through the Headley Bod,
  And flippered as it flew.

One, two! One, two! And through and through
  Excalibur went snicker-snack!
He took its dead and bodless head
  And went jucunding back.

And hast thou slain the Yallerbock?
  Come to my arms, my squeamish boy!
Oh, brighteous peace! Purlieu! Purlice!
  He jawbled in his joy.

'Twas rollog, and the minim potes
  Did mime and mimble in the cafe;
All footly were the Philerotes,
  And Daycadongs outstrafe.

BIOGRAPHICAL
NOTES

BARLAS, JOHN, (1860–1914) was born in Burma and educated at New College, Oxford. A teacher and ardent socialist, he was a demonstrator in Trafalgar Square on "Bloody Sunday" (November, 1886), when, as he wrote, he had "the pleasure of being batoned and floored." In the early Nineties, he was arrested —and bailed out by Wilde—for shooting at the House of Commons, an apparent gesture of contempt for parliamentary procedure. Shortly after, Barlas became briefly associated with the Rhymers' Club. Most of his later years were spent in a mental institution in Scotland. In 1898, John Davidson, a Rhymer and fellow Scotsman, replied to an inquiry from Edmund Gosse as to Barlas' whereabouts:

> No; Barlas is not dead. When I last heard of him he was in Gartnaval Asylum, Glasgow. I am afraid there is little chance of his recovery. His face was very handsome, and he was physically strong; but his head was small, and nothing in it to outweigh insanity.

From 1884–1893, Barlas published eight volumes of verse under the name "Evelyn Douglas," combining his interest in socialism and Swinburnean Decadence.

BEARDSLEY, AUBREY (1872–1898), born in Brighton, England, showed signs of tuberculosis at the age of nine. With his sister, Mabel, who later became an actress, Beardsley gave piano concerts when he was eleven. At sixteen, he was an apprentice in an architect's office in London, but found drafting distasteful. When he left for a clerk's position in an insurance office, he was again troubled by tuberculosis. Meanwhile, he was attending art classes at night. His first commission—and success—came from the publisher J. M. Dent, who wanted drawings for Malory's *Morte d'Arthur*. In 1893, he was elected to the New English Art Club, which brought not only deserved honor but also numerous commissions. John Lane's commission to illustrate Wilde's *Salomé* provided Beardsley with the opportunity to create some of his most strikingly witty and decadent pictures. After working on *The Yellow Book* and *The Savoy*, his health steadily worsened. In March, 1897, he converted to Roman Catholicism, about which Lionel Johnson wrote after Beardsley's death:

> His conversion was a spiritual work, and not a half-insincere aesthetic act of it, not a sort of emotional experience or experiment. . . . He withdrew himself from certain valued intimacies, which he felt incompatible with his faith: that implies much, in these days when artists so largely claim exemption, in the name of art, from laws and rules of life.

During his brief life, Beardsley was a prolific worker, as though he foresaw an early death. The end came rapidly at Mentone in southern France.

BEERBOHM, MAX (1872–1956), the son of a Lithuanian immigrant, was educated at Merton College, Oxford. The "incomparable Max," as Shaw called him, contributed to *The Yellow Book* while he was still an undergraduate. In 1896, in a mock farewell to literature, he published *The Works of Max Beerbohm*, declaring himself a trifle outdated, a member of the "Beardsley period." In 1898, succeeding Shaw, Beerbohm became drama critic for the English *Saturday Review*, a post he held for twelve years. Before World War I, he retired to Rapallo, Italy, with his American wife, the actress Florence Kahn, later to be joined by Ezra Pound. He continued writing witty portraits and drawing his famous caricatures, cultivating what he himself referred to as a modest reputation. A wit and dandy, Beerbohm was admired and feared for his devastating pen.

During World War II, he was in England, but returned to Rapallo shortly thereafter. His wife died in 1951. A month before he himself died, he secretly married his secretary and companion, Elizabeth Jungmann.

CUSTANCE, OLIVE (1874–1944), daughter of a wealthy colonel, was a contributor to *The Yellow Book*: she became friends with Beardsley, who designed a book plate for her. She published several volumes of verse, her last being *Inn of Dreams* (1911).

In 1902, she married Lord Alfred Douglas (see the biographical note following).

DOUGLAS, LORD ALFRED (1870–1945), the son of the Marquis of Queensberry, who provoked a libel suit by calling Wilde a sodomist, attended Oxford, where he was friendly with Lionel Johnson. While still an undergraduate, he edited *The Spirit Lamp*, to which Johnson and Wilde contributed. (It was Johnson who introduced Lord Alfred to Wilde, an act he was to regret. See Johnson's "To a Destroyer of a Soul.") In the years following the Wilde trial, Lord Alfred was constantly in litigation over statements made by his detractors. In 1902, he eloped with Olive Custance, whom he had known as a child: in 1913, she left him. For many years, however, they lived close by so that Lord Alfred might visit her daily. The subject of Oscar Wilde became one of Lord Alfred's most absorbing interests; several of his books concern themselves with their liaison. Like Wilde, Lord Alfred became a Roman Catholic.

DOWSON, ERNEST (1867–1900) was born in Kent of fairly well-to-do parents. His father owned a dry dock in East London; generally the family spent winters in southern France. Dowson attended Oxford from 1886–1888, leaving without a degree. He worked at his father's dock, but spent evenings at literary taverns and restaurants. Through his friend at Oxford, Lionel Johnson, Dowson became associated with the Rhymers' Club early in 1891. In *Everyman Remembers*, Ernest Rhys writes that Dowson was the "one Rhymer whom we secretly believed to be the most potential of the group." In the same year, as a result largely of Johnson's persuasion, Dowson was converted to Roman Catholicism, though there is some question how earnestly he practiced his faith. During his lifetime, he published two volumes of verse, two novels (in collaboration with Arthur Moore), a one-act play which Beardsley illustrated and in which Mabel Beardsley acted, and a volume of short stories. In 1894, both his parents committed suicide; for the remainder of his life—except for brief visits to London—he lived in France, but returned, destitute and ill, to die in England of tuberculosis.

"FIELD, MICHAEL" is the pseudonym of Katharine Bradley (1846–1913) and her niece, Edith Cooper (1862–1914), who were praised by Browning in the 1880's for their drama and verse. Both studied at University College, Bristol, where they were active in the debating society and an anti-vivisection group. Their collaboration resulted in twenty-seven tragedies and eight volumes of verse. Their first play was published under the pseudonym "Arran and Isla Leigh," but thereafter they adopted the name "Michael Field." To their friends, Katharine was Michael, Edith was Field. Though they knew many well-known figures of the Nineties, they were intimate with few. In 1907, they both became Roman Catholics; both died of cancer one year apart.

G R A Y , J O H N (1866–1934), the first of nine children, was born in London but educated in Greenwich. In 1884, he was a clerk in the General Post Office, tracing lost letters; in 1888, he transferred to the Foreign Office. Frequenting meetings of the Playgoers' Club and the Rhymers' Club, Gray became known as a dandy and wit. Because of his friendship with Wilde, it was widely believed that he was the original of Dorian Gray, though Wilde had published the novel before meeting him. In 1892, the London *Star* wrote that Gray "was said to be the original Dorian of the same name. Mr. Gray, who has cultivated his manner to the highest pitch of languor yet attained, is a well-known figure of the Playgoers' Club, where, though he often speaks, is seldom heard." When Gray threatened to bring suit, the *Star* retracted its remark. Later in the decade, Gray entered Scots College in Rome as a candidate for holy orders (he had converted to Roman Catholicism in 1890). Ordained a priest at thirty-five, he was assigned to Edinburgh, where, with his friend André Raffalovich, he lived for many years. His verse was henceforth primarily religious; indeed, by the mid-Nineties, he had already abandoned his devotion to French Symbolism and Decadence, as evidenced in *Silverpoints* (1893). In 1904, he edited *Last Letters of Aubrey Beardsley*, most of which had been written to Raffalovich, who at one time had given Beardsley financial assistance.

J O H N S O N , L I O N E L (1867–1902), born in Kent, was educated at New College, Oxford. In 1890, upon graduation, he lived at the "Fitzroy settlement," the offices and studios of the Century Guild of Artists, and embarked on a journalistic career as a reviewer. In 1891, he converted to Roman Catholicism and contemplated taking orders. Yeats, who at this time became his closest friend, describes him as "determined, erect . . . almost a dwarf but beautifully made, his features cut in ivory." His *Art of Thomas Hardy* (1894) won him acclaim as an important critic, and his first volume of verse in the following year received wide attention. With Yeats, he was active in the Irish Literary Society (he had Irish relatives on one side of his family) until 1895, when he became increasingly withdrawn and alcoholic. In 1902, he died of a stroke after falling off a bar stool.

LE GALLIENNE, RICHARD (1866–1947), son of a brewery manager, was born in Liverpool. After attending Liverpool College briefly, he was apprenticed to a firm of accountants, which he left shortly to go to London. There he met Wilde, Swinburne, Meredith, and other writers in 1889; he became a reader for Elkin Mathews and John Lane, who had just founded the Bodley Head. His *Volumes in Folio* was their first publication. In the Nineties, he was distinctive in appearance, wearing his hair long and sporting a velveteen jacket, a flowing tie, and knee-breeches. One of the most prolific writers of the period, he published over thirty books while in England and in the United States, where he lived for many years (from 1905). He married three times: his first wife died in 1894; his second divorced him; he married his third wife in the United States. He is buried in Mentone, in southern France, near Aubrey Beardsley.

SYMONS, ARTHUR (1865–1945), born in Wales and educated in private schools, was the son of a Wesleyan Methodist minister. His first book, *An Introduction to the Study of Browning* (1886), was favorably reviewed by Pater, who also praised *Days and Nights* (1889), Symons' first volume of verse. Traveling often to France, where he became acquainted with Mallarmé and Verlaine, who was a great influence in his life, Symons established himself as the leading authority on contemporary French literature, contributing many articles on current Decadent and Symbolist writers to the leading journals in England. In 1896, he became editor of *The Savoy*, which ceased publication in December of that year. In 1899, his influential *Symbolist Movement in Literature* earned for him the reputation of the foremost interpreter of the subject in English. On a trip through Italy in 1908, he suffered a nervous breakdown, which resulted in two years of hospitalization. Though he continued to be a prolific writer, his later books lacked the originality and incisiveness of his earlier work. In recent years, Symons, as both poet and critic, has received considerable attention.

WILDE, OSCAR (1854–1900), the son of a distinguished surgeon, was born in Dublin. At Trinity College and later at Magdalen College, Oxford, he had already acquired a reputation for his literary talent and his posing as an Aesthete; indeed, even *Punch* had begun to caricature him. In 1878, he graduated from

Oxford and went to London, where he became famous for his long hair and velveteen breeches. In 1881, he published his first volume of poems, which moved *Punch* to declare:

> Aesthete of Aesthetes!
>   What's in a name?
> The poet is Wilde,
>   But his poetry's tame.

In 1882, he embarked on a tour of the United States and Canada lecturing on such diverse topics as the Aesthetic Movement, house decoration, and the Irish poets of 1848, some two hundred lectures in all. In 1887, he became editor of *The Woman's World*, but abandoned his post two years later. Success came with the publication of *The Picture of Dorian Gray* (1891) and his later theatrical ventures, culminating in *The Importance of Being Earnest* (1895). After the scandal of his personal life resulted in a two-year prison term, he lived in France and Italy until his sudden death in 1900.

WRATISLAW, THEODORE (1871–1933), by lineal descent a Count of Bohemia and a Count of the Holy Roman Empire, was born at Rugby, where his family had lived for three generations. In 1885–88, he attended Rugby School, where his great-grandfather and great-uncle had been masters. He later became a solicitor but in 1893, after publishing two volumes of verse, decided on a literary career. He went to London, where he made the acquaintance of such figures as Beardsley, Wilde, Dowson, Symons, and Beerbohm. Besides *Caprices* and *Orchids*, his two most characteristic volumes of decadent verse, he wrote a play, edited Plato's *Republic*, and contributed to *The Yellow Book* and *The Savoy*. Unable to support himself by his writings, he entered the Civil Service in 1895. In 1900, he published a biography of Swinburne, who was pleased with it. From that time until his death, Wratislaw published only one poem—a lyric written at Swinburne's grave in 1923.

YEATS, WILLIAM BUTLER (1865–1939) was born at Sandymount, near Dublin, the son of John Butler Yeats, a prominent painter and acquaintance of many literary figures. (Yeats's brother, Jack, later also achieved fame as a painter.) His formal education was limited to the Godolphin School in London during his father's residence in London during the 1870's. Later, in Dublin, he studied art. In 1885, he began to contribute prose and verse to Dublin journals; his first book, *Mosada*, a dramatic poem, was published in 1886. His literary career really began in 1887, when his family again moved to London. He was soon founding the Rhymers' Club (1890) and reorganizing the Irish Literary Society (1892), both in London and in Dublin. He was, moreover, a contributor to both *The Yellow Book* and *The Savoy*, which he was later to characterize as "gloomy" magazines. After the Nineties, his development as a poet is astonishing, though some of his friends (for example, Lionel Johnson) had seen his greatness early. In the course of his life, he was a winner of the Nobel Prize and a member of the Irish Senate. Most critics now regard him as the greatest lyric voice of the twentieth century.

SELECTED
BIBLIOGRAPHY ·

GENERAL

Burdett, Osbert. *The Beardsley Period*. New York, 1925. [Contains chapters on Beardsley, Wilde, Beerbohm, The Decadence, and other aspects of the Nineties.]

Buckley, Jerome H. *The Victorian Temper*. Cambridge, Mass., 1951. Published also in paperback as a Vintage Book (Random House). [Contains chapters on Aestheticism and Decadence.]

Carter, A. E. *The Idea of Decadence in French Literature, 1830–1900*. Toronto, 1958.

Casford, E. Lenore. *The Magazines of the 1890's*. Eugene, Ore., 1929.

Charlesworth, Barbara. *Dark Passages: The Decadent Consciousness in Victorian Literature*. Madison, Wisc., 1965. [Contains chapters on Rossetti, Swinburne, Pater, Wilde, Lionel Johnson, and Symons.]

Farmer, Albert. *Le Mouvement ésthetique et "décadent" en Angleterre*. Paris, 1931.

Fletcher, Ian. "The 1890's: A Lost Decade," *Victorian Studies*, IV (June, 1961), 345–54.

Garbáty, Thomas Jay. "The French Coterie of *The Savoy* 1896," *PMLA*, LXXV (1960), 609–15.

Gerber, Helmut E. "The Nineties: Beginning, End, or Transition?" *Edwardians and Late Victorians*, ed. Richard Ellmann. New York, 1959.

Goldfarb, Russell M. "Late Victorian Decadence," *Journal of Aesthetics and Art Criticism*, XX (Summer, 1962), 369–73.

Guerard, Albert. *Art for Art's Sake*. Boston, 1936.

Harris, Wendell. "Innocent Decadence: The Poetry of *The Savoy*,"

PMLA, LXXVII (December, 1962), 629–36. [Discusses Yeats, Symons, Dowson, Beardsley, among others.]

Hough, Graham. "George Moore and the Nineties," *Edwardians and Late Victorians*, ed. Richard Ellmann. New York, 1959.

————. *The Last Romantics*. London, 1949. Published also as a University Paperback (Barnes & Noble). [Includes chapters on Rossetti, the Pre-Raphaelites, Pater, the *fin de siècle*, and Yeats.]

Jackson, Holbrook. *The Eighteen Nineties*. New York, 1913. [Includes discussions of Beardsley, Johnson, Dowson, Wilde, Dandyism, and other aspects of the period.]

Kermode, Frank. *The Romantic Image*. New York, 1957. Published also as a Vintage paperback (Random House). [Contains extensive discussion of Symons and Yeats.]

Le Gallienne, Richard. *The Romantic 90's*. New York, 1925. [Reminiscences of his friendship with many leading figures of the time.]

Lehmann, A. G. *The Symbolist Aesthetic in France, 1885–1895*. Oxford, 1950.

May, J. Lewis. *John Lane and the Nineties*. London, 1936.

Mix, Katherine. *A Study in Yellow: The Yellow Book and Its Contributors*. Lawrence, Kansas, 1960.

Moers, Ellen. *The Dandy: Brummel to Beerbohm*. New York, 1960.

Peters, Robert L. "Toward an 'Un-Definition' of Decadent as Applied to British Literature of the Nineteenth Century," *Journal of Aesthetics and Art Criticism*, XVIII (December, 1959), 258–64.

————. "Whistler and the English Poets of the 1890's," *Modern Language Quarterly*, XVIII (September, 1957), 251–61. [Discussion of *transposition d'art*.]

Praz, Mario. *The Romantic Agony*. London, 1933. Published also in paperback as a Meridian Book (World). [Extensive discussions of themes and images of the Decadence.]

Rhys, Ernest. *Everyman Remembers*. London, 1931. [Reminiscences of the Nineties.]

Robinson, James K. "A Neglected Phase of the Aesthetic Movement: English Parnassianism," *PMLA*, LXVIII (1953), 733–54.

Rosenblatt, Louise. *L'Idée de l'art pour l'art dans la littérature anglaise pendant le période victorienne*. Paris, 1931.

Ryals, Clyde de L. "The Nineteenth-Century Cult of Inaction," *Tennessee Studies in Literature*, IV (1959), 51–60.

Schaffer, Aaron. *Parnassus in France*. Austin, Texas, 1929. [Contains a chapter on Gautier and l'art pour l'art.]

Starkie, Enid. *From Gautier to Eliot: The Influence of France on English Literature, 1851–1939*. London, 1960.

Temple, Ruth Z. *The Critic's Alchemy: A Study of the Introduction of Symbolism into England*. New York, 1953. Published also in paperback by College and University Press. [Contains chapters on Swinburne, George Moore, and Symons, among others.]

————. "The Ivory Tower as Lighthouse," *Edwardians and Late Victorians*, ed. Richard Ellmann. New York, 1959.

Weintraub, Stanley, ed. *The Savoy: Nineties Experiment*. University Park, Pa., 1965. [Contains selections with a historical account.]

————. *The Yellow Book: Quintessence of the Nineties*. Garden City, New York, 1964. [An Anchor paperback containing selections and a brief introduction.]

Wilcox, John. "The Beginnings of L'Art pour L'Art," *Journal of Aesthetics and Art Criticism*, XI (June, 1953), 360–77.

JOHN BARLAS

Looker, Samuel J. "A Neglected Poet: John Barlas," *Socialist Review*, XIX (January, 1922), 28–34; (February, 1922), 78–82.

Salt, H. S. "The Poetry of John Barlas," *The Yellow Book*, XI (October, 1896), 79–90.

AUBREY BEARDSLEY

Beerbohm, Max. "Aubrey Beardsley," *The Incomparable Max*, ed. S. C. Roberts, London, 1962.

Macfall, Haldane. *Aubrey Beardsley, the Clown, the Harlequin, the Pierrot of His Age*. New York, 1927.

Symons, Arthur. *Aubrey Beardsley*. London, 1905.

Walker, R. A., ed. *Letters from Aubrey Beardsley to Leonard Smithers*. London, 1937.

MAX BEERBOHM

Behrman, S. N. *Portrait of Max: An Intimate Memoir of Max Beerbohm*. New York, 1960.

Cecil, David. *Max: A Biography*. London, 1964.

Hart-Davis, Rupert, ed. *Letters to Reggie*. London, 1964.

Riewald, J. G. *Sir Max Beerbohm: Man and Writer*. The Hague, 1953.

LORD ALFRED DOUGLAS

Croft-Cooke, Rupert. *Bosie: The Story of Lord Alfred Douglas, his Friends and Enemies*. London, 1963.

Douglas, Lord Alfred. *Autobiography*. London, 1929. Published in 1932 in New York with the title *My Friendship with Oscar Wilde*.

Sinclair, Marianne. "Bosie, Oscar Wilde, and the Sphinx," *Aylesford Review*, V (Summer, 1963), 162–68. [In part a review article on Rupert Croft-Cooke's *Bosie*.]

ERNEST DOWSON

Flower, Desmond, ed. *The Poetical Works of Ernest Dowson*. London, 1934.

Gawsworth, John. "The Dowson Legend," *Royal Society of Literature Transactions*, XVII (1938), 93–123.

Goldfarb, Russell M. "The Dowson Legend Today," *Studies in English Literature, 1500–1900*, IV (Autumn, 1964), 653–62.

Longaker, Mark. *Ernest Dowson*. Philadelphia, 1944. [A critical biography.]

Plarr, Victor. *Ernest Dowson, 1888–1897: Reminiscences. Unpublished Letters and Marginalia*. London, 1914.

Swann, Thomas B. *Ernest Dowson*. New York, 1964. [A critical study.]

MICHAEL FIELD

Sturge Moore, T. and D. C., eds. *Works and Days: From the Journal of Michael Field*. London, 1914.

Sturgeon, Mary. *Michael Field*. London, 1922.

Symons, Arthur. "Michael Field," *Forum*, LXIX (1923), 1584–92.

JOHN GRAY

Sewell, Father Brocard, ed. *Two Friends: John Gray and André Raffalovich*. Aylesford, Kent, 1963. [Biographical and critical essays.]

LIONEL JOHNSON

Feldman, A. Bronson. "The Art of Lionel Johnson," *Poet Lore*, LVII (Spring, 1953), 140–60.

Fletcher, Ian, ed. *The Complete Poems of Lionel Johnson*. London, 1953. [Contains a biographical and critical introduction.]

Patrick, Arthur. *Lionel Johnson, poète et critique*. Paris, 1939.

Pound, Ezra. *Literary Essays*, ed. T. S. Eliot. London, 1954.

RICHARD LE GALLIENNE

Le Gallienne, Richard. *The Romantic 90's*. New York, 1925.

Whittington-Egan, Richard and Geoffrey Smerdon. *The Quest of the Golden Boy: The Life and Letters of Richard Le Gallienne*. London, 1960.

WALTER PATER

Fletcher, Ian. *Walter Pater*. London, 1959.

Pick, John. "Divergent Disciples of Walter Pater," *Thought*, XXIII (March, 1948), 114–128.

Tillotson, Geoffrey. "Pater, Mr. Rose, and the 'Conclusion' of *The Renaissance*," *Essays and Studies of the English Association*, XXXII (1946), 44–60.

Wellek, René. "Walter Pater's Literary Theory and Criticism," *Victorian Studies*, I (1957), 29–46.

ARTHUR SYMONS

Baugh, Edward. "Arthur Symons, Poet: A Centenary Tribute," *A Review of English Literature*, VI (July, 1965), 70–80.

Fletcher, Ian. "Symons, Yeats, and the Demonic Dance," *London Magazine*, VII (June, 1960), 46–60.

Munro, John M. "Arthur Symons as Poet: Theory and Practice," *English Literature in Transition*, VI (1963), 212–22.

————. "Arthur Symons and W. B. Yeats: The Quest for Compromise," *Dalhousie Review*, XLV (Summer, 1965), 137–152.

Lhombreaud, Roger. *Arthur Symons: A Critical Biography*. London, 1963.

Peters, Robert L. "The Salomé of Arthur Symons and Aubrey Beardsley," *Criticism*, II (Spring, 1960), 150–63.

OSCAR WILDE

Ellmann, Richard. "Romantic Pantomime in Oscar Wilde," *Partisan Review*, XXX (1963), 342–55.

Hart-Davis, Rupert, ed. *Letters of Oscar Wilde*. London, 1962.

Pearson, Hesekth. *Oscar Wilde: His Life and Wit*. New York, 1946. Published also in paperback: Universal Library (Grosset and Dunlap).

Symons, Arthur. *A Study of Oscar Wilde*, London, 1930.

Thomas, J. D. "Wilde's 'The Harlot's House,'" *Modern Language Notes*, LXV (November, 1950), 485–88.

THEODORE WRATISLAW

Ellis, Stewart M. "A Poet of the Nineties: Theodore Wratislaw," *Mainly Victorian*. London, 1924.

Gawsworth, John, ed. *Selected Poems of Theodore Wratislaw*. London, 1935. [With a biographical introduction.]

WILLIAM BUTLER YEATS

Ellmann, Richard. *Yeats: The Man and Masks*. New York, 1948. Published in paperback by Dutton.

Jeffares, A. Norman. *W. B. Yeats, Man and Poet*. London, 1949.

Savage, D. S. "The Aestheticism of W. B. Yeats," *Kenyon Review*, VII (1945), 118–34.

Wade, Allan, ed. *Collected Letters of William Butler Yeats*. London, 1955.

Wilson, Edmund. *Axel's Castle*. New York, 1931.

Yeats, William B. *Autobiographies*. New York, 1956. Published also as an Anchor paperback (Doubleday).